A FAMILY'S PATH IN AMERICA

The Lees
and
Their Continuing Legacy

David S. Turk

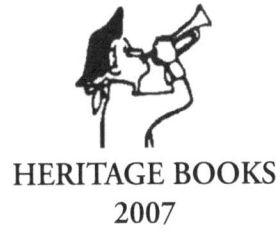

HERITAGE BOOKS
2007

HERITAGE BOOKS
AN IMPRINT OF HERITAGE BOOKS, INC.

Books, CDs, and more—Worldwide

For our listing of thousands of titles see our website at
www.HeritageBooks.com

Published 2007 by
HERITAGE BOOKS, INC.
Publishing Division
65 East Main Street
Westminster, Maryland 21157-5026

Copyright © 2007 David S. Turk

Other books by the author:

Give My Kind Regards to the Ladies: The Life of Littleton Quinton Washington

The Memorialists: An Antebellum History of Alleghany, Craig, and Monroe Counties of Western Virginia, 1812-60

The Union Hole: Unionist Activity and Local Conflict in Western Virginia

All rights reserved. No part of this book may be reproduced or transmitted in any form or by any means, electronic or mechanical, including photocopying, recording or by any information storage and retrieval system without written permission from the author, except for the inclusion of brief quotations in a review.

International Standard Book Number: 978-0-7884-3814-1

**To the Late Shelby Foote, Who Encouraged
Me to Keep Writing**

Table of Contents

Introduction: Variations of Legacy ix

Legacy I: Homes
   Burning History 1
   The Land of Fitzhugh: Ravensworth
      and its Beginnings 3
   Setting Up at Ravensworth 16
   A Centered Society 23
   Companions and Caretakers 30
   Solving the Fire 34
   Postscript: Why Russell Wood? 39

Legacy II: Artifacts and Keepsakes
   The Struggle Over Legacy 43
   Something Turned Up in Alexandria 60
   The Magnolia and the Steward 63
   Access: The Problem of the
      Rocky Mount Manuscripts 67
   One Way of Gathering 71

Legacy III: Family and Military Reputation
   Spreading Branches of the Tree 74
   Romancoke and the Writer 76
   Fitzhugh Lee and Redemption 80
   Fitz the Younger 93
   Alexandria to West Virginia and Beyond:
      Edmund Jennings Lee and his Descendants 100
   The Poet and His Traveling Brood 108
   The Unknown Man: George Taylor Lee 111
   The Poet's Other Children 116
   Spreading Branches, Spreading Legacy 119

Legacy IV: Transition
    A Legacy Dispersed: Post-Mansion
        Ravensworth   121
    The Missing Lees   124
    The Societies   129
    Change   131
    Legacy Today   134

Appendix: Lee Family
    A. "Light Horse Harry" and Partial List of Children
    B. Three Brothers and List of Children
    C. Line of Succession at Ravensworth
    D. Partial Tree of Edmund Jennings Lee Family

Endnotes   140

Bibliography   187

Index   196

List of Illustrations
Center Section

1. Ravensworth in its prime days as a Lee home

2. Ravensworth after the fire, August 1926

3. George Taylor Lee, nephew of Robert E. Lee

4. Graves of Cazenove and Marguerite DuPont Lee, Congressional Cemetery

5. Mrs. Oscar Wood in her forties

6. Former Ravensworth employee Russell Wood in the 1980s

7. Fitzhugh Lee, Jr. readies a mount during the Mexican Intervention, ca. 1916

8. Mr. and Mrs. Fitzhugh Lee, Jr. on vacation, ca. 1930

9. Handbill for concert honoring Mrs. Fitzhugh Lee

10. Campaign card for Edward Campbell "Cam" Sheads

11. Some family legacies held by Mary Middleton Lee: Washington's famous camp chest with his tent from the Revolutionary War

Acknowledgments

To my readers:

I must first state that this book went through a total "reorganization." It was at first intended to be a study on dairy families in the Fairfax area. Then the interest shifted to the Lee Family at Ravensworth, an area close and dear to me. After consulting publishing interests, an editor convinced me that there was extensive interest in the family itself. My book is a comprehensive study on the transition of the various branches of the Lee family to more modern times, as well as a definition of their legacies to the American fabric. It may fascinate some and disappoint others, but I tried to keep to the main points of study. As a historian, the results are not meant as a "scandal" book, but as a time capsule. People are human, and do make mistakes, but there are no real "villains" in the work. What I found was a fascinating group of people and events. I present them as they were, with no attempts at embellishment. If some appear sympathetic, it's because that is how they were in real life.

This book was made possible by many cooperative and patient individuals. First, I must thank the Lee Family, especially Robert E. Lee IV, for their willingness to help. Mr. Lee maintains his proud legacy in his gentle manner and love of history. The late Senator Omer Lee Hirst of Virginia, was gracious in his first-hand account of the 1926 fire and later events. Mr. Bill Sheads sat down with me and told me about the Ravensworth area of the 1920s. Mr. Lee Hubbard and Mr. Mayo Stuntz shared their memories, and I appreciated their assistance.

There are the contributions of my family in this effort. My son Ryan McQuain Turk, now nine years old, worked alongside his dad in his many hours of writing. In addition to his invaluable assistance on "our book," he enjoys playing soccer and the long walks tracing the old Lee wagon road. My wife Janet allowed me countless hours to research and write. My father Howard Turk, a mystery writer himself, fired my interest in history at an early age. My stepmother Karen is a supportive and creative force, as is evident in my stepbrother Brian, a film editor in Los Angeles who recently worked on episodes of "The Osbornes." My mother Ann is my connection to the first families of Virginia and the American South.

My friends are many and all valued. My cousin, William B. Bayne, Jr., and I ran as boys together. Twenty-six years later we share a love of horse racing and the American way of life. His wife Angie and daughters Lanie, Livie, and Allison are a joy. My longtime friend Sunil Setia has been one of the finest friends one could have; Dave Edwards commiserates with my defeats and cheers my victories. I especially thank the Muse who maintains my inspiration and creative processes. My work is a source of joy to me. As a historian, I am privy to much of my life's pursuits. I must thank my boss, Mr. Don Hines, who understands much of human nature, Mike Pearson, who allows me the opportunities, and my many friends at work: Jim Herzog, Dave Turner, Joseph Band, John Noory, Dave Sacks, Mavis DeZulovich, Nick Prevas, and the great Larry Mogovero. Lastly, I wish to thank Frederick S. Calhoun, my predecessor and mentor in the field of public history. His knowledge and patience in indoctrinating a young student into the fascinating world of history will always be appreciated. These people, and so many more not named, deserve credit for dealing with a sensitive historian who obviously is not above poking fun at himself.

David S. Turk
September 2005

Introduction

The Lee family had successive generations of great statesmen and military men. Through those generations, they acquired artifacts, lands, homes, and reputations. From Thomas Lee's colonial business mind in the mid-1700s until General Robert E. Lee's death in 1870, the family's rapid ascent in national politics and military prominence received national attention. The accumulation of wealth and reputation, passed on to descendants in a changing American society, guarded it. Collectively, the inheritance was both their legacy and their burden. This is the story of how the Lees maintained and guarded their artifacts, lands, homes, and reputations through successive generations.

The general population perceives legacies as an inheritance. The Lee family provided America with an inheritance that took shape in several different forms. General Robert E. Lee's personality, like that of George Washington, transcended art and literature. Busts, plates, and postcards portrayed him as the aging warrior. He was a gentlemanly, gracious soldier--a man seemingly void of demerit. In fact, several modern historical accounts focused on this one aspect of his personality. During the Civil War, he was the cause the southern people rallied behind. Lee's family had a burdensome task of protecting the name and reputation of a man redefined in perpetuity. The difficulty was that each new generation of the family had less in common with the old general. Lee's military gift was a legacy in itself, and someone in the family was bound to inherit it. Another indirect legacy was formed through Lee's marital ties to the Custis and Washington families. Through purchase and inheritance, the Lee family maintained the stewardship of many of Washington's personal objects. The national value of the objects, reputations, and lands were important to generations of Americans.

Human frailty being what it is, most of the Lees gingerly carried the heavy burden of legacy. Appearances showed an ideal aristocratic southern family, yet their letters and lives revealed different attitudes than the genteel deference for which they were famous. Reality was found in the written words of Robert's eldest son, George Washington

Custis Lee, as he described his own deteriorating health. Grandson George Bolling Lee was deposed in several embarrassing court cases to salvage the family fortune. Such examples cast little doubt that the Lees faced the same burdens many upper class southern families did. In fact, they sharecropped their land after the trying times of the Civil War, selling parcels of land to the timber and development industries. They also found their neighborhoods increasingly occupied by poorer neighbors. Without the Antebellum plantation system in place, the Lees suffered as much as the general population.

The legend of the Lee family gave southern families something to take pride in. The "Lost Cause," defined in print by Richmond editor William Pollard, enshrined the Lees. Struggling southerners, some from fine homes, looked to the survival of the Lee bloodline. As its family possessions and homes passed from generation to generation, it reflected on the South's survival as a culture. The Lee heritage was a positive symbol that southerners clung to in the lean years after the Civil War.

The family home was the most accessible legacy of southern pride. Following the Civil War, the Lee family spread across Virginia. However, Mrs. Robert E. Lee spent much of her time at Ravensworth in central Fairfax County, Virginia. Prior to the war, the estate passed through successive generations of her mother's family, the Fitzhughs. The grounds initially contained vast acreage of land for planting tobacco. The estate's glorious rise under the Fitzhugh family lasted through the Civil War, and the house was a centerpiece of Virginia's aristocracy. In its early years, the Custis and the Lee families visited often. A young Robert E. Lee courted Mary Anna Randolph Custis in its gardens. Family members lived and died at Ravensworth. Until the outbreak of the Civil War, the estate represented aristocratic southern life.

War changed the fortunes of the Lees and Ravensworth. The widow proprietor of the mansion, Anna Maria Fitzhugh, defiantly stayed throughout the war. The U.S. government removed certain heirlooms of George Washington from Mrs. Lee's former home, Arlington House. For years, the family fought for the return of the relics. The Arlington House estate was unusable to the family as its grounds had become national cemetery. Due to its location, Ravensworth became the primary seat for the Lee family following the

Civil War, although they also inherited other Virginia estates; the Lees owned the old Custis estate along the Pamunkey River, known as the "White House," and the nearby manor of Romancoke.

By the 1870s, the younger generation of Lees appeared to drift further afield. In 1874, Robert's second son William Henry Fitzhugh Lee, known as "Rooney," inherited Ravensworth from "Aunt Maria." From the onset, Rooney Lee's neighbors rallied around him as a famous celebrity. Rooney's brother Custis ascended to the presidency of Washington and Lee University in his father's stead, while his surviving sisters constantly traveled. Only brother Robert E. Lee, Jr., maintained the same lifestyle as Rooney. Robert, Jr. avoided most comparisons to his father until late in life. He converted his estate at Romancoke into a legitimate family seat, and wrote one of the most complete and accessible volumes of family history.

The family legacy changed direction as Robert E. Lee's children passed away. The precious heirlooms of the family fell to fewer descendants. Rooney's widow, Mary Tabb Lee, extensively added to her own collections in mixing Washington pieces with newer custom-made pieces. Mary Tabb Lee maintained the items for her children, despite the custodianship of a growing number of valuables.

On August 1, 1926, the Lee family legacy permanently changed. The grand manor house at Ravensworth, the prized estate and a chief historical seat of the family, burned. With its demise, the careful construction of its immediate community, along with its associated treasures, was permanently damaged. The fire reminded Americans that heritage was vulnerable. The priceless historical paintings, furniture, porcelain, and other family effects were lost forever.

At the time of the Ravensworth house fire, the Lees found themselves in court battles over a portion of their legacy. Tabb Lee's surviving son, George Bolling Lee, defended the family's control over their heirlooms. As depositions filled the courts, the stakes grew. Lawyers questioned the intent of the Lee family wills. Only the destruction of Ravensworth forced an end to the long court struggles. The surviving heirlooms were scattered, many distributed outside direct family control for the first time.

The burden of legacy fell to other branches of the Lee family. General Fitzhugh Lee became a hero of a reunified nation. By virtue of the Spanish-American conflict in 1898, Lee bridged the old divisions by being both patriotic and southern. He conjured the martial image of his uncle in the American mind. Following his death in 1905, his son Fitzhugh, Jr. emerged as the heir-apparent of the military legacy, serving as an aide to President Theodore Roosevelt. This appointment was one of the last powerful public offices for a Lee. By the time of his retirement in 1939, Fitzhugh Lee, Jr., had faded into the political memories of a changing world.

The Lee family has become a matter of historical interest rather than a political and societal force in the twenty-first Century, yet the living members maintain the deference and style that characterized them from the start. They realized the connections to George Washington and Robert E. Lee were special ones, and because of this they were treasured. New associations and societies were formed in the family's memory, and the ancestral home at Stratford Hall was reopened for eager public eyes. The legacy has passed to the American people through historical societies and museums.

Legacy I: Homes

Burning History

On August 1, 1926, young Omer Lee Hirst observed the reddish night sky. Pillars of smoke were visible in the distance down Braddock's Road. The source of the smoke was Ravensworth mansion, owned by the Lee family.[1]

The residential seat of the Lee and Fitzhugh families was built in the late 1700s by William Fitzhugh, but by 1926 the white painted wood structure was tinder. House fires were commonplace and often hard to extinguish, due to the long distances between volunteer fire units and their inferior equipment. Upon arrival, Alexandria Fire Chief J.M. Duncan found the Lees' neighbor, Kansas Senator Joseph Little Bristow, directing the placement of family items into neat rows on the lawn. He had rushed from his home at nearby Ossian Hall and directed that pictures from the walls of the ground floor be saved first. The heat of the blaze blocked access to the second floor, and smoke permeated the walls and filled the stairs. Shortly thereafter, an entire wing of the house was fully ablaze.[2]

Omer Lee Hirst witnessed the fire from a short distance, watching the blaze with his neighbors and family. The house smouldered for hours. He recounted,

> I was twelve when Ravensworth burned, but I was there. It burned on a Saturday night into Sunday morning. We all piled into the family car. Things were popping here and there. Ashes...hot glowing scraps..."[3]

Douglas Dove, who worked at the estate, arrived a half hour after the fire started. He recalled,

> We couldn't get nothin' out of the main part of the house. We just saved the stuff in the east wing. I don't recall what was saved, they had it all piled out there on the lawn. I helped carry that stuff out. There was a lot of people there helpin'

out. Mr. [Segessenman], he was a Swiss fella that lived in the neighborhood, he was there and he kinda took over and told people what to do and watched us.[4]

Bristow, Duncan, and Segessenman did their best. Many artifacts formerly belonging to Robert E. Lee and President George Washington were saved from destruction. Duncan and the other men could do little else but contain the fire within a zone.[5]

Many items connected to American history were lost that night, and the nation suffered for it. The owner of the house, Doctor George Bolling Lee, was in New York with his family. Ravensworth was a little-used summer residence, although still a treasured architectural gem that the family visited for a few weeks every year. During their absence, Nelson was employed as the caretaker of the estate. The grounds functioned as a horse and dairy farm and George Bolling Lee bred horses there.[6]

Although a diminished estate with absentee owners, Ravensworth had remained the centerpiece of its community, and its loss shocked the surrounding community. Once a visual masterpiece, the flamed-licked brick chimneys stood surrounded by heaps of charred ruin. The bed where General Robert E. Lee died was a casualty. A few outbuildings, such as the stables, escaped the flames.[7]

Upon hearing that his house burned, Doctor Lee rushed to Virginia from New York. In appreciation of his neighbors' efforts, he published a note of thanks in the local newspaper, *The Fairfax Herald*.

> Through the Fairfax Herald, I wish to extend my sincere thanks to each and everyone who assisted in saving from complete destruction many portraits and other effects from the house at Ravensworth the night of the fire. I am deeply grateful to them and also to innumerable friends inVirginia, and elewhere, from whom I have received expressions of sympathy.
>
> GEORGE BOLLING LEE[8]

The old Ravensworth mansion was irreplaceable, and Doctor Lee did not rebuild it. Instead, he erected a smaller frame house on the property to serve as the family's summer residence. Soon Doctor Lee returned to New York, and the rescued oil portraits painted by members of the Peale family, and most of the antique silver, was neatly packed and shipped to Alexandria. With a reduced estate, Nelson continued to care for the property.[9]

The estate's caretaker, Andrew Nelson, experienced his second house fire in one week, having lost his own house the previous Monday. Nineteen-year-old dairy farm worker Russell Wood had sounded the alarm in that case, allowing Nelson enough time to escape. The thin gap in time between the first blaze and the burning of Ravensworth was noted by the *Fairfax Herald* that it "makes all the stranger the suspicion that the fire was of an incendiary origin."[10]

A search began for the fire's origins. Official inquiries were opened by the Fairfax County Police, which studied Fire Chief Duncan's report. Two deputies, Haywood Davis and Virgil Williams, conducted inquiries at the request of the Commonwealth's Attorney Wilson W. Farr. The young prosecutor barely returned from a vacation to receive the news of the fire. For some days, the two officers questioned Nelson, Wood, and others. From their inquiries, they discerned that the fire started in the attic at about 1:30 a.m. on Sunday morning. Several hours later, Russell F. Wood was arrested in connection with the fire.[11]

It appeared the case was closed. Wood was held in the Fairfax County Jail, but the investigation mysteriously began to unravel. As suddenly as he was apprehended, Wood was released. Chief Duncan's report disappeared from the files, and the official inquiries were purged. There was a discernible silence about the fire. Following Wood's release, the fire was treated as an accident. The August 6th *Fairfax Herald* reported there was no connection between Wood and the Ravensworth fire.[12]

The Land of Fitzhugh: Ravensworth and its Beginnings

The fire essentially ended the symbolic relationship between the Lees and Ravensworth. From the very beginning, the southern family's interconnected society was symbolized by several divisions.

Their ancestors sub-divided their land between heirs or a family line simply died out. In the case of the Fitzhugh family, both happened. In a society where bloodlines determined the settlement of large tracts of land, the Lees survived the large number of divisions and produced generations of heirs. The Ravensworth estate, or the southern portion of the original tract, made a family passage of possession from Fitzhugh to Lee. The land was carved from a large grant to John Mathews in April 1684. In turn, the tract was sold to Colonel William Fitzhugh of Stafford County, Virginia, in August 1685. The original Fitzhugh purchaser was the son of a woolen draper, but a sharp businessman. The large tract of land, one of the largest grants in the region, was near water and conducive to the growing of tobacco. "Rolling Roads," which were little more than pathways cut in the forest to access ships in the rivers, provided a ready route to market.[13]

William Fitzhugh shipped tobacco to Europe as early as April 1686. Shortly after, he leased some of his land to French Huguenots, and stated:

> 150 or 200 familys upon one Dividend wch contains 21,996 acres, which I will either sell them in fee at 17 (pounds sterling) for every hundred acres, or else lease it to them for three lives paying 20 shillings per annum for every hundred acres...[14]

His success was slower than expected, and by 1690, Fitzhugh accepted less money or a hogshead of tobacco a year as payment from the settlers. Despite these incentives, many of the French Huguenots departed for lands in Maryland.[15]

Upon his death in 1701, a 22,000 acre estate was split between the Colonel's two sons: William and Henry. Henry took the northerly tract, and William the southern. The 1701 inheritance proved a permanent split, and the land was further dispersed over the years. Neither brother lived on the large holdings, renting segments of the land to a number of tenant farmers. Colonel Henry Fitzhugh's surviving ledgers included Ravensworth's rents for the years 1759 and 1764. The number of renters in the northern section of Ravensworth were numbered at 43.[16]

Aside from renting lands, the Fitzhughs planted the seeds of their residential seats. Several large estate houses were constructed on the northern tract. The first was built about 1779 and called "Oak Hill." A second manor house, later called "Ossian Hall," was built in 1783. Henry's son Nicholas was the first Fitzhugh family member to move permanently to the land. However, there were four other brothers who owned a slice of the northern tract. Richard, Mordecai, Battaile, and Giles Fitzhugh each received about 2,000 acres. This was the beginning of the inevitable outcome--the northern tract's disappearance from family hands.[17]

Unlike the fate of the northern lands, the southern tract of the estate had a history of concentrated ownership. Henry Fitzhugh's cousin was William of Chatham, named for a distant house he owned near the town of Falmouth, opposite Fredericksburg on the Rappahanock River. He moved his primary residence from this location to the 9,000 acre southern tract of Ravensworth. Known for his business acumen as well as his one blind eye, William Fitzhugh's move was motivated by profit of the tobacco trade. By living on the tract, he personally supervised the cultivation of the fertile product in Northern Virginia. About the year 1796, construction began on the new mansion that would be called Ravensworth.[18]

Lee descendant and writer Eleanor Lee Templeman remarked the new structure at Ravensworth was "exceedingly handsome." Of its early appearance, she wrote,

> It was...approached through an oak park where peacocks flashed their brilliant plumage. To the south or "family side," the open view from the slight elevation stretched above the box-lined flower beds into the countryside, and caught the summer breezes. The wide, pillared, two-story verandas which extended the entire length of the house were decorated with tubs of tropical shrubs and flowers from the conservatory...The spacious rooms were about twenty-seven feet square.[19]

William moved his wife, Anne Randolph Fitzhugh, and his young family to the house. A woven family sampler made from this period documented the presence of three daughters and a son. Martha Carter Fitzhugh died at the age of seven; Anne married lawyer William Craik of Maryland in 1800; Mary Lee Fitzhugh married young George Washington Parke Custis, the President's step-son, in July 1804. The only son of the union, William Henry Fitzhugh, was born in March 1792.[20]

Mary Lee Fitzhugh proved a suitable mate for the spendthrift George W.P. Custis. Prior to his marriage, George Washington Parke Custis spent a considerable sum collecting the personal effects of his step-father, regarding their importance to his family heritage as paramount. A second large purchase was the grand estate overlooking the Potomac River, called Arlington. George W.P. Custis had little interest in a career with the military or the practice of law. Instead he became a gentleman farmer. Mary's money management skills saved her husband from deepening debts, and she gave birth to the only surviving child of the union, Mary Anne Fitzhugh Custis, born in 1807. Mary Custis would eventually marry her cousin, Robert E. Lee.[21]

In contrast to her sister, Anne Randolph Craik was mentioned little in existing records. One remark written by her cousin Maria Calvert castigated her as a "fool."[22] She was probably undeserving of the characterization; Maria Calvert was not fond of her other Fitzhugh relations either. Anne married into the family of President Washington's physician, placing her in high standing. Tragically, she died suddenly near Martinsburg, Virginia in September 1806. Descriptions of the details of Ann Craik's death highlighted its unexpected nature.

> This lady had accompanied her husband to Bath for the benefit of his health. Soon after their arrival there she was attacked by symptoms of nervous fever which induced them to endeavor to return, but by the time-they had reached Martinsburg..in defiance of every possible exertion of medical skill, the irresistible mandate of death summoned her...[23]

There were no children of this union. Her widowed husband William

Craik received a tract of land adjacent to the property of Ravensworth in the Spring of 1807. This tract remained in the Craik family until 1836.[24]

Upon the death of old William Fitzhugh in 1809, the heirs of Mary and Anne each received 800 acres of the family's southern tract. The bulk of the vast estate was left to his 18-year-old son, William Henry Fitzhugh.[25] The younger Fitzhugh was an ambitious man, well versed in Virginia politics. He married into an upper class Maryland family when he took Anna Maria Goldsborough as his bride. In July 1813, William Henry wrote his sister Mary at Arlington with undisguised glee,

> Rejoice, my dear Sister, in your brother's fortune --An angel has consented to unite her destiny with his--And from her father, he has this morning received the final sanction of his hopes--I can not join you until they leave Washington...God bless you & make you as happy as your Brother.[26]

The family further increased its local ties upon Fitzhugh's marriage to Anna Maria Goldsborough on January 11, 1814. His father-in-law, Charles Goldsborough, was a former Maryland governor and state delegate. Anna Maria's grandfather was the Attorney General of Maryland and a member of the American Constitutional Convention. Although the couple had no children, they adopted Anna Maria's relative Mary Caroline Goldsborough and delighted in the numerous visits of relatives. William Henry Fitzhugh sympathized when his cousin, Ann Carter Lee, was abandoned in Alexandria after her husband, General Henry "Light-Horse Harry" Lee, left the family for the West Indies. She became a frequent guest at Ravensworth over the next fifteen years.[27]

The young Fitzhughs established Ravensworth as a grand estate. By 1812, they expanded the house and its garden to greater proportions. The estate was modeled into a working farm with a number of supporting outbuildings. Well-to-do relatives with their children in tow visited often. Anne Carter Lee brought her children, including a young Robert Edward Lee, to see her generous relatives. William's sister, Mary Lee Custis, brought her young daughter Mary from Arlington.[28] A largely fictional account of the Lee family, Marguerite Vance's *The Lees of Arlington*, provides a commendable if somewhat enhanced portrait of a visit to Ravensworth.

> "Welcome, welcome to *Ravensworth*," he [William H. Fitzhugh] greeted them, taking Mary's place at Mrs. Lee's side. Then, "Luke--Horace--Ben--here, all of you, come take the bags, and you, Nat, tell th' boys down at th' stable to fix you up with whatever you need for yourself or the horses."[29]

Vance's work noted the presence of slaves at Ravensworth. William Henry Fitzhugh's concern over slavery led to his membership in the American Colonization Society. Founded in 1816 by a group of like-minded gentlemen including his cousin, Robert H. Goldsborough, Judge Bushrod Washington, and politician Charles Fenton Mercer, the Society encouraged the mass movement and resettlement of slaves to Africa. Fitzhugh ascended to the Vice Presidency of the organization in the 1820s. His dedication to the ideal of colonization was noted by South Carolinian John C. Calhoun in 1828 In his last will, William Henry Fitzhugh wanted all his slaves freed by the year 1850; however, his family found that wish to be unrealistic. Four years after Fitzhugh's death that he saw two remedies for the evils of slavery: sell the slaves as a group for the best price obtained or send a partial number to a large plantation and buy them lots of land to farm.[30]

> The objections to the former are, that, conduct the transaction in the gentlest manner you can, it is, inevitably to a certain degree inhumane & offensive to ones own feelings. It cannot be effected without violence, and without handcuffs & chains...The latter involves no violation of humanity. Remaining the property of their present master, there is no possible severance of connection...To them the removal is just the same as the emigration of any poor white family seeking their fortune in the Southern or Western Country.[31]

After a debilitating illness, Ann Carter Lee died at Ravensworth in 1829 and was buried on the estate. Robert E. Lee painfully remembered the event toward the end of his life. Following the death of his Uncle Sydney Smith Lee, Robert E. Lee, Jr. wrote that his famous father stood at the room where his own mother passed away "and said to one present: 'forty years ago, I stood in this room by my mother's death-bed! It seems now but yesterday!'"[32]

Robert's oldest brother, Charles Carter Lee, continued his mother's tradition of staying for long periods at the estate. When not lodging there, he corresponded with Anna Maria Fitzhugh. The writing between them spanned for decades. A young Charles Carter Lee penned one of his first poems to William Henry Fitzhugh.

> Now as in savage time the mead of fame
> Crowns those who slaughter beasts or monsters
> tame, but when security surrounds a state
> Teachers of wisdom & the arts are great...
> Or other fragrant blossom which the dew slip
> Or seen the glow of cousin Anna's two-lips.[33]

William Henry Fitzhugh blossomed as a politician and farmer, yet his health was poor. In the 1820s, he was named as a possible Virginia gubernatorial candidate. Sensing his rising fortune, he participated in the Virginia Constitutional Convention in 1829-30 and worked feverishly in leadership roles for the proceedings. Exhausted after the convention adjourned in early 1830, Fitzhugh visited his wife's relatives in Cambridge, Maryland. He died unexpectedly in May, shortly after his arrival. Charles Goldsborough wrote a short letter describing Fitzhugh's death to Charles Carter Lee.[34]

> Dear Sir--
>
> We have sustained, suddenly, & unexpectedly
> without a moment's warning to prepare us for it..
> in the loss of our most dear & valued friend Mr.
> Fitzhugh-He was taken from us in friday morning
> the 21st Inst. at my house, almost in a moment,
> by an attack which the physicians presumed to

have been apoplexy...All is grief and confusion here.³⁵

The terms of William Henry Fitzhugh's will gave his widow life tenancy at the Ravensworth Mansion. The bulk of his estate went to his sister Mary Lee Custis. By doing so, the Lees became the eventual heirs of Ravensworth. Aside from the Lees, her Goldsborough relatives visited regularly. Her father supported her greatly until his own death on December 15, 1834.³⁶

One of the most frequent visitors to Ravensworth was Mary Anne Custis. She grew up at nearby Arlington House overlooking the District of Columbia on the opposite side of the Potomac River, and her "Aunt Maria" hosted a honeymoon visit after Mary Anne's marriage to Lieutenant Robert E. Lee of the U.S. Engineers in July 1831. Soon after their visit, the young couple began a family in 1832 with the birth of George Washington Custis Lee. Six more children followed: William Henry Fitzhugh Lee, Mary Custis Lee, Agnes, Robert E. Lee, Jr., Annie, and Mildred.³⁷ Ravensworth became a primary recreational destination for the Lee family. One daughter of Robert and Mary Lee, Agnes, kept a diary to track her daily activities. Her entry of August 6, 1853 stated:

> We returned yesterday from Ravensworth. Last Wed. evening Pa, Ma, Rob & I started for R--- arrived about six. Rob & I immediately set out for the rock & ran all over over the garden. The pangs of hunger assailed us sorely on our return but we were soon gratified by a most excellent supper.³⁸

In addition to her Lee relations, Mrs. Fitzhugh welcomed friends of her neighborhood. Ossian Hall, a home built on what was formerly the northern tract of the property, was occupied by Francis Asbury Dickins and his family. Considered part of the area's estate aristocracy, the Dickins family enjoyed a cordial relationship with Maria Fitzhugh. Mrs. Dickins was from the Randolph family, another revered name in Virginia. Existing letters revealed the class and community bonds between these two families of the area aristocracy.³⁹

My dear Mrs. Dickins,
   I had intended to prepare to Mrs. Lee to walk over with me this afternoon to Ossian Hall but the arrival of more company to dinner prevented our doing — I am again alone, but it is too late to go--It is long since I heard anything of you--I hope you are all well...I have had the stile put up opposite the point where you fit into the road & it is all dry now...If you will come, may let it be early & consider it entirely an informal visitation, you will find us almost altogether...I hope it is not one of Mr. Dickins Washington days, and that he will be disposed to join you--tell Miss Clara that I am sorry her acquaintance Eliza Kerr is not here, but she will find some wild little boys...[40]

The letter highlighted several points of interest. The first, and most obvious, was the ease and friendly nature of the Fitzhugh and Lee households to others. Far from isolated, they reached out to other families surrounding them. The "wild little boys" were none other than George Washington Custis Lee and his brother William Henry Fitzhugh Lee, aged eleven and six respectively. Another point of interest was more stylistic in nature. There was the mention of a "stile" in the letter, an allusion to an entry turnstile built along the estate's front fence, which was painted a bright red color. The fixture existed for many years, but this letter was the first written evidence of its time of construction. Neighbors remembered the unusual feature several generations later.[41]

   Despite neighborly connections, the 1850s and 1860s brought tragedy to the Lees. Both of Mrs. Lee's parents died--her mother in April 1853 followed by her father four years later. As it happened, the Lees resided at Arlington House only four more years. As the nation prepared for war in early 1861, Colonel Lee sided with his home state of Virginia rather than with the Federal Government. The Union forces contemplated the capture of Arlington Heights as an appropriate safety measure to protect Washington, D.C., and when Robert E. Lee left to join the Confederate army, Mrs. Lee took refuge with Maria Fitzhugh at Ravensworth. Despite the convictions of her relations, Mrs. Fitzhugh considered herself a Unionist and incorrectly assumed the military would simply pass her home. After a short time it was not considered safe for Mrs. Lee and her children at Ravensworth, and they moved on to Richmond for the duration of the war.[42]

As a Confederate general, Robert E. Lee rose to the heights of military fame in the South, and one of his three sons distinguished himself as a horse soldier. Although oldest son Custis served as aide to Confederate President Jefferson Davis, his second son William H. Fitzhugh, or "Rooney" Lee, became a cavalry general. His military career began after an 1854 visit to New York, which encouraged the young man to attend Harvard University. While he was a student, General Winfield Scott secured his appointment in the 6th U.S. Infantry Regiment. Rooney Lee was assigned to Colonel Albert Sidney Johnston, who later served as commander of the Confederate forces in Tennessee and the West for the first years of the Civil War. During his prewar service, Rooney spent time in Texas and Utah. In 1859, he married his cousin Charlotte Wickham and retired to civilian life.[43]

Rooney Lee abandoned the military life for a short time. In 1860, he raised his own volunteer cavalry company, known as "The Lee Rangers." Upon the outbreak of the Civil War, Rooney Lee joined his father in the mountains of Virginia and steadily rose in the ranks. By April 1862, he was Colonel of the 9th Virginia Cavalry. During the Seven Days Campaign in the summer of 1862, Rooney led his cavalry around Richmond as part of General Jeb Stuart's force. The force completely circled Union General George B. McClellan's entire army, although the young Lee was captured shortly after the fabled event.[44]

In Rooney Lee's absence, his relations paid a terrible cost. One of his homes was set afire by advancing Federals. Two infant children died, followed by the illness and death of his wife Charlotte on December 26, 1863. It likely explained Rooney's willingness to take personal risks in battle.[45]

Arlington House was another war casualty to the Lee family. The house was quickly occupied by Union troops in 1861. Some family heirlooms usually kept under lock and key at Arlington House were taken to the Patent Office in Washington as war trophies by the Union soldiers. As a final degradation to its owners, the property became a national cemetery.[46] The disgust of the family was related by Mary Lee to her friend Mary Macon.

> ...Rob stays with us & his grandpa brought him a likeness of himself...framed & I gave him my first oil painting sent from Arlington with other <u>debris</u> of what the Yankees had left of an once happy & well filled home upon the receipt of those two pictures...several boxes of old letters have also come & it is so sad to destroy the records of those bright & happier times...[47]

The Lees never resided at Arlington again. They focused their attentions to their numerous other land holdings. Miraculously, Ravensworth was spared the torch during the fighting. Many visitors stopped at the estate on their way to Richmond. Although largely shut inside the estate, the widow Fitzhugh experienced some contact with nearby Union forces throughout the Civil War. When she ventured out to Alexandria by carriage in the summer of 1861, there was an alarm that Confederate troops were streaming north in the aftermath of the First Battle of Manassas. She was temporarily refused a pass to her own residence. When she finally arrived, she found soldiers quartered at the house. They vanished the following day. Only Mrs. Dickins visited on a regular basis during the war.[48]

During the Civil War's first winter Union troops camped nearby and chopped down a good many trees. Anna Maria Fitzhugh was irritated by their brash actions, and contacted the commanding officer. She insisted that she was loyal to the Union, and that removal of her wood was not a friendly act. The troops stopped cutting for a time, then resumed when the officer asserted a great need for the cords. In turn, she was promised payment for the wood.[49]

Mrs. Fitzhugh depended on neighbors and friends for her vital needs for the remainder of the Civil War. George Burke, her friend and agent, saw to her needs until his own death on October 20, 1864. Thereafter a tenant farmer named Alfred Bayless took Burke's charge.

One of her former neighbors, County Justice Daniel W. Lewis, administered the Oath of Allegiance to Mrs. Fitzhugh at Ravensworth and considered her a loyal citizen.[50]

Lee Family resided in several places after the war, but always remained close to Maria Fitzhugh and Ravensworth. Robert E. Lee accepted the presidency of small Washington College in Lexington, Virginia. Robert E. Lee, Jr. moved to a tidewater farm named Romancoke, located near Rooney's "White House" property in King William County, Virginia. Despite their distance, the Lee family visited back and forth frequently.[51] Rooney Lee wrote in June 1870 that he would "...go to Alexa to see my Aunt Mrs Fitzhugh who is too infirm to come to me & who is anxious for me to come to her once more."[52] Robert E. Lee visited Maria Fitzhugh several times until his death. When the old hero arrived, he always drew a crowd. His son Robert, Jr. wrote,

> So many of his friends called upon him at Mrs. Fitzhugh's that it was arranged to have a reception for him at the Mansion House. For three hours a constant stream of visitors poured into the parlours. The reception was the greatest ovation that any individual had received from the people of Alexandria since the days of Washington.[53]

On November 28, 1867, Rooney Lee married Mary Tabb Bolling of Petersburg, Virginia. She was the daughter of George W. Bolling and his wife Martha Nicholls. "Tabb," as she was often affectionately called, was an energetic woman who made a fine companion for Lee. The Bollings of Petersburg were from Virginia aristocratic stock, and her father was pivotal in Reconstruction politics after the close of the Civil War. Robert E. Lee wrote to his son from Lexington with some premarital advice. Given the impending nuptials, the old scion pointedly wrote Rooney not to tend the estates prior to his wedding, as "You & Robt; Could hardly pay the necessary attention to business matters, with your heads filled with love & matrimony."[54] On February 11, 1869, Robert Edward Lee III, "Bob," was born at Petersburg. Three years later, on August 30, 1872, George Bolling Lee, or "Bolly," was born in Lexington, Virginia.[55]

The inevitability of death was obvious to Robert E. Lee. He weakened after years of war and worried for a beloved wife crippled by arthritis. General Lee died in Lexington on October 12, 1870. Following the death of her daughter Agnes in 1873, Mary Custis Lee longed for a last view of her old home at Arlington. A carriage from Ravensworth carried her to the former estate, yet she would not enter the grounds. She died shortly thereafter on November 5, 1873.[56]

Like her niece Mary Custis, the final years of Anna Maria Fitzhugh's life were filled with declining health and admiring visitors, suffering a number of serious rheumatic attacks during 1869. General Lee remarked in a letter to his wife in July 1870 that,

> I arrived here yesterday from Alexandria and found Aunt Maria well in general health, but less free to walk than when I last saw her. She is cheerful and quiet, but seem indisposed to try any of the healing baths, or, indeed, any of the remedies resorted to in cases of similar character, and seems to think nothing will be of avail. I hope in time that she will be relieved.[57]

In November 1870, Anna Maria Fitzhugh filed a federal claim for the timber cut during the war's first winter. She asked for three dollars per cord with a total claim amounting to $375,000. She received no satisfaction to her initial claim, so she applied again in May 1872 with the newly-formed Southern Claims Commission, which considered claims of loss to loyal citizens during the Civil War. The Commission questioned her connection to the Lees, noting her heir apparent was Mary Custis Lee. Mrs. Fitzhugh became flustered over the severity of the questions, and she cut short the question if she thought the interrogation too intense. She insisted she was loyal, and she denounced "two republics in one country." The issue was still in dispute until long after Mrs. Fitzhugh's death, three years after the testimony of a former Union soldier confirmed the claim.[58]

The Commission's questions stemmed from Anna Maria Fitzhugh's will. The document was written at Ravensworth and dated August 23, 1870. Anna Maria Fitzhugh formalized her intentions, stating that her niece Mary Lee inherited her "present residence at

Ravensworth, and I add to it whatever furniture, books, & c., may be in the house at the time of my death..."[59] The complexity of the inheritance issue intensified when Mrs. Lee died. Rooney Lee inherited the estate despite his ownership of the "White House" property. Custis remained in Lexington, although he was the eldest son. A transition of legacy came with the inheritance. After almost sixty years of residence at Ravensworth, Anna Maria Fitzhugh passed away in April 1874.[60]

Setting Up at Ravensworth

Within four years, the three elders of the Lee family were deceased. Rooney Lee arrived to find an efficient estate. For the first few years, his wife Tabb primarily stayed at the White House estate. The new proprietor of Ravensworth wrote meticulously, and he immediately informed Tabb about their new neighbors. From the existing letters, Rooney Lee was an observant writer who accurately described the happenings around him.

> I have been getting on very well-under the circumstances-visiting my neighbours-Herbert and his wife have been very attentive-and now Dickens has been over to see me-Mrs. Dickens was a Miss Randolph-Ella Poldestar's niece and says she is very anxious to see you-will take care of you...[61]

In 1874, the Dickins family of Ossian Hall included the parents and three older children: Frank, Randolph, and Albert. Patriarchal lawyer Francis Asbury Dickins supported civic works at the budding Annandale church. He kept an active journal and, in October 1872, he wrote of a dream he had.

> Had a dream that Margaret [his wife] and I were in a desperate situation and the only possibility of escape was to make the horse we were on jump off a high precipice into a stream of water, it appeared hopeless Margaret said 'don't do it' but

> I said said God have mercy on us and dashed over
> fell much hurt, saw Margaret a short distance
> bleeding by not seriously hurt...[62]

Oddly, the dream proved prophetic six years later. Francis Asbury Dickins fell from his horse, and died from internal injuries. With the death of Dickins on October 27, 1879 one of the large landowners vanished from the area.[63]

Changes in the Fitzhugh family created more divisions in the original land tract. By the 1870s, many of the "northern tract" Fitzhughs faded away. Following the death of large landowner Richard Fitzhugh, the divided tracts passed through many hands. H.A. White obtained 497 acres in the easternmost portion of the tract, while other land allotments passed to Berkley Ward; William M. Fitzhugh; David Fitzhugh; Maria M. Fitzhugh; and Ann Fitzhugh Battaile. A large number of lawsuits between the members of the Fitzhugh family ensued in the mid-1850s, further devaluing the family holdings.[64]

David Fitzhugh, who was held as a suspected Confederate sympathizer in the Old Capitol Prison during the Civil War, died in 1868. This reopened legal challenges from the other heirs. In the fall of 1869, Ann F. Battaile moved from her residence in Culpeper, Virginia, to her portion of the Ravensworth tract, which contained the Oak Hill mansion. The tract also contained some extra old outbuildings. The prolonged legal tangles resulted in financial difficulty, which in turn meant the Battailes sold portions of the property. Oak Hill mansion became vacant for a time after the family moved into an old schoolhouse on the property.[65] By 1875, desperate times were evident in the writings of Ann's daughter Sue, who wrote a local grocer,

> My Dear Mrs. Watts,
>
> please lend me one dollar for a few days, as I have
> no provision in the house of any kind I will sell
> my interest in my corn crop in a day or two and
> pay you up faithfully. I paid paid [sic] up before
> when you lent me a dollar--and please sell me a
> lb of butter <u>fresh butter</u>...in my deep affliction and

distress of mind I will die if I go without food any longer.[66]

Other Fitzhughs in the "northern tract" fared little better. Union troops encamped on Edwin Fitzhugh's property near the Little River Turnpike. In the spring of 1862, General Winfield S. Hancock's men pulled bricks for their own use from the foundation, eventually causing the house to collapse.[67] Ms. Dolly Fitzhugh resided at Cool Spring, the fourth Fitzhugh home on the original tract. In March 1878, she asked attorney Thomas R. Love if her father was entitled to "the Balance of the Legacy left him by Uncle David Fitzhugh, if so, would it be possible for you to arrange so that even a small amount might be given him at this time."[68] She remarked that the family wished to supplement their house with boarders "during the coming season...we will be oblige to make some provision absolutely necessary for their accommodation."[69] Attorney Love responded with bad news. He noted a large sum was previously paid to her father, but debtors obtained judgments to divert money from the Fitzhughs to satisfy liens.[70]

Further changes in the neighborhood occurred on the western border of the Ravensworth estate. Upton Herbert purchased a large tract of land in 1852, building his own stately home on the acreage. "Bleak House," named for the title of a Charles Dickens novel, was occupied by its owners for just a few years. Herbert was a secessionist during the Civil War, and he moved into Mount Vernon, acquired from the Washington family two years before.[71]

The lives of the Lee family while separated was well documented. Mrs. Lee traveled frequently between their two estates. Both of Rooney Lee's children, Bob and George Bolling (known as Bolly), regularly wrote their mother while she was on extended visits throughout Virginia. Like his father Rooney, eleven-year-old Bob was a prolific and insightful correspondent. He wrote often to his mother, as when describing his experiences in February 1880.

> I hope you are having a nice time. I am sorry papa and yourself are sick, but I hope you will soon be well. George was eleven years old last Thursday. The ground is covered with snow here.

> We miss you very much here at Ravensworth.
> ...I thank you for my birth-day basket I have not
> got it yet. We went to church yesterday it was
> communion Sunday. Bolly will tell you about
> the ice-house. Miss Fanny says the doves she
> spoke of were hawks when you left, but were
> only in the chrysalis state; after the transformation
> scene, they come out gentle turtle doves, and still
> remain...[72]

Young Bob's writings often took a humorous turn, as when he related that his brother was making "sliced animals" on the floor of the house, and that "Bo just now he jumped on the arm chair and it tumbled over on the floor with him he said O!"[73] In one of the many communications, the boys wrote of the interaction with servants on the Ravensworth estate. Bob wrote,

> We miss you very much here at Ravensworth...
> Bolly will tell you about the ice-house. Miss
> Fanny says the doves she spoke of were hawks
> when you left, but were only in the chrysalis
> state; after the transformation scene, they came
> out gentle turtle doves, and still remain so, which
> she hopes they will continue to do at least until
> your return.[74]

Their young foreign-born coachman, Andrew Nelson, was included in Rooney's letters to Tabb. Despite his marriageable age, the pursuit of a wife proved awkward for the servant. Rooney was sympathetic when he wrote Tabb in late March 1881,

> Yesterday was a beautiful day...so springlike that
> we thought Winter had completely gone...to find
> it snowing hard this morning when Robbie went
> off to school. <u>He</u> was well wrapped up and went
> off as cheerily as ever...Two postals for you
> yesterday, one from your Mama - and one from
> Miss Fanny..Poor Andrew is doing all he can. I

> really feel sorry for the boy. And he seems very sad. So much for making a fool of one's self! Ladies do not know the sensation-as they never do anything that is foolish!!!⁷⁵

In his reports to Tabb, Rooney Lee revealed much of his own kindly character. Two days later he again wrote Tabb, commenting on the Methodist Church in nearby Annandale.

> We are getting on-as well as we could hope-with <u>you away</u>. Yesterday Rob & Bolly [George Bolling Lee], with Andrew as coachman, went to Annandale to hear the new Methodist preacher. It was a blustering cold day, and the church was not crowded as far as I could gather...The boys are very good, and getting on very nicely. Bolly goes down into the green house every morning and attends to the flowers.⁷⁶

As with Nelson, Rooney was kind to his laborers. When an employee named Burles suddenly departed without notice, then reappeared after a month with no money, Lee advanced him a month's wages. The growing dependence on the salaried servants was indicative of a change in social trends. The "new settlers" during this period, or small farming families, took the place of the "large tract" owners such as the Dickins family in most activities. However, the small landowners dovetailed into the carefully-constructed social structure of the Lees. Large clusters of newly-arrived Europeans specialized in a trade. The Swiss Segessenman family specialized in gardening. The Irish-born family of Michael Coffey ran a dry goods store in nearby Annandale. Omer Hirst recalled their house farther up Braddock Road as "an old structure--clapboards over logs."⁷⁷

Following the Civil War, a number of small farmers settled near the Lee's community circle. One such farm was owned by the Newmans, an African-American family. Farmer John Newman lived with his wife Lilly and three children. Farmer Owen Jones and his family of seven rented their house. Their reverence for the Lees was evident in naming their youngest child Bolling. Neighboring the Jones family was schoolteacher William Watt, a Scottish immigrant. His wife Elizabeth sold dry goods to a mixed class clientele which included the Lees.[78]

As much as Rooney Lee enjoyed life at Ravensworth, he dutifully traveled to promote the family heritage. His brother Custis remained in Lexington as President of Washington and Lee University, so second son Rooney carried out many of the ceremonial duties exampled by the presentation of a remembrance flag in the Military Hall in Charleston, South Carolina in February 1878. His notable speech on this occasion foreshadowed a career in politics.

> In accepting your invitation please be assured of my grateful appreciation of the kind sentiments expressed therein for one whose highest ambition was to serve his country, in her time of need, and whose heart, in the days of her humiliation and sorrow, had no throb not in sympathy with his suffering countrymen. I shall look forward with great pleasure to my visit to your battle-scarred city, being certain of a hearty welcome, as among your citizens I shall meet many comrades who followed Jackson and rode with Hampton in the memorable campaigns in Virginia.[79]

While Rooney Lee carried on the family legacy, his sister Mary Custis Lee traveled extensively, often accompanying her sister Mildred on adventurous and sometimes harrowing journeys. A tour in 1879 stopped in Norway during the summer; aboard a ship in the Arctic Circle, Mildred penned a description of the friendly people of the area.

> Mary & I are travelling alone, & are both in a wretched cabin together-we live on fish, & are generally uncomfortable - but we are amply compensated by the wonders of this strange Arctic [sic] land. We crossed the Arctic Circle yesterday - does it make you shiver to hear of it! I have already seen some Laplanders...As we

cannot go further, that being the most northern
point of land in the world, we turn our faces
southward then, & return to see the rest of
Norway - travelling in Carrioles (?) driving
ourselves, & carrying our own provender. So
you see this journey is not child's play, especially
in a country where we speak not a word of this
language. But the Norwegians are the most
polite & honest people in the world - & so we
have no trouble.[80]

Coachman Andrew Nelson and his brother were recruited from neighboring Sweden on a visit by Mary and Mildred. In 1881, seventeen-year-old Nelson became an American citizen.[81] Andrew's presence and duties increased in Rooney's correspondence. While visiting the Bollings in Petersburg, he wrote his wife:

send the wagon for me Thursday night to meet
the said-night train-let them leave the house at
12 ½ m-and build a fire-nor close the road-Let
Andrew go down-I will leave Thursday at 12 pm..."[82]

Rooney Lee was the political heir to his father's legacy. After serving several terms in the Virginia House of Delegates, he represented the state's eighth district in the Fiftieth Congress in 1885. He served two additional terms, in the elections of 1888 and 1890. One of his colleagues commented,

[Lee was] as true to his constituents as any subject
to his sovereign, laboring in season and out of
season to serve them, and even when his strong
frame began to weaken and the germs of disease
had been planted in his system he disregarded
the warning calls for rest and continued to bend all
his energies in the discharge of his trust, and I but
speak the truth when I say that he fell a martyr to
duty.[83]

Another colleague remarked that Lee was called out to talk, or "carded out a dozen times" per day, and he showed remarkable patience at the large number of constituents demanding his time. To ease the tensions often present in Capitol debates, Lee brought large bunches of flowers from Ravensworth's garden to distribute among the members. Representative Joseph Washington of Tennessee remarked on Rooney Lee's efficient guidance on a bill for the relief of Alexandria's Episcopal High School. In doing so, he utilized his father's oft-used tactic of quiet persuasion. In convincing the most boisterous detractors to the bill, his speech made up in substance what it lacked in rhetoric.[84] However effective, the years of Congress wore hard on Rooney Lee. He was afflicted by a series of illnesses in the summer of 1891. His once-athletic frame was gone, and his busy schedule offered little time for exercise. Rooney's rich diet aged him more than his actual 54 years. He died on October 15, 1891 at the same age that his father took command of the Confederate army. His pastor wrote of the things most important to the patriarch.

> Of his home life, it is too sacred to speak. It was simply beautiful. He lived for his family. All, including the servants, were devoted to him. His reading of family prayers before breakfast was very impressive. Sunday nights, after tea, he liked to hear the old hymns sung...[85]

A Centered Society

Rooney Lee's death came at a time of new arrivals at Ravensworth, but the event evoked sympathy and enduring respect from the family's small farm neighbors. Ravensworth and its residents remained the centerpiece of the community despite the passing of the patriarch; they became societal curiosities. The new occupants of the surrounding tracts interacted even more with the Lees. They worked, sold goods, tended the mansion's gardens, or attended church services with the family members. The local newspapers reported on the Lees and their neighbors. The society pages wrote about the family with more frequency, including reporting the numerous guests to Ravensworth. At times, the stories took a fantasy quality, and were often embellished by the press. For example, the *Fairfax Herald* observed a northern paper's erroneous report that "Genl. Robert E. Lee was a cousin of Abraham Lincoln...is denied emphatically by members of the Lee family."[86]

The Lee family promoted commerce in the growing community. Outlying villages from the estate emerged as business centers. Annandale, Springfield Station, Burke Station, and Ilda flourished in a post-war environment. The main road that connected the villages was Braddock Road, a century-old route which started in the City of Alexandria and ended in Pennsylvania. The road was named for General Edward Braddock, whose men reportedly traveled the route on his ill-fated campaign against the French and Indians near Pittsburgh in 1755. Braddock's men were ambushed, and the general was killed. Braddock Road was a natural dividing line of the Fitzhugh grant between its northern and southern sections. One of the longest known existing segments of the road stretched from Annandale, some three miles northeast of the house, to the wilderness of Loudoun County, about thirty miles west.[87]

The new residents along Braddock Road provided closer community ties and labor for the Lees. Veterinarian and teacher William Watt, a native of Banff, Scotland, purchased Oak Hill from the Battaile Family in 1883. His wife sold groceries to her neighbors, which included milk, butter, and other household items. John David Sheads and his family arrived from Culpeper County in 1884, settling near Ossian Hall. Mary Tabb Lee approached Sheads as a potential employee in Ravensworth's burgeoning gardens. Despite several attempts, Sheads kindly repeated, "I have a farm to run."[88]

The surrounding farms brought about a neighborhood schoolhouse that the Lee family facilitated. William Watt, a young school teacher, taught several of the Lee and Fitzhugh children in a small structure set close to Braddock Road.[89] The schoolhouse dated from about 1895, as Bob Lee mentioned it in a letter to attorney R.W. Burch over the matter of a fence. Owen Jones, who rented from the Lees, was the man who built the fence. When the county ordered the fence's removal, Bob defended his neighbor's interests.

>Mr. O.W. Jones the lessee of the Ravensworth
>farm requests me to write to you to the following

effect-he understands that a complaint has been made to you about a certain fence built and maintained by him in front of the "Ravensworth School House" which you have ordered to be taken down in consequence of the said complaints. Mr. Jones begs leave to submit the following facts. The fence was erected with the permission of Mr. Geo. Auld, at that time a member of your board. Mr. Jones does not object to the fence coming down if you direct if the School Board will defray their part of the expense..[90]

To some neighboring families, Ravensworth was a second home. British gardener Jonah Ayres moved into the area as a young man in the early 1870s. He was mentioned in Rooney Lee's correspondence as an employee at Ravensworth in 1884. The inclement winter weather made Rooney remark that "Andrew [Nelson] and Ayres had the wagon" and a good deal of trouble transporting the family to a dinner at Mrs. Eppa Hunton's house. The following spring Rooney wrote that "Ayres has planted his peas and radishes, and will finish his potatoes today, or early tomorrow."[91] Jonah Ayres purchased ten acres of Fitzhugh land from the Battailes in 1887 with money from his gardening, and later added a second fourteen-acre tract. Of his three boys, oldest son Samuel later became Ravensworth's butler. By 1910, Tabb Lee entrusted local servant Laura Wheeler with the daily care of Custis Lee and Mary Tabb's sister Sarah Melville Bolling.[92]

Another local resident who worked for the Lees was Lilly Payne Newman, the resourceful mother of the mansion's carpenter. In 1894, she sought firewood from Ravensworth for the cold winter. From his Washington, D.C. law office at 330 4 ½ Street, Northwest, Bob Lee wrote Mrs. Newman of his approval, and he had "heard from Gen. Custis [his uncle] and he says that you can cut some dead pine wood off of his land near Accotink Hill" provided no new roads were created from her efforts. The Lees wanted no wood cut during the spring, and were concerned over the growing timber trade.[93]

Growing business interests and progress affected the family. For example, the Lees had their own train stop at Ravensworth. In November 1877 five members of the Lee family contracted for the construction of a railroad stop along the neighboring Washington City, Virginia Midland and Great Southern Railroad. For $825 and "other considerations," the railroad company built "a Switch Siding and open shelter for passengers as the 'Ravensworth crossing,' and shall establish at said point a flag station at which all trains shall stop" with the use of a signal. The only exception was express vehicles. When the Southern Railway Company acquired the track of the old Washington City, Virginia Midland and Great Southern in 1894, their management wanted to "correct the curvature" of the track line "near Ravensworth." In September 1901, Custis Lee sold the railroad a wedge of land for a "bypass curve" for $432.81. However, the grade reductions routed the track further south, rendering the old Lee station as a useless structure. The curve correction decreased the risk of accidents over several hard and dangerous turns. Access to the train stop was always awkward. Edward Campbell Sheads, known as "Cam" to area residents, noted the Lee coach forded a wide creek and some bumpy road to the railroad track. The road was dangerous after a hard rain flooded Accotink Creek. In one instance, Bob Lee was obligated to leave his luggage on one bank of the swollen creek, crossing the water on a fallen log.[94] Although the trains provided an alternative mode of transport, they were often late. In July 1903 Custis Lee wrote of the delays.

> Yesterday, my train, that should pass here about
> a quarter past one, went by at about a quarter before
> five; and the day before, it passed about 6 P.M.
> It is hard to know what to do with regard to them;
> I shall have to try for the Manassas train, which
> passes earlier.[95]

Although an astounding academic, Custis had found administrative tasks stifling in Lexington, and resigned as president of Washington and Lee in 1896, after a 26-year tenure. He remained until the end of that academic year, and then departed to permanent retirement at Ravensworth. His increasing rheumatism and depression made for a gloomy existence, but not without the senses of humor and purpose. Custis remained President Emeritus of Washington and Lee, and he was frequently visited by old professors at the house He joked to his brother Robert, Jr. of his nephew Bob as "Bellerophon," and he needled the constant travel of his sister Mary.[96] Other Lees came and went from Ravensworth frequently, but Custis viewed the estate as his permanent headquarters. He commented in a letter to a friend that "Rob [Robert E. Lee III] goes to Washington City every day except Sunday; and his mother goes very often."[97]

Although her son was an accomplished lawyer, Tabb Lee handled special business affairs on her own. She sought details on family real estate matters. The best evidence of her business acumen was an exchange of letters to Richmond businessman N.W. Bowe on the subject. After a decision to purchase property in Richmond, she was "shocked to hear of the low valuations of the houses."[98] Tabb showed interest in the city lots, which later became a point of contention in the family inheritance. In February 1893, she even implored Mr. Bowe to come to Ravensworth.[99]

Left to his own devices in the mansion, Custis indulged his scholarly activities, including the observation of temperatures. In January 1900, he noted the collection methods of ice by Ravensworth servants.

> Our self-registering thermometer, here, marked
> 0 (Fah.) last Saturday night, that was the lowest
> we have had...Tabb's force began to cut ice on
> the Accotinc, near Andrew's house, on New Year's
> Day, and continued the cutting Tuesday;
> yesterday (Wednesday), they began hauling the
> ice to the ice-house, and are doing the same to-day.
> The ice is reported to be 6 in. thick, including some
> two inches of snow-ice.[100]

Custis exercised in the garden and took a daily walk around the estate. He read extensively in Ravensworth's library researching the construction of sewers and cisterns. Unwanted books and excess family items went to Washington & Lee, but not without some comment; even French author and philosopher Jean Jacques Rousseau was not above his criticism. In July 1902 he wrote that an "unexpurgated edition" of *Rousseau's Confessions* was not worth reading because of the lurid content in various parts.

> I had intended sending the book to the Library of W.& L. U.; but have hesitated between doing so and destroying the book (an expensive one). It might answer for the part of the Library that is not circulating; but it is not fit for young people to read-possibly not fit for anybody.[101]

Apart from this, Custis' activity rarely went beyond the fence at Ravensworth. Occasionally he assisted the neighborhood, as when he designed the belfry for the local Episcopal church.[102]

Though Custis was a constant presence at Ravensworth, his two nephews often went well beyond the gates. Bob Lee spent a good amount of time in his downtown legal office. His Washington, D.C. law practice moved several times. His brother Bolly recalled that Bob graduated from Washington & Lee in 1892 to enter his chosen profession.

> ...I am not clear just what his first office was..he had another office with Mr. Gordon, I think somewhere in Georgetown...Then he had an office at the Wyatt building for many years.[103]

In 1902, he started the first of three terms as a Fairfax County delegate. His brother Bolly pursued the occupation of medicine. Like his brother, his formal education began at Washington & Lee. Subsequently, he attended the School of Physicians and Surgeons in New York City, specializing in the field of gynecology. Both brothers were single for a long time.[104]

Like Rooney Lee, Colonel Bob's weight problems increased with age. Bolly advised his brother to "take more exercise than occasionally going into his office in Washington and clip coupons..."[105] Wakefield Chapel churchman John N. Link later wrote,

> So Col. Bob said 'I have decided to get some exercise feeding the chickens. Come on outside and I will show you.' I went with him expecting to see a large chicken house crowded with

chickens. Instead I saw a brood hen and about eighteen newly-born chicks. I can still visualize him shaking with laughter and chuckling at having put one over his brother.[106]

Instead of physical exercise, the Ravensworth circle found more cerebral and social pursuits. Bob was religious and well read, sharing books with his neighbors on various religious topics. As matriarch at Ravensworth, Mary Tabb was known for her generosity and good humor. She often gave out chocolate bars to the laborers. The steady diet of candy fattened the Lee brood at Ravensworth over the years.[107]

Another generation of Lees passed. Mildred, the youngest daughter of Robert E. Lee, died in New Orleans in 1905. In 1911, Custis Lee slipped on the stairs at Ravensworth, badly fracturing his hip. He never walked again and moved by use of a wheelchair until his death at Ravensworth on February 18, 1913. Like most of his siblings, his body was removed to the family crypt in Lexington.[108] Of his death, sister Mary Custis Lee wrote,

> I wish you could have seen him before he was taken to Lexington. Death had smoothed away all traces of pain suffering and even of for he looked like a man of 30, with his handsome features, and almost a calm smile on his noble face! After all his prolonged suffering...The desolation is for those left behind. I closed his poor tired eyes and straightened the attenuated fingers before they stiffened in death...[109]

Even in the event of death, the Lees were gracious in their handling of grief. Responding to a well-wisher's letter of sympathy on Custis' death, Bob Lee stated, "Thank you so much for your kind letter of sympathy on the death of my Uncle Custis. He was a long, patient and noble sufferer..."[110]

Companions and Caretakers

Like many former plantations, there was a considerable African-American community. The 1860 Census revealed that Ravensworth had thirteen slaves and three recent manumissions. Compared to most of the area residents of the time, Anna Maria Fitzhugh owned more slaves than most of her large-estate neighbors. One known slave, Ben Jeffries, was born on the estate and lived to the age of 100 years. In the years following the Civil War, African-American families comprised a portion of the small farmer class. When not working on his carpentry, Linwood Newman assisted the Sheads family with the shucking of the corn crop. Large bib overalls were used for the tedious work, which was not without its adventures. On one particularly hot summer day, Cam Sheads recalled that Newman grew tired after hours of shucking the cornfields. During a break the carpenter fell asleep under a large shade tree. While sleeping, a black corn snake made its way into his bib overalls and curled up inside. Newman awoke and gestured to Sheads. Careful to not excite the snake, Newman called out in a quiet tone, "Mr. Sheads!!" The tactic worked. Cam Sheads noticed, and he removed the snake.[111]

Linwood Newman's mother Lilly was born a slave in March 1859. After her marriage to John "Custis" Newman, she worked as a laundress for the neighborhood. However, there was much tragedy for the Newman family. In January 1881, four-year-old son Richard died of burns. Her husband died of a spinal affliction at the age of forty-four on November 25, 1895. Another daughter, Elizabeth, died of whooping cough in October 1897. Three children survived infancy.[112]

Lilly Newman contributed to area folklore, relating one of the region's most famous ghost stories. The account centered around a previous occupant of the Oak Hill estate named Ann Fitzhugh. Just before the American Revolution, young Ann traveled with her father to London. While there, she met a young British officer named Captain Charles Hawkins. They fell in love, but troubles back home in Virginia necessitated the family's return to America. A few years later, Hawkins' ship landed at the nearby port of Dumfries. The young captain located Oak Hill and visited Ms. Fitzhugh. The family welcomed their old friend, but the repeated presence of a British officer alarmed the surrounding community. The local militia was alerted by vigilant neighbors, and the soldiers surrounded Oak Hill while Hawkins was present. Luckily for the British officer, the house had a secret room in the attic. The couple hid above the militia as they searched the home. Just before departing, one of the soldiers thrust his sword directly into the ceiling, fatally stabbing young Ann. Although Captain Hawkins escaped, the tragedy inspired a local legend that Ann's blood repeatedly stained the dining room ceiling.[113]

Some of the local African-American residents were inventors as well as laborers. Glenn Newman designed a snowplow that cleared Braddock Road in a four-foot winter storm. Dennis Fox was known for his unusual experiments in his home further down Braddock Road. About the time the Wright Brothers flew at Kitty Hawk, North Carolina, Cam Sheads recalled Fox built a homemade flying machine. He recalled,

> Dennis Focs [sic], a black man, decided that he could build an airplane and fly. He got an engine and made his contraption, and then got up on the roof of a shed near Sideburn to see if it would fly. It didn't.[114]

Custis' death prompted more changes at Ravensworth. For Mary Tabb Lee, three Lee deaths within a short period made her the focal point of the community. The neighborhood rallied to her. While Tabb was respected, her family's influence over neighbors lessened. The new tenants and owners were not stewards or employees. Some of the families consisted of former Union soldiers, mostly of the middle or lower class. One remarkable exception was the arrival of Senator Joseph Little Bristow of Kansas in August 1914. A progressive with money to spend on land acquisitions, Senator Bristow purchased Ossian Hall and its existing six hundred acres. He later added tracts to his land. A natural ally for his neighbor, Bristow assisted Bob Lee's lobbying efforts with the Fairfax County Board of Supervisors for private access roads through their farms. In doing so, they built new logging roads for easier timber transport. Then Bristow sold his Salina, Kansas property to finance his new enterprise.[115]

As was his sudden purchase of Ossian Hall, Bristow's life was surprisingly impressive. He was born the day after the Battle of

Manassas to a Kentucky Methodist minister and his wife. Married at eighteen, Bristow focused on the political and business circles in Kansas. He owned and edited several local newspapers. In his late thirties in 1897, Bristow was appointed the Fourth Assistant Postmaster General. He entered Congress as a senator in 1905, and decided to purchase a country estate after tiring of the commute.[116]

Senator Bristow's personal life was as exceptional as his political stature. He and his wife had six children. Edwin, the youngest son, was most interested in the Ossian Hall property. A Bristow biographer noted the Senator, Edwin, and four assistants "set out to rebuild the land. They spread lime on the soil, built woven-wire fences, set up a sawmill, and experimented with farm tractors."[117]

Despite being large landowners, relations between the Bristows and the Lees were primarily of a business nature. There was one exception. Edwin Bristow was smitten with Mrs. Lee's new traveling companion, Arneita Sheads. His love went unrequited, although it showed a rare social connection between the houses.[118]

Arneita Sheads came to Ravensworth after the death of Custis Lee. She frequently accompanied Mary Tabb Lee for her coach and rail rides. With her companion in tow, Tabb Lee traveled to Florida and Europe. One particular visit to Richmond provided an interesting story. Mary Tabb Lee had bought Arneita a baby alligator. After the creature outgrew its initial home in a shoe box, the alligator's new residence was the garden fountain of Richmond's Jefferson Hotel. On their next visit to the hotel, "Miss Nita" inquired about her former pet. She was told the alligator scared patrons and was removed.[119]

Arneita assisted Mrs. Lee in many practical ways. As an accomplished artist, Arneita rendered detailed sketches of Ravensworth furniture pieces, and the drawings were sometimes used in ordering prospective pieces for the house. One sketch required a visit to the Arlington mansion, where Arneita drew the likeness of a certain chair. Subsequently, Tabb Lee sent her sketch to a furniture maker for a model replica. Arneita's daughter Virginia Moore remembered one amusing errand at the Florida Avenue market in Washington, D.C., when, by then quite hard of hearing, Mary Tabb Lee yelled over the noise of the city streetcars, she yelled about the amount of starch in her underclothes-much to the astonishment of the other passengers. Despite her undisputed devotion to Mrs. Lee,

Arneita Sheads left Ravensworth in 1919 to attend Mellon Art School in Washington, D.C.[120]

The Ravensworth community experienced more changes by the 1920s. Owen Jones moved his family from the area, and a Swiss gardener named Frederick Segessenman arrived. He moved his family into a simple frame house across from the red gate at Ravensworth. Segessenman had a garrulous nature, as longtime resident Bill Sheads recalled. Cam Sheads often drove his horse-drawn wagon past the Swiss gardener's house and the gentleman would continue talking as they rode away. The schoolteacher, William Watt, had died in April 1911, but Mary Tabb Lee still depended on his widow. She once asked Mrs. Watt to bring several of her children to the estate, including "borrowing Jack for a few hours" to fill up her wood boxes for the winter. Tabb sent workers up Braddock Road to Mrs. Mary Marshall's house to purchase butter. According to Douglas Dove, Mrs. Lee claimed "nobody could make butter like she did and we used to have to go over there and get the butter every Monday."[121]

There were great changes within the Lee family during this period, as well. Bolly and Bob were married by 1920. Tabb and Bob spent a greater amount of time in the city so, at the time of Bob's marriage, she moved her primary residence to the Stoneleigh Apartments near Connecticut Avenue, N.W. In addition, Bob purchased a downtown residence.[122]

While the family spent less time at Ravensworth, there was still activity. Andrew Nelson's grandson Douglas Dove was baptized in a font on the front porch of the house on August 21, 1921. Although the Lees were not Catholic, a font was borrowed from St. James Church in Falls Church for the ceremony. The ceremony demonstrated how close community ties were despite religious differences Although living primarily in Washington, Bob Lee made an appearance at many area gatherings. He was a regular lay reader at the Episcopal Church of the Good Shepherd, east of Ravensworth along Braddock Road. In addition, he served as the superintendent of the Sunday School. His appearance at a housewarming party for Joseph E. Willard's new Fairfax home caused consternation. Weighing some 250 pounds, Lee slipped on the mansion's slick floors and literally shook the structure.[123]

Sadly, 1922 began a downward spiral for the community and the

Lees. On September 7, 1922 Bob Lee suddenly died of apoplexy. He was married less than two years and sired no children. He willed his Washington home at 1733 Riggs Place, N.W. and tracts of property next to Ravensworth to his wife. However, while executing the will, it was found to contradict that of Rooney Lee. Per his father's wishes as the eldest surviving male in the family, Bolly legally controlled Ravensworth despite his busy practice in New York. A lengthy court battle ensued with Bob Lee's widow over the estate, along with various Lee and Washington family heirlooms. Tabb Lee spent her last years mired down in legal tangles until her own death on May 5, 1924.[124]

Unlike the unfortunate circumstances of her son's last will and testament, Mary Tabb Lee's own will reflected generosity toward servants and friends alike. She willed the Ravensworth butler, Samuel Ayres, 200 dollars. Andrew Nelson received 100 dollars. She left several smaller legacies to Virginia Letcher Stephens, Kate Stewart, Bolly's wife Helen, and Mrs. Ben Nash, who were companions and friends. The bulk of the estate was willed to her surviving son Bolly.[125]

Solving the Fire

By 1926, Ravensworth was no longer the Lee's primary residence. The deaths of Bob and Mary Tabb Lee removed important representatives of the Lee legacy. Bolly worked at a thriving medical practice in New York with his young family, and spent little time in his childhood stomping grounds. Although the house retained its regal splendor, its contents were at the center of a legal battle issued by Bob's widow, Mary Middleton Lee. In Bolly's absence, daily stewardship of the estate fell to coachman Andrew Nelson. He resided in the house above the stable outbuilding. On the wall above their wood stove hung a gift from Tabb Lee. It was a painting depicting the Virginia fox hunt, and it hung in the same spot for many years. In the first months of 1926, life at Ravensworth went on as usual. Then in late April, Mrs. Nelson died. After years of financial setbacks, her death marked a personal decline for Andrew Nelson.[126]

Following her death, a moody Nelson maintained an uneasy control over the staff at the dairy, which provided the bulk of income for the estate. There was much employee turnover. However, there was some stability provided by 47-year-old Oscar Wood, who oversaw dairy operations with his two young sons, Carl and Russell.[127]

The Wood Family contributed greatly to the estate's dairy enterprise. Oscar Early Wood was one of eight children born to Davis and Elizabeth McCauley Wood of Albemarle County, Virginia. Born in January 1879, Oscar grew up on the dairy farms of the Virginia piedmont. During the Spanish-American War, he almost joined Theodore Roosevelt's "Rough Riders." Instead, he married Grace Marrs from his home county and sired four sons. Oscar found work at Sam Jessup's bottle works and Payne's Dairy in nearby Charlottesville, and doubled his income by moonlighting as a cabinetmaker. After some years working with Jessup and Payne, he saw revolutionary changes in the industry such as safer pasteurization processes in dairy products. Combining business acumen with local connections in Virginia, he ventured north as overseer for dairy operations for the Portner farm in Manassas. It was there he met Doctor George Bolling Lee, who hired him away for the Ravensworth dairy farm.[128]

Ravensworth was a family experience for Oscar Wood and his sons. Carl Wood drove the dairy truck to and from distributors. When not working on the farm, he drove a taxi in downtown Washington, D.C. Russell worked odd jobs before joining the Army as a private in January 1924. He learned considerable welding skills, but his drinking affected his service. After six months, on July 12, 1924, Russell received an honorable discharge. He became a permanent dairy worker at Ravensworth. Unfortunately, Russell's propensity for alcohol continued.[129]

Evidence of Russell Wood's drinking was found in Fairfax County court records. In May 1926, Wood was named in one of thirty-eight "true bills." His repeated charges of liquor law violations blotted the ledgers, but Wood was not alone in the age of Prohibition. Many in the neighborhood were charged with like offenses, but most defendants were not prosecuted; instead, they were lightly fined. To make matters worse, Wood would have had easy access to the Lee's stock of old wines, said to be non-existent in the era of Prohibition. Carl Wood's successful taxi business may even have had its roots in liquor, as he was reported to have supplied city hotel bellhops with ready spirits.[130]

The accessibility of spirits to Russell Wood, the missing owners, and a hot dry forest endangered Ravensworth. Andrew Nelson's wife Mary died at the end of April, and diverted the coachman's attention from the management of the estate. In the last week of July 1926, the *Herndon News Observer* reported that Nelson and Russell Wood argued over an unreported matter. The next day Nelson's house was on fire. Two officers "brought up three men from the Accotink Valley, near Ravensworth, on various charges. All three were fined and two committed to jail for 30 days."[131]

The following Sunday morning, at about 1:30 a.m., flames arose in the attic of Ravensworth. The fire was undetected until it spread to the floor below. However, the flames spread slowly enough to allow the workers to repeatedly run into the parlors on the first floor, saving valuable silver, paintings, and china from generations of Lee, Fitzhugh, and Custis families. The nearest fire fighters were in Alexandria, and it was questionable whether their assistance mattered after the first hours of the burning.[132]

> A group of less than two dozen persons stood around and the flames eat up one half of the priceless furniture in this house, powerless to render further aid in saving the effects. However, the onlookers had been busy for nearly an hour previous, removing what effects they could. They saved seventeen handsome oil paintings from the flames, together with most of the silverware, historic dishes and various other things, including considerable valueable [sic] mahogany furniture...The oil paintings were carried to the home of former Senator Joseph L. Bristow and the remainder of the salvaged goods were placed on the lawn surrounding the home and brought here yesterday for storage.[133]

An inventory revealed the items from the first floor rooms: the office, the billiard room, and the library. Much of the china was spared from the south room and chamber on the second floor. The central hall and nursery, on the top level, lost the most items. The total loss in personal and real property amounted to $70,000, yet it was insured for only $40,000.[134]

The paintings, china, and silver saved were of national importance. Custis Lee's heirlooms were included among them, having come to Ravensworth upon his retirement from Washington and Lee University. There were also some personal effects formerly belonging to George Washington. Even the *Alexandria Gazette* emphasized the importance of saving the artifacts.

> It is for these relics that the greatest concern will now be felt. Gen. Robert E. Lee's military papers fortunately had been removed from "Ravensworth" and are now perfectly safe. Most, if not all, the private letters of General Lee had been in the custody of Captain "Bob" Lee and are now in possession of his heirs. The chief personal relics of the Confederate chieftain-his Appomattox sword and uniform, his field glasses, his camp equipment and his horse furnishings-are in the Confederate Museum. But it is possible that at least one of his other swords was at "Ravensworth," and it is certain that the famous portraits of the Lee and Washington families were there, among them Peale's Washington and the pictures of Robert E. Lee and of Mary Custis, made about the time of their marriage. The Washington silver from "Mt. Vernon" was usually kept at "Ravensworth," but it may have been sent recently to Washington. Most of the silver is believed to have been saved, anyway. The bed in which General Robert E. Lee died has almost certainly been destroyed, as it was in that wing of the building from which little or nothing was salvaged. This bed had been given to Washington and Lee University, but it had not been shipped there. The papers of General "Rooney" Lee, which have never been examined by any historian, probably have been destroyed...[135]

In fact, Bolly remembered that many historical papers burned in the fire, including those kept by his Uncle Custis. He wrote a friend years after the fire that most letters belonging to Custis "were burned in the fire at Ravensworth about fifteen years ago as were many of my father's [Rooney Lee] and General Robert E. Lee's letters and historic papers."[136]

It is unknown how much historical insight was lost. After the flames were extinguished at 9 a.m. the following morning, the investigation immediately began. *The Fairfax Herald* reported there was "only a pile of smoldering ashes and standing chimneys" and that the fire was "of incendiary origin." Those nearest the house early in the blaze reported "a strong smell of coal oil about the place."[137] Ravensworth was not wired for electricity, so there was no short that could have caused the blaze. The *Fairfax Herald* did a thorough investigation on the possible motives for the fire, and featured Special Agents Virgil Williams and Haywood Davis of the Fairfax County Police as the case detectives. The two policemen were sent under the direction of Commonwealth's attorney Wilson W. Farr of Fairfax, who had just returned from vacation to learn of the fire. Suspicious about the nature of the Nelson house fire the previous week and its connections with alcohol-related activity, it was not surprising that Farr sent for the two young officers. Naturally, alcohol was immediately seized upon as a motive in the *Fairfax Herald's* report. The Lee stock of valuable wines was stored in a cold cellar for some years on the estate, however the family insisted those same wines vanished in the first years of Prohibition. There was no further mention as to whether the wine had been destroyed, sold, or redistributed elsewhere. The *Fairfax Herald* proposed that the fire was set to cover the theft of any existing bottles. Undoubtedly Williams covered this angle and found little to support it.[138]

The officers found enough evidence of alcohol usage to have Russell Wood arrested on violation of the liquor laws on August 13. He was reported by the paper to be held "regarding the burning of Ravensworth mansion."[139] The subsequent "prohibition violation law hearing" resulted in the temporary incarceration of Wood and Linwood Newman, Ravensworth's carpenter. Newman was quickly released on bail. The *Fairfax Herald* later reported, "Nothing was developed, it is stated, to show the cause of the Ravensworth fire."[140]

News sources never pursued the cause of the fire, and Fairfax Fire Chief Duncan later admitted that the official reports went missing. Court records indicated a lack of evidence. On September 30, 1926, the Commonwealth of Virginia indicted Russell Wood for maintaining a still. Wood never showed at court, and his bail was later forfeited. At every court term from September 1926 to September 1927, the clerk's criminal docket showed Wood as a "fugitive from justice." Finally, in the November term of 1927, the charges were quietly dropped.[141]

In the investigation's wake, events began to settle at Ravensworth. The Wood family quietly removed themselves to Alexandria. Cutting his losses, Bolly Lee rebuilt a summer home on a much smaller scale, retaining the dairy concern and horse farm. In late September, Bolly settled the suit brought on by Bob Lee's widow using the insurance money.[142]

The burning of Ravensworth brought an end to an era of social grandeur for the community. Without its architectural centerpiece, the Lee legacy sustained itself through other homes. Ironically, the largest of these is Arlington House and the surrounding cemetery which holds the remains of American servicemen.

Postscript: Why Russell Wood?

Although briefly connected with the Lee legacy, Russell Wood and his family remained an interesting postscript to the fate of Ravensworth. There was little surviving information to indicate his involvement, yet the *Fairfax Herald* was unsparing in its investigative reporting. The news reports, like most of the official reports of Williams and Duncan, simply disappeared. It indicated that the *Herald* may have been premature in blaming Wood, and the authorities released the suspect after a short period of incarceration.

Despite the lack of evidence to hold Wood on an arson charge, there is a later chain of events that further implicated him. Oscar Wood and his family began work at Alexandria's Thompson Dairy, located on the grounds of a large estate known as Hollin Hall. Both were possessions of Harley Wilson, a director of the North American Company and the Washington Railway and Electric Company, and his wife. Like Ravensworth, Hollin Hall's storied history included previous owners in the family of Virginia statesman George Mason.[143]

The Wilsons purchased the 297-acre estate in March 1913. As the initial mansion burned in the War of 1812, they lived in the spinning house. The outbuilding was known as "Little Hollin Hall," and it served as a temporary residence while their elaborate new manor house was under construction. The Wilsons searched Virginia for old brick to use in their garden walls. Once an adjoining farm was added to their existing property holdings, dairy manager James Brown departed. Oscar Wood arrived at Hollin Hall to replace him, and Russell worked with him.[144]

The dairy operation under Oscar Wood was remembered by another worker at Hollin Hall. Fifteen-year-old Gardener John Stephens began work at Hollin Hall in 1926. While his primary duties included the guest house and the walled terrace garden, he occasionally visited the dairy operation. Among the historic structures immediately surrounding the operation was a 75-year-old barn. It was regarded as one of the finest structures of its kind, containing 250 tons of feed and hay inside.[145]

On or about November 3, 1928, the noted barn, dairy, and carriage house all burned to the ground. It was four o'clock on a Saturday afternoon when the fire was discovered. Although five miles away, fire engines from the City of Alexandria lacked a ready source of water. The dairy operation was engulfed in flames, but this time Oscar Wood saw the crime happen. Though misidentified as "James Wood" in the *Fairfax Herald*, it was the father who was the key witness against his own son in the ensuing court action.[146]

> It is stated that James Wood, foreman of the Hollen [sic] Hall dairy, and father of the accused man, told Sheriff Kirby he saw his son start the fire to the barn. Russell Wood was later found by Sheriff Kirby and County Policeman Hill Davis, hidden in a cornfield, and brought him to jail here to await the action of the grand jury at the November term of the Circuit Court which opens Monday next, November 19.[147]

Russell Wood was indicted for arson. Sheriff Eppa Kirby confined Wood to a small holding cell until the next grand jury met. The total loss was tabulated at an estimated forty-thousand dollars. Upon his plea of guilty to the grand jury, the 22-year-old Wood was sentenced by Judge Howard W. Smith to ten years in the state penitentiary. It was a shock to the Wood family, but his former prohibition charges in Fairfax weighted the sentence.[148]

> ...upon an indictment of the Grand Jury for felonious arson. Russell Wood...pleaded guilty thereto and submitted the case to the Court for trial, and thereupon, in compliance with the Statute in such cases made and provided and by and with the consent of the attorney for the Commonwealth and of the prisoner, now given in open Court and entered of record, the Court hears and determines the case on his said plea guilty without the intervention of a jury, and after hearing the evidence in the case is of opinion that he is guilty as indicted and gives judgment that he be confined in the Penitentiary house of this Commonwealth for the period of ten years.. subject to a credit of 17 days served by him in said jail from November 3, 1928 to November 20th,1928.[149]

Russell Wood's life declined into incarceration, drifting, and drinking. Wood spent almost seven years in the state penitentiary near Richmond. Prison records confirmed his arrival on December 18, 1928, and his term expired on July 29, 1935. Subsequently Wood was conditionally pardoned, and upon his release, drifted aimlessly around the region. He was estranged from the rest of his family. In the 1950s, Wood met a Martinsburg, West Virginia auctioneer named Raymond N. "Casey" Jones at the Newark, New Jersey Salvation Army. Jones brought him back to Martinsburg as a maintenance man for his auction house. He was known as "Pappy" Wood, a lovable alcoholic who occasionally disappeared from town, only to reemerge at a Hagerstown, Maryland charity mission for months at a time.

However, the years of drinking and drifting took their toll on the 79-year-old Wood. On November 10, 1986, Russell Wood died of prostate cancer in a Veteran's Administration hospital.[150]

The rest of the Wood family also lived quietly. Oscar and Grace retired to a small frame house only a few scant miles from Ravensworth. Shortly after the couple's 68th wedding anniversary, Grace Wood died on October 29, 1970. Oscar Wood followed three years later on July 19, 1973. Carl Wood moved to Virginia's Northern Neck peninsula, and died there on July 25, 1993.[151]

The sad postscript of Russell Wood's life after the burning of Ravensworth depicted a sympathetic, but self-destructive, young man. His argumentative nature, combined with a willingness to set fire to the dairy operation at Hollin Hall, was indicative of the earlier two blazes. However, authorities chose not to indict Wood on the Ravensworth fire. In hindsight, it was probably sympathy that spared him at the Lee estate. If Russell Wood did not start the fire, there can be little doubt he knew how to commit arson. His argument with Andrew Nelson, followed by the burning of the caretaker's quarters, insinuated a pattern. Those who knew the answers are gone, and so was the Lee legacy known as Ravensworth.

Legacy II: Artifacts and Keepsakes

The Struggle Over Legacy

Ever since the Civil War had thrust Robert E. Lee and his family into the limelight, the Lees had to deal with various parties laying claim to Lee family artifacts, including their valued Washington silver, paintings, and furniture. However, in the 1920s the battle was personal and the opponent formidable. The claimant was married to one of their own. Mary Middleton Lee was a shrewd Charleston, South Carolina belle. She was the wife of Robert E. Lee III for just over two years; after the unexpected death of her husband, the legal battle she waged over the precious Lee and Washington artifacts lasted longer than the union itself-four years. Mary Tabb and Bolly Lee dealt with constant legal issues and grudges, including the internment of Bob Lee's body in a South Carolina cemetery rather than placement in the family chapel. However, the battle for the family heirlooms had become part of a larger war--the decision of final disposition of them. Various museums and family members vied for the keepsakes. Some of these same problems crossed over into the stewardship of the family papers, which spread to another branch of the family. Interested historians, rather than the family, began shaping the legacy. Part of the struggle over legacy was who controlled the publications and image of the Lees. Needless to say, the family had two camps on the subject; some encouraged the historians, other preferred a much more closed access. The one thing all could agree on was that the argument over the objects and papers began long before Bob Lee's death in 1922.

The dispersion of family artifacts began during the Civil War. After the occupation of Arlington House by Federals in May 1861, some of George Washington Parke Custis' choice collection of family artifacts and furniture were open to removal. Some of the items never made it into storage at Ravensworth, and it fell to a handful of remaining servants to watch over them. General Charles W. Sanford took possession of the property and ordered the removal of most contents. While most of the items went to the Patent Office in downtown Washington, soldiers kept some items as souvenirs or plunder of war. Even the items sent to the Patent Office were trumpeted as being "captured from Arlington" and set in a display. Some of the exhibited inventory included General Washington's Revolutionary War Tent, punch bowl, and the blanket covering him at death.[1]

Mary Custis Lee had attempted to move all of the belongings, but she found that the captors were reluctant to release them. The crass nature of the "capture" contributed to Mrs. Lee's early efforts to regain the items quickly after the close of hostilities in 1865. Alexandria lawyer and Lee relative Philip Fendall assisted in attempting to regain the family items the following year. Daughter Mary Custis composed a list of items to forward to Fendall. She wrote that Mrs. Lee wanted "the things removed to [John] Green's warehouse in "Alexandria," & as Mr. Francis S. Smith, of that place, has been in the habit of attending to business for us..."[2]

In reassembling the items from Arlington, a long battle followed. Another Lee relative, Francis Smith, was entrusted with the storage and transport of the items claimed from the Patent Office to Green's warehouse. Mary Lee sent Fendall an inventory of missing items compiled by her daughter. It was a descriptive work of sharp memory which included:

> Two mahogany knife cases
> Old fashioned was[h] stand
> Old green silk window curtain fringes
> White hooked curtains & counterpane
> Blankets
> Washington Coat of Arms
> Old andirons
> Old stick chair
> One large china bowl
> One green china tea pot. Two others
> One flat dish. Blue India China
> 3 glass finger bowls[3]
> Cincinnati China
> 40 plates. 10 flat dishes
> 6 small pieces
> 3 pieces of M.W. China[4]
> Two china vases with tigers and leopards

      on one side, landscapes on the other
2 large mahogany bureau, brass [-]
Small oval mahogany tea table
Two glass chandeliers (old fashioned)
One oval mirror, gilt frame
Small mahogany cabinet with little drawers
      (One drawer gone)
7 Washington tents & tent poles
One suit of Washington clothes
      (Buff worked with blue)
One green chintz sofa cover
10 iron framed glass hall lamps
Old iron chest[5]

Mary Lee instructed Philip Fendall to locate her family Bible and other "missing" items. She was bewildered by the loss of empty picture frames and crimson silk brocade curtains left behind. With the instincts of a detective, Mary assisted Fendall in every way possible, naming several suspects behind the missing items. Major General Nathaniel Banks was named by Mrs. Lee as the procurer of the family linens and "many articles from Mt Vernon."[6] It was suspected that a Lieutenant Ingalls took the family books. To add further insult, the family's Smith Island property was missing much of its livestock and wood. The family contacted Colonel Hancock Taylor and pleaded the family's case.[7]

Some of the items were returned and placed into John Green's care, but the Patent Office relics were a different story. The changing political temperament in Congress prevented their immediate return. Although President Andrew Johnson was a moderate, it took until 1869 for him to be able to publicly request the return of the Lee artifacts to the family. Congressman John A. Logan, a one-time Union General, opposed the return of the Washington items with a public smearing of the Lee name. On March 3, 1869, the radical element in Congress officially denied the family their heirlooms by declaring the Washington items the property of the "whole people." President Ulysses S. Grant ignored further claims during his term. Litigation outlasted the lives of both Robert E. Lee and his wife. Only Custis Lee's suit against the Federal Government, backed by a sympathetic

President Grover Cleveland, procured the items. However, it took almost thirteen more years to ship most of the Washington items back to the Lee family.[8] Custis wrote of the travails to his brother Robert E. Lee, Jr. in 1900. He passed the quest for the Mount Vernon relics to his sister after seeking them for 18 years.

> With regard to the "Mount Vernon relics":
> When Presdt. Johnson ordered them returned
> to our Mother. Congress passed a joint resolution
> that they should not go back to the hands of
> Rebels, &c. I think there was a list of them made
> and reported at that time. Some years after that,
> I gave my consent to the Mt. Vernon Regents to
> take the relics to Mt. Vernon if they could get the
> consent of the U.S. Govt. to do so. As the relics
> have not been taken to Mt. Vernon, I presume the
> consent of the Govt. could not be obtained. Some
> years after that (probably, the last time our sister
> Mary was in this Country), to stop her incessant
> nagging on the subject, I told her that she might
> have the Relics if she could get them, and gave
> her the necessary papers to that end...[9]

As Robert E. Lee's children passed away, the collective ownership of the heirlooms and portraits concentrated into fewer hands. The death of Mildred Childe Lee in March 1905 meant that only Mary Custis Lee and her brother Custis were left to claim the legacy on their father's behalf. Perhaps knowing the precarious situation and the long legal battle to reclaim some of the old family effects after the Civil War, ownership of some items quietly slipped away from their possession.[10]

The real custodians of the Washington family artifacts were Custis Lee and his sister Mary. As the eldest son, Custis felt the keen responsibility to maintain the family's dual legacies: the two famous families of Washington and Lee. Mary Custis felt the same obligations, although their tactics of stewardship were different, as was seen in their recovery efforts concerning the family Bible. In 1904, *the Richmond Times-Dispatch* reported the details of Custis' passive battle over the possession of the Lee-Washington Bible, one of the items removed by soldiers from Arlington House. The Lees forgot the Bible in their rush to leave Arlington, and the soldier who took it believed it abandoned property. In the subsequent 40 years the Bible passed to the man's son and was later sold to Philadelphian George W. Kendrick, Jr. in about 1882. A news account appeared in 1903 of the Bible's "discovery" in Kendrick's possession. Mary Custis followed up on the account and demanded that the Philadelphian return the family tome. Kendrick refused, even though legal action was threatened. In March 1904, reporters interviewed Custis Lee at Ravensworth. His tactics proved different. Mindful of his father's quiet influence based on leadership and charm, the son followed his example. Rather than demand the Bible, Custis took the high road. He told the reporters,

> I shall make no formal request to Mr. Kendrick for the Bible's return...and shall for the present take no legal action. I have decided to let Mr. Kendrick work the matter in his own mind and come to a decision as his conscience directs. He knows my right to the book and I believe that he will ultimately turn it over to me.[11]

There was always demand for the Washington and Lee family portraits and other artifacts for museum exhibits and special events. Custis helped organize many of the exhibits, although the family pictures were widespread in ownership. Several were owned by Custis, but some remained on an extended loan to Washington & Lee University. A number of oil paintings were jointly owned by Custis, Mary Custis, Robert, Jr., George Bolling, and Bob Lee. In April 1907, Custis was asked about lending a number of portraits for the Jamestown Exposition. The grand display, situated not at Jamestown but Norfolk, marked the 300th anniversary of Virginia settlement. Many of the paintings were under the care of Washington & Lee University and required permission to be loaned. Custis wrote Washington & Lee Treasurer John L. Campbell that he did not oppose the request made by the daughter of Colonel John A. Washington on behalf of the Virginia Daughters of the Revolution, "although I should prefer the pictures to remain where they are."[12] Six of the 31 paintings were loaned for the Exposition, but Custis withheld a portrait of John Parke Custis and his sister Martha, because he felt four paintings of the Custis relatives would be too many. The oils sent to the celebration included: portraits of Colonel Daniel Parke, Daniel Parke Custis, Martha Custis, and Nellie Custis as well as two landscape type pictures of morning and evening, both of which had hung over the mantel in George Washington's home at Mt. Vernon.[13]

When memorials and statues were proposed, it was Custis whose opinion weighed heaviest. He wrote his brother that he felt appreciative of the proposed statue of their father near the U.S. Capitol in Washington, D.C. in 1909. However, he feared angry reprisals by members of the Grand Army of the Republic, which was comprised of Union veterans. Custis wrote that if the "people of Washington city do not want a statue of Genl. Lee in the city, it will always be liable to damage or destruction..."[14]

Reflecting his concerns over the family legacy, Custis wrote his will in February 1912. It was this will that defined some of the contentious issues that arose later in civil suits.

> First: I give and bequeath to the Washington and Lee University, to be held by the trustees thereof, the original portrait in oil of General George Washington by Charles Wilson Peale, painted in 1772, the original portrait in oil of General La Fayette by the same artist, painted for General Washington in 1779; all my books and office furniture that I left in Lexington upon my departure there from in the summer of 1897, and all my interest in a certain claim against the United States Government on account of wood gotten from Ravensworth by representatives of the Government during the Civil War. By an agreement in writing this claim was placed in the hands of Mr. Charles Kerr...I also give and bequeath to the Washington and Lee University, to be held by the Trustees thereof, the sum of Five Thousand Dollars ($5000.00), which sum is to

be invested and the interest used in the preservation and improvement of the Lee Memorial Chapel.

Second: All my pictures and portraits, of every kind and description, except the two given to the Washington and Lee University, are to be divided as nearly as may be, into three equal lots, considering number and value, both intrinsic and from the standpoint of sentiment: and I give and bequeath to my sister, Mary Custis Lee, one of the said lots; to my brother, Robert Edward Lee, one of said lots; and to my two Nephews, Robert Edward Lee, Jr. and George Bolling Lee, the remaining lot, to be equally divided between them.

I have heretofore given to my said sister, Mary Custis Lee, the "Mount Vernon Relics," and as further evidence of her title to them I now give and bequeath the same to her absolutely.

Third: I give and bequeath to my sister-in-law, Mary Tabb Lee, widow of my deceased brother, William Henry Fitzhugh Lee, the sum of Five Thousand Dollars ($5000.00) and all the furniture of which I may die possessed, except the office furniture given the Washington and Lee University.[15]

The will went on name the two nephews at Ravensworth as recipients of all Custis Lee's Fairfax County lands and large cash sums. Robert E. Lee, Jr., the brother of Custis, received the "rest and residue" of the estate. When Custis died at Ravensworth in early 1913, the wording of individual items were decidedly vague. While Custis had described the Washington family oils in detail, the "Mount Vernon Relics" was largely unexplained. Did Custis refer to the heirlooms from the first President's home? Or was there a more select grouping?[16] In 1935 historian John W. Wayland asked George Bolling

Lee on the precise terminology of "Mount Vernon Relics" as phrased in the will of Custis Lee. The doctor replied,

> these so called 'relics' were pictures, furniture, etc., taken from Arlington at the beginning of the war and stored in Washington, by the United States Government...These 'relics' were returned to my aunt, Mary Custis Lee, by President McKinley, by the advice of his Attorney-General, and were in her possession at the time of her death.[17]

Mary Custis Lee, the last surviving child of Robert and Mary Custis Lee, died on November 22, 1918. Earlier that year she filed a detailed will. Although she had made a previous will in 1908, the death of her two remaining brothers and two executors necessitated a new legal distribution. As per her usual manner, she had made large bequests to memorials in her family's stead. She left her two nephews from Ravensworth sizeable monetary sums, gently chiding that the money should go to charity or to other Lee relatives, if both continued as bachelors.[18] Her disposition of family items had conditions, even an objection of sorts, drawn up within the text of the will.

> To <u>Washington and Lee University</u>, Lexington, Virginia, the sum of ten thousand dollars ($10,000.) to assist in building what I know has been in contemplation, a <u>Fireproof Room</u> in which I should especially wish deposited <u>my</u> share of the Family Pictures from "Mount Vernon" and "Arlington." The division of them was made some years ago without consulting <u>me</u> at all, my due I think, as I was the last surviving child of my parents, and having been brought up at "Arlington," was the one living person who knew much about them. Consequently, many <u>mistakes</u> were made regarding both the <u>subjects</u> and the <u>artists</u> which I shall endeavor to have corrected, most of them still in the College Library at "Lexington." I hereby bequeath those belonging to me, as a personal gift to said "College," of

which my father and oldest brother were the consecutive presidents and who both lie buried there. I sincerely hope that as soon as practicable the pictures may be securely hung in this fireproof building, as most of them are a part of the history of our Country, and especially of Virginia. I have already donated them to the College, and given them a list of them.[19]

Mary Custis Lee minced; she was dissatisfied with the disposition of the artifacts as decided by the will of her brother Custis. However, until Custis' death, Mary Custis spent most of her time abroad and therefore was not readily available to give input on crucial decisions involving the artifacts. Following her return to America, she felt her personal choices for the disposition of family heirlooms were preselected. However, her decision was rooted in logic. She felt that the relics should rest at the college her father loved so much.[20]

Both Lee boys took Mary Custis Lee's remark about their bachelorhood seriously, and within two years they were both wed. Robert E. Lee III's late marriage to Mary Middleton Pinckney in early July 1919 at the Church of the Epiphany in Washington, D.C. was reported by the *Fairfax Herald*; attendees were limited to family and a few friends.[21] Likewise, Doctor George Bolling Lee waited a long period, and he preferred his marriage kept private. In announcing his January 1920 engagement to Helen Keeney of New York, he asked his mother not to announce it at the time, except to his brother and new sister-in-law. From Atlantic City, New Jersey, he wrote "there will be no announcement until just a short while before we are married--so please don't tell any one..."[22] They married on April 17, 1920. By that time, Bob Lee and his new wife were the primary residents at Ravensworth, and Mary Tabb had removed to her urban quarters on Riggs Place, N.W. in the District of Columbia. She took a number of Lee and Washington family artifacts with her, keeping them safely stored in a trunk on the premises. This proved to be a problem for Bob Lee's new wife.[23]

Mary Wilkerson Middleton was born in 1874 to Ralph Izard and Virginia Memminger Middleton. Through her father, she was descended from two South Carolina luminaries: Henry Middleton, first President of the Continental Congress; and Arthur Middleton, who signed the Declaration of Independence. Her father grew up at Belle Isle Plantation near Charleston and was educated at Dartmouth College. During the Civil War he served in Confederate South Carolina's Marion Artillery. He married Sarah Virginia, daughter of Confederate Secretary of the Treasury Christopher Memminger, in December 1867. Being one of numerous siblings, Mary split her time between Charleston and their summer residence at Flat Rock, North Carolina. Her Uncle, Doctor Allard Memminger, owned the family estate at Flat Rock, known as "Enchantment."[24]

Mary married her cousin, Gustavus M. Pinckney of Charleston, in 1909. The young man was an intellectual, descended from a famous family also involved in the formation of the nation. As a second son of wealthy parents, Gustavus had time for academic pursuits. His book, *The Life of John C. Calhoun*, was a definitive biography of the South Carolina politician. His sudden death in Charleston on December 5, 1912 at the early age of 40 left Mary available for remarriage. However, she did not marry again until she wed Bob Lee almost eight years later.[25]

The family's relations with Bob Lee's new wife were never established due to the union's brevity. Like her previous marriage, there were no children. By March 1922, Bob Lee was in poor health. His illness lingered on through the summer, so the couple traveled to the healing waters at Hot Springs in Bath County, Virginia. In September, Bob Lee rallied enough to take a train to the Shenandoah Valley region; however, en route he became gravely ill near Roanoke, Virginia and died on September 4, 1922.[26]

By way of railroad car and hearse, the body of Bob Lee went to Lexington for the funeral. He was placed in the R.E. Lee Memorial Episcopal Church on the Washington & Lee University campus for the funeral ceremonies. Two Episcopal churchman, one from the Episcopal Theological Seminary in Alexandria and the other from Washington & Lee, presided over the sad services. Afterward, the body was taken to the Lee Chapel and interred.[27]

Mary Middleton Lee was in a precarious position. She was married to Bob Lee for only two years, had no children, and was the wife of the primary resident of Ravensworth. Doctor George Bolling Lee and his wife had a daughter, Mary Walker Lee, born in June 1921.

A son, Robert E. Lee IV, followed three years later. Under terms of the will of her father-in-law, Rooney Lee, Mary Middleton Lee began a series of claims for family heirlooms. It began while Mary Tabb Lee was still alive.[28]

When Bob Lee died, Mary challenged the will of her long deceased father-in-law, Rooney Lee. Under the terms of the elder Lee's will, should one of the sons die before their mother, the deceased son's share would revert to the surviving sibling. Had Mary Tabb Lee died before Bob Lee, the property would have divided evenly between the two sons. Bob Lee's will stated different terms altogether for his wife. She retained ownership of their Riggs Place residence in the District and his share of the Lee estate. Upon her remarriage or death, the younger Mrs. Lee's share would move back to George Bolling Lee's family.[29]

> Second:--Whereas, my father, William H. F. Lee, died about thirty years ago, leaving his estate to my mother for and during her life, with the remainder in fee in said estate to myself and to my brother, George Bolling Lee, I hereby devise and bequeath to my wife, Mary M. Lee, my interest in the estate so left by my father, until she re-marries, or, should she not remarry, then during her life time, with the remainder after her re-marriage or her death, as the case may be, to my said brother, George Bolling Lee.[30]

The fourth provision of Bob Lee's will mentioned certain precious items of the Washington and Lee families. In other words, some of the those items formerly stored on the grounds of Ravensworth and the other surrounding Lee properties were being posthumously decided for several generations by the confusing wills. It was problematic on the surface, for if Bob Lee believed he was settling all potential problems on estate division, he was wrong.

> After the death of my wife, I bequeath to Washington & Lee University, at Lexington, Virginia, three (3) portraits now in said residence at 1733 Riggs Place, Washington,

D.C. - one being a portrait of Robert E. Lee; one of Mrs. Robert E. Lee; and one of George Washington Parke Custis. And, after her death, I bequeath to my brother, Dr. George Bolling Lee, of New York, the silver now in said residence, known as the "Mount Vernon Silver" and the "Lee Silver"-the possession of the said portraits and the said silver to remain with my wife during her lifetime.[31]

The confusing wills fostered bad feelings between Mary M. Lee and her in-laws. Shortly after Bob Lee's death, an appraisal was made "as has beem [sic] presented to us by Mary M. Lee, Executrix.." The appraisal was complete, but probably too detailed. The listing appraised portions of the estate that would have been distributed to other Lee relations. Also, there was no monetary impact on the young widow, as Bob Lee owned a good deal of stock in different railroads totaling over $33,000.[32]

The appraisal also indicated Mary M. Lee's interest in the family antiques at Ravensworth, however scattered they were by late 1922. Several Lee relics, including a silver waiter and one dozen dessert spoons, were stored at the Riggs Place residence. The following Washington articles were there as well: a wine cooler, a small silver tray, and one pair of candle sticks "presented to Daniel Parke by Queen Anne for carrying dispatch at battle of Blenheim."[33] The appraisal cataloged a list of items at Ravensworth: a collection of books, a toilet case, a broken gramophone, an unworn pair of shoes, a chafing dish, military boots, clothing, and half interest of mahogany wardrobe and bureau. The method of listing made assumptions of another interest in the estate of Mary Custis Lee, who died in 1918. The items on this section included three miniatures of General Robert E. Lee by Brinak, a gold pendant, and buttons taken from the velvet coat of General Washington. From this latter estate at Ravensworth was listed a small silver urn, an antique pitcher with a hinge top, a silver coffee pot, two tankards, four candlesticks, an "extra large" antique serving spoon, two broken silver ladles, and broken silver sugar tongs. Prominent items included on Mary Custis Lee's estate inventory was an iron chest given to George Washington Parke Custis by General Washington and two tents owned by the General during his Revolutionary War campaigns.[34]

If the appraisal was not enough to raise some family hackles, the next legal move was far more divisive. In the Supreme Court of the District of Columbia, the younger widow entered a suit against George Bolling Lee and his mother over a trunk of family heirlooms transferred to the care of the National Savings and Trust Company. In April 1919 the trunk was transferred to the Lees in order to discern the ownership of its contents. In reaching a decision over the division of the trunk's contents, Mary M. Lee declared that her in-laws did not give her a share. In addition, she hired attorney Sidney F. Taliaferro to file the suit in order to keep the trunk's contents, valued at $15,000, within the physical limits of the District of Columbia.[35]

> Among the contents of the trunk are said to be a sword belt, camp stool, gauntlets, flasks and brush used by Gen. Lee during the civil war; a red sash worn by Lee while a cadet at West Point; his commission as lieutenant general signed by President Pierce, his razor, a red cravat and a knife. The trunk also contains a gold watch once owned by George Washington and two pistols said to have belonged to the "Father of His Country."[36]

In the subsequent appraisal of Bob Lee's estate, an entire section was devoted to the contents of the trunk. In addition to the items mentioned above, there were additions and some corrections to the expanding inventory. The red sash was worn by Custis Lee at West Point, not General Robert E. Lee. There were several books, including an opera book presented by a member of the Custis family, a silhouette portrait of a Mrs. Archer, and an ink stand owned by Washington.[37]

In order to reassemble the two old wills to find real intent, a court injunction was quickly entered by George and Mary Tabb Lee, which Mary M. viewed as an attempt by the Lees to block her share of the family estate. Specifically, the Lees were fearful that the extension would include their lands, including the Ravensworth tract. Newspapers published an official statement from the family. The legal pronouncement said that if Bob Lee's widow was entitled to land, it was not to be the Ravensworth house.

> ...the share of the said Mary M. Lee may be allotted to her in the real estate other than the Ravensworth tract of land; that the said Mary M. Lee may be enjoined from occupying or attempting to occupy any of the real estate belonging to the estate of the said W.H.F. Lee, until it is adjudged in this suit that she is entitled to a share of the estate of the late W.H.F. Lee, and that she may be especially enjoined from occupying or attempting to occupy any part of the said Ravensworth tract of land mentioned in the bill until the Court in this suit has decided that she has an interest therein and not then unless she is allotted the said tract of land under the proceedings in this suit; and to obtain general relief.[38]

The injunction elevated legal confrontation. Shortly thereafter, Rooney Lee's will was extensively reexamined. 82-year-old retired Judge James M. Love, who had written the will in 1891, was the only living witness to the document. He expressed little doubt as to Rooney Lee's intent:

> I received a message from Gen. Lee to come down to his house at Ravensworth. I went down. I found Gen. Lee in bed. When I went into his room he told me he wished to make his will. He first spoke of giving his entire estate in fee simple to his wife, Mrs. Lee...The General told me that he wanted to make his will. He first said that he wanted to give everything he had to his wife, Mrs. Lee, although he did not want it to appear that he wanted to cut out his boys. I told him he could give her a life estate in everything. He thought for a minute or two and he said, "Yes, that answers it."[39]

Love recalled that he penciled in the second clause of the will, which mentioned the disposition of the estate among his two sons. It was Rooney Lee who chose the wording, and the dying man even proofed Love's work before approving the change. Although ailing, General Lee insisted on copying his own will.[40]

While the courts toiled over the Lee artifacts, Mary Tabb Lee fell ill when visiting friends and relatives in Richmond after a winter's stay in Summerville, South Carolina. Bolly had advised her to stay in the mild southern climate, but it did little good. She was in Richmond several weeks before dying on May 6, 1924. A number of people traveled south to attend the funeral, including coachman Nelson and Glenn Newman. The *Fairfax Herald* reported that Mary Tabb Lee's funeral was held at Richmond's "St. Paul's P.E. Church, Wednesday, and the body was taken to Lexington, where her husband and son are buried, and laid at rest."[41]

Despite her death, the court cases continued. After the initial court actions of 1923 and early 1924 worked out in favor of George and Mary Tabb Lee, Mary M. appealed the decision. Mary Tabb Lee's will had further complicated the matter; small bequests were made to the Ravensworth butler Ayres, coachman Nelson, and other friends. Her daughter-in-law Helen Keeney Lee, received "one of my pins and a string of pearls."[42]   Mary Tabb Lee made item six of her will so detailed it was clear where the remainder of her estate was going.

> All the rest, residue and remainder of my estate, of whatever kind or character, and wheresoever located, real, personal or mixed, including the portraits of General Robert E. Lee, General W. H. F. Lee and my father, George Bolling, and Mrs. R.E. Lee and Mrs. Bolling, my grand-mother, and including all furniture and silver which I have bought and every character and kind of personal belongings which I may own at the time of my death, I give, devise and bequeath to my son, George Bolling Lee, in absolute estate, in the event he survives me. Should he predecease me, then all the property hereby given, devised and bequeathed

> to the said George Bolling Lee, I hereby give,
> devise and bequeath to any grand-child or
> grand-children who may be living...[43]

The Court of Appeals of the District of Columbia ruled in favor of George Bolling Lee concerning the disputed contents in the trunk, upholding the argument that Mary Tabb Lee intended to give the trunk to her surviving son. Mary M. was legally outmaneuvered, and the ruling gave her no interest in the trunk contents.[44]

With Mary Tabb Lee's death, the dispute over heirlooms evolved into a battle over Ravensworth itself. Three citizens, A.C. Ritchie, R.R. Buckley, and J.U. Kincheloe, were selected as appraisers of her estate. The three met at Ravensworth on September 5, 1924, and labeled the contested items as "Articles of Controversy." The appraisers wrote:

> ...there were many articles in this house which,
> we were informed by the Executor, belonged to the
> estate of Mary Tabb Lee, but which are claimed
> by Mary M. Lee, widow of Robert E. Lee, Jr. were
> the property of the late W.H.F. Lee."[45]

Mary M. Lee claimed many items under the same pretext as her previous efforts. From the south room of the house she claimed a framed tapestry and two engravings--one depicting the Washington Family. From the upper floor's central hall, she claimed two caned chairs. She claimed the wardrobe, clothes rack, and desk from the nursery. From other rooms, she claimed a writing desk and a book stand with oval glass from the mansion's billiard room.[46]

One of the biggest disputes was not over personal property, but a lease made by Mary Tabb and George Bolling Lee to the Thalheimer Brothers of Richmond in October 1923. With the terms of Bob Lee's will in dispute, Mary M. Lee was party to a 50-year lease on several land lots in Richmond upon the death of Mary Tabb. Knowing nothing of the deal, she was infuriated that no attempt was made to include her on the decision on the lease. There appeared to be little alternative but to settle the issue in the courts. In order to defend their interest in the lease, it was necessary for the Thalheimer Brothers to get legal representation.⁴⁷

The Supreme Court of Appeals for the state of Virginia heard one of the cases in session at Wytheville, in the western portion of the state. Mary M. Lee filed suit in Richmond, believing it to be a proper legal venue. The Supreme Court of Appeals disagreed, deciding that the Circuit Court of Fairfax County maintained jurisdiction over the reconstruction of Rooney Lee's will. This might have been the case because the Lee properties for which Mary filed suit included interest in the "White House" and 609 Broad Street in Richmond.⁴⁸

By 1926 the battle over the heirlooms grew burdensome. Ravensworth caught fire, and the enthusiasm of the parties dampened. With the primary estate in ruins and George Bolling Lee pondering its future, Mary M. Lee's claims became a secondary matter. Both parties pressed to settle the issue. A $30,000 settlement from the insurance money transferred to Bob's widow. She maintained half the interest in the Richmond property, but the contract with the Thalheimer brothers remained in effect. *The Fairfax Herald* reported that the settlement required Mary M. to renounce any interest in the Ravensworth and "White House" estates. The same newspaper reported that she had no interest "in many historic heirlooms of the Lee and Washington families."⁴⁹

The suit settled, George Bolling Lee donated or sold some of the artifacts. In May 1927, he gave the portrait of his father to the Fairfax County Board of Supervisors. The Board gladly accepted it, and Hon. R. Walton Moore gave an address to commemorate the gift. Farming implements and livestock were sold at auction at the Ravensworth estate on December 9, 1926. Among items advertised were grain drills, plows, Holstein bulls, and wagons. A few notable heirlooms were advertised as "NICE FURNITURE which belonged to the late Mrs. W.H.F. Lee. This furniture consisted of a bedroom suite, bookcases, chairs, etc."⁵⁰

However, Bolling Lee was not legally "out of the woods." In early 1928 the state's attorney, W.W. Wall, contended that the transfer of the Richmond property from Mary Tabb Lee to Bolly was not exempt from inheritance tax as it was a deal made just prior to her death. This implied Mary Tabb Lee knew she was dying, and made the transfer to avoid taxes. Fairfax attorneys Thomas R. Keith and Charles Pickett noted the transfer was made six months before her death and was a result of the Mary M. Lee suits. This information was enough to release George Bolling Lee from the extra tax burden of 900 dollars, a substantial sum at the time.[51]

Something Turned Up in Alexandria

While the lawsuits dwindled, Ravensworth valuables were being moved illegally. In February 1929, recognizable pieces of the Lee holdings appeared in a few Alexandria antique shops. The items were identified by friend and Alexandria banker Taylor Burke, and he brought the case to the attention of local police. Chief William Walker Campbell acted vigorously once he found that the items in question were indeed those of the Lee family. The items were reported stolen from Ravensworth, and they were missing from previous inventories since its treasures were crated and stored after the 1926 fire. The trail led Campbell to two area families and workers from the estate.[52]

Rumors had surfaced within the Alexandria police department in early 1929 about stolen china, brass work, and glass in the city's fashionable antique shops. By February, Campbell was aware of the finds. Small monetary amounts were exchanged for the treasures, yet several of the pieces moved into new hands immediately. One antiques dealer related his find to banker Burke. As the latter included the Lee family among his clientele, he asked the antique dealer for his source. The answer was two local women. The trail led them to coachman Andrew Nelson.[53]

The two women were identified as Mrs. Matilda Minter and her daughter, Mrs. Jessie Derosier, and daughter-in-law Mrs. Eva Garland. All had ties to Charlottesville, Virginia. Charlie Garland and his wife Matilda had three children; Clarence; Jessie; and Russell. In 1920, the family moved to Alexandria without Charlie as head of household. Matilda married Raleigh Minter, a painter at the Alexandria shipyard, and supplemented the family income by working as a seamstress. Jessie Garland married Charles Derosier, a leather worker from the District of Columbia, and was living at 422 2nd Street, N.W.[54]

As the case unraveled, it proved to be more an embarrassment than an organized fencing operation. The three women were not wealthy; Nelson was equally sympathetic, a man who was down on his luck and attempting to reverse a mass of misfortune that befell him. Although Linwood Newman was charged, his involvement was unlikely. After a divorce, he moved his family to Alexandria prior to the appearance of the stolen items. Because of their connections to Ravensworth, both Nelson and Newman were thought to have inside knowledge of the thefts.[55]

Clearly an amateur effort, there were some obvious errors on the part of the theft ring. Antique stores in Alexandria were too close to the estate and subject to recognition by antique dealers, friends, and local family members. Both Nelson and Newman would have known this. Taylor Burke had intimate knowledge of the Lee holdings through his business and personal connections with the family. Burke was named as second executor in the will of Mary Custis Lee, as her "particular friend and banker...who long had charge of my money affairs and knows all about them."[56]

When Doctor Lee returned from New York to appear in front of Judge A.C. Ritchie in Fairfax, the trial took on a tabloid atmosphere. On February 23, 1929, the preliminary larceny proceedings necessitated gathering the notable artifacts together in the courtroom to be used as exhibits. The *Fairfax Herald* later reported that "many of the articles stolen were brought into court to be used as evidence and attracted much attention lying on the tables inside the bar."[57] Doctor Lee identified the items for the record. A grand jury was given until March 18 to consider a verdict.[58]

The story of the arrests revealed the cooperation of police forces from both Alexandria and Fairfax County to recover the Lee property. While it was Captain Campbell who led the investigation in Alexandria, Fairfax policeman Virgil Williams assisted in the arrest of Eva Garland. Two baskets loaded with chinaware, cut glass, and silver were recovered from the Garland and Minter homes. Virginia police arrested Derosier in Washington, finding one painting at her home.[59]

Despite the high profile detective work by Campbell and other law enforcement officials, the whole matter was treated as an embarrassing blight that needed to be erased. As early as February 12, the *Alexandria Gazette* reported that, as the objects were recovered, the whole matter might be dropped.

> While nothing definite as to what disposition will be made of the cases, it may be, according to reports, that the entire matter will be dropped, inasmuch as most of the loot had been recovered. The dishes and cut glassware were taken from a period before the fire which destroyed Ravensworth in 1927, according to Sheriff Kirby. Ravensworth is located eight miles southwest of Alexandria in Fairfax County, and the home of the distinguished Lee family of Virginia. After the fire, of incendiary origin, which destroyed the colonial home, the silverware, glassware and other heirlooms were packed in barrels and placed in the cellar.[60]

Effort to settle the matter quietly were further complicated by the grand jury indictments of all six defendants in the "taking or the selling of the relics." Judge Howard W. Smith presided over the sentencing in Fairfax. While it initally looked grim for all six people despite any confirmation of individual roles, the court disposed five out of six of the indictments by March 26. Three were given suspended sentences pending good behavior and two were "nolle prossed," which signified marginal or no proven connection. The *Alexandria Gazette* reported that the "only case remaining undisposed of is that of a colored man named Newman."[61]

Linwood Newman was left as the lone defendant. Puzzling by today's standards of justice, as it was doubtful he had any influence over the other defendants. However, being African-American in the 1920s South, the racial factor cannot be ignored. The weight of decision might have been tipped by prior liquor offenses or racism. On March 30, the case against Newman ensued. Some of the artifacts were again displayed, including several vases and Robert E. Lee's pistol case. After deliberating two hours, the former estate carpenter was found "not guilty." By this time, Nelson disappeared from the area. The grave of his wife Mary at Sharon Chapel in Alexandria had a empty plot next to it. The *Fairfax Herald* related that Doctor Lee had not wished any of the defendants to be prosecuted.[62]

The Magnolia and the Steward

As a result of her legal actions, Mary Middleton Lee received some of the family heirlooms. The artifacts she received were glasses, finger bowls, silver, and miniature portraits. Supported by her $30,000 legacy, she moved to a residence on Wyoming Avenue, Northwest, Washington, D.C., in the center of a fashionable international neighborhood of embassies and old statesman's homes. Her life at home, adorned with old antebellum-style columns, was completed by a servant named Oscar Maynard. The African-American was fiercely loyal to Mrs. Lee, acting as both chauffeur and butler. When Mary issued invitations for one of her numerous soirees at the residence, it was Maynard who personally delivered them--on a silver tray.[63]

In many ways, Maynard fit the type of servant the Lees always depended on. He was foreign-born, clean, and satisfied with his employment. The immaculate chauffeur immigrated at the age of seven from his native Haiti. After some years in Newark, New Jersey, his family settled in Washington, D.C. Upon his graduation from Francis Junior High School, he came to work for Mrs. Lee in February 1927. If it was difficult to understand Maynard's sense of loyalty to a living symbol of the Confederate South, he enjoyed the benefits his job provided. The two were always on good terms, and it appeared Maynard was something of a old-style servant.[64]

Maynard was part of the entourage that traveled with Mary to her summer retreats at Enchantment. One of her close friends, a German neurologist named Count Friedrich August de Blackmere, often accompanied them. Mary Lee was known for her eccentricities and arguments in the nearby town of Flat Rock, North Carolina, and Blackmere was the gentleman who fired a rifle into the estate's large lake to discourage young trespassers from swimming. Mary's primary obsession at Enchantment was planting lilacs. The flowers grew from large beds at the estate's stone gates to the walls of the house. The presence of lilacs did not soften her reputation with the local children, who knew of her two deceased husbands. One resident remembers a rhyme they concocted: "Here comes Mary Lee...looking for number three."[65]

Despite every precaution, the guardianship of the Lee artifacts were far from secure. Mary M. was abroad in the summer of 1932 when several of the articles were reported stolen. While sailing to Europe she had entrusted her keys to a friend, Mabel Ashley, asking her to obtain a tin box for the keys and "look into the closet" where the heirlooms were kept. The items listed as missing were a set of glass casters and two salt stands from the Washington family; "two salt spoons, worth $500; three fingerbowls, five port glasses, and four claret glasses, valued at $3,000."[66] A Washington plaque by sculptor Antoine Houdon valued at $25,000 was safe, as was another Washington caster set and Society of the Cincinnati plates. Although application was made with the Automobile Insurance Company of Hartford, Connecticut, no payment was forthcoming. Mary sued them in the District of Columbia Superior Court.[67]

Mary M. Lee remained a social force in Washington. In June 1935 she threw a party whose guests included the Ambassadors from Italy, Germany, Brazil, China, and Turkey; Secretary of the Interior Harold Ickes and wife; Secretary of Labor Frances Perkins; and Francis I. du Pont. The paper reported that she had an orchestra play "Southern airs and Strauss waltzes, favorites with the hostess."[68] She decorated her Wyoming Avenue house in "pink roses, delphinium and lilies," and her guests wore costumes, sipped St. Cecilia Charleston punch, and ate Virginia ham. Even more interesting was the chance to see the Lee artifacts from Ravensworth.[69]

> Guests were given a rare opportunity to inspect Mrs. Lee's famous and valuable collection of miniatures, the portraits of General Lee, of various distinguished Middletons, and Pinckneys. Among the miniatures are those of Robert E. Lee and his wife, of George and Martha Washington-gems, all of them-and a miniature of Mrs. Lee's grandfather, Secretary of the Treasury in Davis' Confederate Cabinet, by Frazier, which is considered priceless.[70]

The times brought about major changes in society and life. Count de Blackmere died on an extended visit to Mary Lee's Wyoming Avenue home in January 1941. Afterwards, members of her family moved in. By 1948, Mary Lee lived with her nephew Ralph Izard Middleton at both the Wyoming Avenue house and Enchantment. George Bolling Lee died July 14 at the age of 76. Up to the end, he lived in New York as a visiting surgeon to Bellevue Hospital. Despite occasional visits to the former Ravensworth estate for horse breeding or summer visits to his scaled down frame house, Doctor Lee maintained his life as a resident of New York.[71]

Mary Lee's last years were not as quiet, remaining sharp-tongued even in old age. After hearing of federal intervention at Little Rock, Arkansas in 1957, she sent President Dwight D. Eisenhower a memorable telegram: "Abe Lincoln got his. You'll get yours. Signed Mrs. Robert E. Lee Ill."[72] However, her most memorable deed came in June 1938 when Mary removed the remains of Robert E. Lee III from the family chapel to Magnolia Cemetery in Charleston. Mary made this request of the Board of Trustees, who could not stop her as she was Bob Lee's widow. Once approved by court order, the body was removed from the Lee crypt in Lexington and transported to Charleston for reburial. Both her husbands were buried in the cemetery, on a sloping hill outside the city. Her friend the Count de Blackmere was buried there as well. Mary was not long in joining them.[73]

Mary's decline was rapid in her final two years. She broke her hip in a fall while at Enchantment, leaving her unable to walk; Oscar Maynard had to physically carry her from place to place. While in Asheville, North Carolina on May 19, 1959, Mary died at the age of 84. Funeral services were held in the Church of St. John's in the Wilderness, and she was buried with her husband at Magnolia Cemetery.[74] The *Washington Post* particularly mentioned the family treasures in her obituary.

> Several years after she and her husband came to Washington they purchased a house at 2140 Wyoming Ave. The house was put up for sale several times in the last 10 years but still remained in her name at the time of her death. It was the scene of many social evenings for the diplomatic and smart set in Washington. A portrait of General Lee and his wife and other

relics of the Lee family and her own Middleton forbears were kept in the house.[75]

Mary had changed her will several times between 1950 and 1959. The Register of Wills in Washington, D.C. recorded three versions: June 23, 1950; April 15, 1953; and February 5, 1959. The only consistency was her request to be buried in Magnolia Cemetery in Charleston. Heirs to the estate and the distribution constantly changed. In the first will, the "rest, residue and remainder" went in equal parts to her nephew Ralph Izard Middleton, friend Hans von Dreyhausen, and Oscar Maynard. She mentioned specifically that she was including,

> ...any and all interest which I may have, under said will of said Robert E. Lee, in and to certain silver known as "Mount Vernon Silver" and "Lee Silver" in the residence of said Robert E. Lee at 1733 Riggs Place, Northwest, Washington, D.C., at the time of his death, which silver was bequeathed to me for my life-time and after my death to said George Bolling Lee.[76]

In the April 1953 will, the Wyoming Avenue house and Enchantment were to be sold and the profits split between Ralph Middleton and Oscar Maynard. The 1959 will was much broader. She directed the executor to sell the Wyoming Street house, send her books to Georgetown University, and give her clothing to her servants. The "remainder" went to her two nephews Beverly M. Middleton and Ralph I. Middleton. Some notable items went to her nephew Beverly, who spent most of his life in the Carolinas. After a colorful career as a radio personality in Hendersonville, North Carolina, he divorced and moved to Northern Virginia. While there, he displayed Lee items in a benefit for the Alexandria Hospital in October 1963. One such item was the Ravensworth Vase. The sterling silver vase was made by Samuel Kirk and Son on special orders from Mary Tabb Lee, and the vessel featured a base-relief of the Ravensworth house itself. A female figure depicted beside the home was thought to be Mary Tabb Lee. The *Washington Star* reported the presence of the vase and other objects.[77]

> The vase was returned to Virginia with Mr. and
> Mrs. Beverly Middleton, who recently moved to
> Alexandria from Charleston, S.C...Also on display
> at the Middleton house are original Miley and
> Brady photographs of all members of the Robert
> E. Lee family, the books and prayer books of
> the Lee family, silverware of George and Martha
> Washington and other memorabilia of historic
> Americans.[78]

Beverly Middleton died in 1973. In a final irony of his role as protector of the Lee heritage, he chose to be buried in Gettysburg Cemetery, the site of General Robert E. Lee's most bitter defeat. Middleton would have been buried in Flat Rock, but gave up his burial plot during divorce proceedings. The items Beverly possessed were scattered.[79]

Access: The Problem of the Rocky Mount Manuscripts

By the 1930s, historians and archivists such as Douglas Southall Freeman and Burton J. Hendrick wrote extensively on the family. Part of the Lee legacy was found in the family letters, covering successive generations of the Lee family. As the Lee families grew larger and more distant from each other, letters penned by "Light Horse Harry" and Robert E. Lee had a higher risk of accidental destruction or loss.

In the midst of resurgent interest in the old family residence of Stratford Hall, a Westmoreland County, Virginia resident discovered that a large cache of Lee papers was in the possession of C. Carter Lee of Rocky Mount, Virginia. The young gentleman was the Commonwealth's Attorney in Franklin County and had a brilliant legal mind. He and his siblings inherited the letter grouping in a mixture with that of his paternal grandfather, Charles Carter Lee. In two old trunks were his grandfather's unpublished poetry and memoirs.[80]

However, there was additional historical material from "Light Horse Harry" Lee and Robert E. Lee. As the eldest son of his father's second marriage, Charles Carter Lee received the letters of "Light Horse Harry." He also inherited the remainder of his half-brother Henry's correspondence after his early death in Paris in 1837. As the two brothers were the last of the Lees to live at Stratford, it was natural that historians sought these letters. The Robert E. Lee material was limited to letters written to Charles Carter Lee, some in wartime.[81]

Word spread of the surviving correspondence, and historians inquired about citing or copying the material. According to archivist Edwin Hemphill, C. Carter Lee gave permission to historian Ms. Ethel Armes, representing the Robert E. Lee Memorial Foundation, to search the contents of the trunk for a book on the ancestral family home of Stratford Hall. Douglas Southall Freeman was denied permission to search the same contents, and the reason given by Carter Lee was that the material was too recent for public airing More to the point was that Carter Lee had a general dislike for one of Freeman's articles on the Lees. "Lee and the Ladies," published in *Scribner's Magazine* in October and November 1925, was viewed negatively by the family.[82] In February 1933, scholarly Cazenove Lee, descendant of "Light Horse Harry's" brother, and secretary of the decade-old "Society of the Lees in Virginia," offered his opinion on the Freeman issue.

> I might add that I am familiar with the use made of similar material by Dr. Douglas Freeman in an article "Lee and the Ladies," (Scribner's Magazine, Oct. and Nov. 1925). I consider his treatment of his subject as unethical, unkind and in places I know it to be untrue. I am satisfied that the Lee Foundation will never be guilty of such conduct. I trust that no fear of this character is causing the withdrawal of the manuscripts.[83]

While C. Carter Lee allowed Foundation members at Yale University to begin copying the papers, he was distrustful of Miss Armes. He also felt he had lost control of the letters in the matters of publication, as indicated in a February 20, 1933 letter to a Foundation official. In the letter, he asked for the immediate return of the contents on loan. Carter Lee was vague in his reasoning. He wrote,

> ...the rest of the family have very definite ideas upon the subject...We have certain urgent reasons, which are causing us at this time to get together all of the unpublished letters of General Light Horse Harry Lee, and of General R.E. Lee..."[84]

The "certain urgent reasons" was the most puzzling part of the letter, and historians worried. Stratford Hall was being purchased by the Robert E. Lee Memorial Foundation and most interested parties were casting about for important family papers to restore the structure to period appearance. Knowing the historical value of the papers, Cazenove Lee interceded. Historians were concerned with the outright sale of the collection, which would put the papers out of reach before the copying was finished. There was some confusion over the possible intent of C. Carter Lee, so Cazenove decided to find out. He sent an inquiry to his cousin, who answered that he was considering a bulk sale of the collection to Yale University. Although C. Carter did not dwell on the subject of Freeman's article in his response to Cazenove, he recalled that he refused the historian access because of "Lee and the Ladies."[85]

Cazenove Lee acted quickly to preserve access to the Rocky Mount papers. He suggested holding the letters at Yale until he inspected them. As he had some idea of historical value, he offered assistance for a future "sale." In the meantime, C. Carter Lee's brother Henry, a doctor in Cincinnati, expressed his wish that the letters be sent to Stratford Hall. By July 1933 the shift to the estate as a repository looked favorable. The letters were returned from Yale, while the Foundation made final overtures for Stratford. When in late 1936, Edwin Hemphill inquired about the framing and care of the papers to prevent their deterioration, C. Carter Lee maintained their stewardship.[86]

By January 1935, Freeman was back in favor after he wrote his multi-volume biography of Robert E. Lee to great critical acclaim. After some of the Lees observed a reading, Cazenove remarked,

> he [Freeman] arose in the National Cathedral and thrilled 2000 people for 40 minutes. He brought tears to many an unrepentant eye, he preached the

best sermon that spot has heard in many a day. He held the attention of the Bishop of Washington and Carter Glass--some task."[87]

Other historical projects required access to the Rocky Mount papers. In 1934, author Burton J. Hendrick was commissioned by *Atlantic Monthly* to write a book on the Lees. He required access to the same Rocky Mount manuscripts to complete his research on several generations of the family. Instead of receiving cooperation from fellow historian Ethel Armes, Hendrick was rebuffed; she had her plans for her own book focusing on the life of Henry Lee. There might have been personal difficulties between the two writers, as Cazenove noted they were "working within 100 ft of each other in the Library of Congress."[88] In February 1935, Cazenove intervened again. Feeling he could not approach his cousin C. Carter Lee for a second researcher, Cazenove decided on bargaining with both potential authors. He reasoned to Ethel Armes that Hendrick's book would be of benefit to any future research she undertook on her proposal. Cazenove further wrote Mrs. Emerson Root Newell, who chaired the Foundation's Committee on research, to allow Dr. Hendrick access to the copies. Privately, he sharply criticized Ethel Armes. In a letter to a friend, Cazenove acknowledged Miss Armes as a valued member of the Foundation, but that she "needs a spanking."[89]

Cazenove Lee early ensured public access to the letters, and therefore saved the family legend through scholarship. Hendrick finished his book by October 1935, when Dr. Freeman credited Hendrick's book in his remarks at the dedication of Stratford Hall. The book was a great success with the public because of its genealogical bent. C. Carter Lee possessed the Rocky Mount manuscripts for almost a decade longer, finally donating them to the Virginia State Library in two parts, the first in December 1944 and the second in March 1945. By this time, Carter Lee's health had steadily declined. He died on New's Years Day, 1958, at the age of 51. Cazenove Lee's negotiations had ensured future access to the Rocky Mount manuscripts, and maintained the Lee legacy in the most important family studies of the 1930s. Cazenove continued his work with the Society of the Lees of Virginia until his death in 1945.[90]

For historians, a larger question remained. How much of the Lee family legacy was in its belongings, and how much in its collective descendants? The destruction of Ravensworth and decline of the mansion society, the death of the Lee children, and formation of memorial societies contributed to the transfer of legacy to inanimate objects. These facilitated a new period of biography from prominent historians as Freeman, Armes, and Hendrick. As C. Carter Lee knew, the owners of the objects and papers controlled the legacy. As long as the Lee descendants controlled the papers and objects, the direction of legacy was at their disposal. Cazenove Lee realized that outside eyes meant giving up part of that control. Perhaps he knew that historians were kinder through a peaceful transfer to public access.

One Way of Gathering

Eleanor Lee Templeman was a noted author and historian by the 1970s. Her book on the history of Arlington County, Virginia, called *Arlington Heritage*, described her family legacy in the area. In addition, her contributions to the Society of the Lees of Virginia, particularly after the death of Cazenove Lee, were commendable. As Northern Virginia furnished a second family home, Sully Plantation, Templeman planned a transit of a number of family artifacts to that location and the restored Arlington House. By 1971, she was on a course to do this.[91]

Mrs. Templeman's personal lineage came from Richard Bland Lee, Robert E. Lee's uncle. She was a personal tour-de-force of legacy-building. Her personal attachment to the precious heirlooms of the Lees was well known. In other words, Eleanor Lee Templeman was a guidepost of legacy for several decades.[92]

Eleanor faced a daunting challenge in locating scattered family heirlooms. In addition, she wanted a proper placement for each item. However, most underestimated her fortitude, and her battle with Mrs. Marie W. Weitzel showcased her tenacity. The episode began in March 1948, when J. Collins Lee, a descendant of Richard Bland Lee, passed away. His neighbors at the time of his death were Dr. John Weitzel and his wife Marie. Templeman wrote decades later that J. Collins Lee was an alcoholic incapable of maintaining his own affairs. For the last two years of his life, the Weitzels rented him a room and drafted his will. Eleanor Templeman believed it was signed under duress. The will gave the Weitzels possession of a large number of antiques from the Sully Plantation house, and featured items personally belonging to Richard Bland Lee.[93]

Eleanor Templeman sued for her family heirlooms in 1952. The range of items, from card tables to Martha Washington's silk bonnet, stirred her desperation to keep them within the family's grasp. She monitored the Weitzel's actions before and during the long settlement proceedings, including several sales made by Mrs. Weitzel and her friend Torrey McKenney. One of the actions, she wrote later, was a "sneak sale" near Charlottesville before settlement of the suit. There was an auction in New York in January 1952 that featured some of the Lee's silver items. Eleanor wrote her Richmond attorney that her cousin Mary Rust attempted to purchase some family silver. While offer and counter-offer bounced back and forth, Eleanor believed the silver was intended for the Parke-Bennet sale in New York. She asked her attorney to subphoena any record of sale in the auction for the five Lee lots being offered.[94]

Despite her enormous efforts, Templeman lost the case. She felt the judge's remarks about the statute of limitations mislead the jurors. In reality, she lost the case because her evidence was not verifiable. She drew an elaborate family tree, showing a six generation inheritance chart for the contested items. It was an impressive effort, but Eleanor Templeman's genealogical case was a stretch in legal terms. Firstly, her Aunt Anna Washington Reading was killed in a California train wreck on December 30, 1906. Templeman claimed Reading's will would have included Eleanor at the beginning of the following year. Instead, her Aunt Alice Matilda Reading claimed the estate under the existing will. Eleanor further claimed Alice verbally promised her items, or at least some family china, from Anna Reading's estate. Indeed she was the only child of her generation, and she expected to receive a large inheritance. However, Alice Reading sold a number of items prior to her death in 1939, especially those items belonging to the Washington family; letters written by President James Madison were sold to the Library of Congress, and half of the old Lee Canton china was sold to another relative. There was enough proof of prior intent of distribution, so Mrs. Templeman's inference to Alice Reading's promise was doubly hard to verify in the settlement.[95]

Eleanor Templeman continued her battle to regain family articles. Her efforts flared after Sully Plantation was placed on the National Register of Historic Sites. She was still bitter at Mrs. Weitzel in 1971, when she wrote John Melville Jennings of the Virginia Historical Society. In the communication, she informed Jennings that she had a "large box of testimony" to deliver him--and that she appreciated that he had "direct knowledge of the character of Mrs. John Weitzel!"[96] Shortly thereafter, Mrs. Templeman began arranging for family loans of artifacts for Sully and other Lee homes. In her painstaking way, she brought the correct items into the houses to which they formerly belonged. However, getting loans for museum display was an issue. Relatives provided china, but even donations were scrutinized. Donated pieces needed to meet the period standards at the very minimum. In 1977, she attempted a "reciprocal loan" between the Lee Society and the Fairfax County Park Authority to move two items from the Sully lineage to that location. Mrs. Templeman owned the two items in question: the firescreen of Mrs. Edmund Jennings Lee and the spinning wheel of Mrs. Richard Bland Lee. One of the parties balked at losing the pieces on loan. In reaction, Eleanor sold the two items outright to the new Sully Foundation.[97]

Until her death in 1984, Mrs. Eleanor Templeman was the "great recoverer" of Lee legacies. From her Arlington home, she arranged her papers and writings for archives. Her own contributions were vast, but one must question the desperation of her quest. It was endless, practically hopeless, to rearrange the artifacts as they were from a myriad of relatives and strangers. Her legacy--which she felt her right as a Lee descendant--was to bring those lost heirlooms "home." Her efforts did exactly that, but not without its failures. Without the overall effort, it was doubtful that the clusters of items in various museums would number as many. The answer to her struggle for legacy, the latest of many, was contained in the words of her July 1977 letter to Frances Shively on the loan. Templeman wrote that "these heirlooms will be 'going home' to where we and our descendants could enjoy seeing them in our ancestral home."[98]

Legacy III: Family and Military Reputation

Spreading Branches of the Tree

The Lee family boasted a large family tree. Several notable members sprang from its branches. Often overlooked by historians, the collateral lines of the family served as the bearers of the family legacy. One example was the line of Robert E. Lee, Jr., known as "Rob" in the family letters. He was one of two married sons of the famous General, although he wed later in life. Rob Lee's influence on historians derived from his biographical work on his 1904 book on his father's life, *Letters and Recollections of General Lee*. However, his quiet existence as a country squire at the old Custis estate of Romancoke belied his active role in promoting the Lee legacy. Although one of his postwar homes was located close to the "White House," Romancoke soon eclipsed the older home in daily activity. The new life of the estate paralleled the changes in Robert E. Lee, Jr. himself. As a young man, he embraced the foot soldier's life and a single man's existence. However, once he matured and married, Rob's wife and two daughters grounded him. He focused intently on his heritage until his death in January 1916.[1]

Although he excelled in his writing, Rob Lee shunned any thoughts of military glory. He decided against war service in 1898, giving the military representation of the family to his Cousin Fitz Lee. In doing so, Rob Lee unknowingly passed on furthering a direct legacy from father to son. However, it was in keeping with the view his father held on wars. He noted that America was,

> ...anxious to forget the past estrangement [the Civil War]-& I have seized this opportunity to try & make it all inclusive-I have done with wars-save in defense of my country-& I take very little interest in what is going on now."[2]

Although Robert E. Lee, Jr. carried his father's full name, a good portion of the military glory of the Lee name fell to his first cousin,

Fitzhugh Lee. Like their cousin Rooney Lee, Fitz promoted the image of a dashing cavalryman during the Civil War. Sydney Smith Lee's son redeemed not only the family's military reputation, but the entire Southern military stature. Fitz Lee later emerged as an "Renaissance Man" in his postwar life, as a businessman, politician, author, and soldier. Knowing the value of political propaganda as a source of regional pride, he wrote a book, *General Lee*, in 1894. While the writing provided one of the first family accounts of the Confederate general, it was an unstable Cuba which gave Fitz Lee the opportunity for which all Southerners waited-military glory and redemption of Southern pride. The Spanish-American War enhanced his rise in popularity as a military hero. As a result of his inspired leadership, President Grover Cleveland appointed Fitz Lee consul general in Cuba. Soon after the American victory in Cuba, the elderly Fitz Lee's image graced ash trays, paper fans, and sewing kits distributed across America. His death in April 1905 saw mourning that echoed General Robert E. Lee's own funeral some 35 years before.[3]

The same military potential graced his son Fitzhugh Lee, Jr. Like his ancestors, the younger Fitz had a genuine love of horsemanship. He began his career with great strides, serving President Theodore Roosevelt as a presidential aide. However, Fitz Jr. faded from his early prominence into a modern military consisting of tanks and machines. Never again would a family member make the Lee name synonymous with military prominence.[4]

Just as the military role of the Lees faded into obscurity, other branches of the family drifted from their traditional family seats. Two examples were Robert E. Lee's poet brother, Charles Carter Lee, and his youngest uncle, Edmund Jennings Lee. Charles Carter Lee's sons and grandsons often saw Robert's children, but their generations suffered from constant wanderlust. Additionally, the descendants of Edmund Jennings Lee adhered to religious service. The consistent family ties to Alexandria's Theological Seminary and other religious missions frequently required movements. A portion of the family moved into West Virginia, where this line of Lees centered around an estate near Shepherdstown, called Leeland. Their ties to Alexandria never ceased, but change widened the distance between family members. Even with the modernization of society, combined with the American habit of looking to its heroic roots, America needed the Lee legacy. Despite their constant movement of residence, fame found them as protectors of the family legacy through ownership and representation of vital family documents dating back to the time of "Light Horse" Harry.[5]

Romancoke and the Writer

In King William County, Virginia, the old Custis estate of Romancoke was described as a "dependency" or "overseer's house" of the more prestigious "White House." The house's farm buildings were a necessity because of the estate's enormous acreage. It was a large tract when George Washington purchased the land from a gentleman named William Black about 1773. The name "Romancoke" was on English explorer John Smith's first map of Virginia. It was an Indian phrase defined as a "large bend in the Pamunkey River." The terrain was flat and marshy, although it was fertile for corn cultivation. George Washington Parke Custis kept a careful inventory of stock, corn, and slaves working on the property. Romancoke usually provided a plentiful corn crop to adequately supplement Custis' income.[6]

Before his marriage, Robert E. Lee, Jr. was restless following his move to Romancoke in 1866. A bachelor attracted to postwar business schemes, he was often in Lexington with his father. After a few years, the second marriage of his brother Rooney Lee enticed Rob to fix up Romancoke. With the help of his sister Mildred Childe Lee, Rob made the old house fashionable. It was modest in size, yet suitable for entertaining guests. Some friends stayed for long lengths of time; a fellow veteran who originally intended to stay two days ended his visit after two years. In 1871, Rob's marriage to Charlotte Haxall of Richmond changed his bachelor habits.[7]

Rob settled down into the role of husband. However, his life abruptly changed when Charlotte contracted tuberculosis and died on September 22, 1872. The family worried over both Rob's mental and physical condition following Charlotte's death. Events drove Rob to drink heavily, and he fell back upon his old bachelor habits. In 1875, his sister Mildred arranged for his passage on a vessel to Europe. In London, Rob's name alone brought people from all over Great Britain to simply catch a glimpse of him. Young officers who heard the surname of "Lee" came to see him ride English horses. The ladies were impressed with the Captain's southern manners. The British saw him as the best of American society.[8]

After his uplifting travels, Robert E. Lee, Jr. pursued business opportunities at home. In 1890, he moved to Washington, D.C., and joined the real estate and insurance firm of Dulany, Fleming and Lee. The office was at 1320 F Street, N.W., close to his nephew Bob Lee's law firm. Always close to his family, he spent much time with Bob at Ravensworth. However, he returned to domestic life when he married his cousin Juliet Carter on March 18, 1894. As the couple prepared to move back to Romancoke before the wedding, Rob's brother Custis sent a deed of release for the property. For their housekeeping needs, Rob and Juliet retained a servant couple who had previously worked for his parents, Bob and Sarah Meredith. Within a few years, the Lees had two daughters, Mary Custis and Ann Carter.[9]

Rob Lee found new life and literary focus in compiling a volume of his father's letters. In 1896, he began writing letters to various family members and friends to gather research material. One of the first people Rob consulted was his oldest brother Custis. Still President of Washington & Lee University at the time, Custis assisted Rob in gathering the disparate letters.

> I shall be very glad to do anything in my power to assist you in your article on Genl. Lee. I have but few of his [letters] with me, and do not know that they would be of much use; but will send them if you desire. There are, or were, a number of his letters to our mother; Mary had them to look over with Fitz. Lee, when the latter was preparing his book...I have, also, in Genl. Lee's letterbooks, copies of letters (not personal and private ones) written while he was in Lexington, Va; some of them are in the Rev. J. Wm Jones' "Personal Reminiscences." These letter books are now in the hands of Dr. Henry A. White, of W.& L. U., who is preparing (or thinking of so doing) a biography of Genl. Lee.[10]

Dutifully devoted to the work, Rob Lee created a full life account of his father that reached beyond his Civil War campaigns. He canvassed friends for further material, creating one of the most personal accounts of the General. He wrote to one of his sources,

> I also wish to ask you whether I could get a copy of letters to, & of a paper, written by Genl R E Lee, now in his office, having been undisturbed since his death...I hope to complete & publish some time in 1900-& I am anxious to make the collection of letters as complete as possible..."[11]

The literary efforts started by others culminated in Robert E. Lee, Jr.'s own work. Some of the papers he possessed remained in one of sister Mary Custis Lee's trunks following their use in his cousin Fitzhugh Lee's book. Fitz had written a wartime account that held a measure of personal content, but none of Lee's children had yet recorded their memories. Other accounts were written by authors of his father's generation, such as General Oliver O. Howard and former Confederate General Thomas Rosser. Cousin Edmund Jennings Lee, grandson of Rob's great-uncle, prepared an article on "The Character of Lee." Despite all the writings on his father, Rob Lee was in no hurry to publish. Frank Leslie's Publishing House proposed a series of articles in their illustrated magazine *Popular Monthly*. His original intentions was an article, but the material grew expansive. The correspondence and reflection comprised an entire book. By October 1896, Rob's finished work became embroiled in the publishing house wars. *The Illustrated American* was interested in it, but Lee hedged in sending it there.[12]

The extensive research and a profusion of letters made for a thick volume. Other publishers had bolder ideas for the Lee biography. Harper & Brothers of New York wrote Rob Lee proposing to feature the work in both magazine and book forms. The firm offered to send their literary representative, Walter Hines Page, to Romancoke to discuss a full publishing deal. Page was the former editor of the *Atlantic Monthly* magazine and considered a "heavyweight" in the publishing world. By late January 1900 Page felt he had an understanding with Rob Lee on book royalties: 10% on the first 1,500 copies, 12 ½ % on the next 1,500, and 15% above this number. However, this proved negligible as Lee had lost interest in the offer.[13]

The appearance of *Recollections and Letters of General Robert E. Lee* in 1904 resounded well with the book-hungry public. The honor of publication fell to the Garden City Publishing Company. Letters arrived from admirers and former Confederate soldiers, such as B.W. Green. On October 25, Green wrote Rob Lee that "it is a good story, well told; plain and straightforward; no flourishes, no gush or exageration [sic]" and that he planned to give a copy to each of his grandsons. The book made a lasting impression, and it encouraged other authors on the subject. A Richmond resident named W.J. DeRenne wrote Rob of his ownership of "some two hundred letters" of General Lee to Confederate President Jefferson Davis. As a monument to the man, DeRenne proposed sending them to historian Doctor Douglas Southall Freeman for examination.[14]

Rob Lee's book sold well in both America and Europe. Not until Douglas Southall Freeman's multi-volume work several decades later was Rob Lee's work equaled as the primary work on the family. His brother Custis guarded the family name from any undesired publication, but gave his brother cautious optimism upon receipt of the thick volume. He wrote Rob, "...your book did not reach me until yesterday. It seems to be an imposing volume, with good paper and print; and I thank you for it very much. I hope it may bring you some compensation as well as credit."[15]

Unmoved by his sudden popularity, Rob Lee's interest centered on life at Romancoke and Washington, D.C., focusing little on the outside world. Daily routine was described by Captain Lee's one-time doctor, Bathurst Bagby, as a "very secluded. He would never allow his friends to nominate him for any office, as he did not want any position or honor given on account of his name and ancestors."[16] While at Romancoke, his bachelor nephew, Bob Lee, visited him "once or twice a year." His closest associates were immediate family and house servants; when one of Juliet Lee's former slaves fell ill with severe pneumonia in late 1905, the Carter family paid for the 90 year old woman's numerous medical bills.[17]

Despite limited appearances and a failing constitution, Rob Lee maintained contact with the Willard Family of Fairfax. In January 1914 Rob visited Ravensworth where he learned his old friend Belle

Willard married Kermit Roosevelt, one of President Theodore Roosevelt's sons. He wrote, "I had not the slightest suspicion of any thing of the kind. I hope I may meet Mr. Roosevelt..."[18] It was about this time that the heart problems which plagued his father began with him. As early as 1906, he wrote a friend, "I have felt my age for the first time this winter - Have not been well & have lost much of my activity."[19] Doctor Bagby recollected that he "visited often" to treat Lee's angina. He had the condition for several years. By the winter of 1912, Rob referred to his condition as a "disease." However, he remained upbeat and minimized its presence. He recalled his miseries as "originating in a gland in my neck takes some liberties with the nerves of my legs & hands. I am hardly a invalid & do not suffer any pain."[20]

Robert E. Lee, Jr. died in January 1916. After his death, Romancoke was sold out of family hands. Later owners gave the mansion a more regal appearance. The Lee's residence at the estate, while lasting for decades, was never generationally rooted as it was at Ravensworth. The descendants of Rob Lee resided north of Romancoke, many settling outside Washington, D.C. Today they represent one of the most active lines of direct descendants of Robert E. Lee.[21]

Fitzhugh Lee and Redemption

In *Memoirs of a Poor Relation*, Marietta Minnigerode Andrews related her memories of General Fitzhugh Lee. She recalled her father Charlie Minnigerode ran away from home at the age of sixteen to serve under Lee in the Confederate army.

> ...he had seen the cavalryman in a saddler's shop looking at equipment, and had been thrilled as a young hero worshipper by the encounter. Fitz Lee noticed him and said to him, "Boy, why aren't you in the Army?" And a few nights later the boy was in the Army..[22]

Fitzhugh Lee was born on November 19, 1835 in Alexandria, Virginia. He was the eldest son of Robert's brother Sydney Smith Lee and his wife Anna Maria Mason. His godmother was Ravensworth's Anna Maria Fitzhugh. In addition, Fitzhugh Lee had not one legacy, but two. He was the grandson of Henry "Light Horse Harry" Lee, but also the great-grandson of George Mason of Gunston Hall, the founding father of the Bill of Rights to the American Constitution. The same daring and ambition that characterized his paternal grandfather dominated Fitz Lee. "Light Horse Harry" Lee was the ideal of the horseback soldier. His green-jacketed cavalrymen saw glory in the American Revolution in fights at Paulus Hook, New Jersey and Eutaw Springs, South Carolina. "Aunt Maria" observed the young Fitz Lee had an early "desire to become a dragoon like his grandfather, Light Horse Harry."[23]

Knowing legacy as he did, Sydney Smith Lee's (often called "Smith") naval career disallowed any centralized homestead. Like Robert, Smith was a "Stratford orphan." They were both young boys when "Light Horse" Harry Lee died. Their mother was forced to live far from their estate seat at Stratford. On February 5, 1835, Smith's marriage to Anna Maria Mason was not held at Stratford, which had sold out of immediate family hands, but at the fashionable home of his future father-in-law, Clermont. If there was an Arlington or Ravensworth for Fitzhugh Lee, it was this Alexandria estate. The fields of Clermont were located several miles west of the bustling port of Alexandria, but Fitz enjoyed them only a few years. When John Mason moved there in 1833, he was aged and financially troubled. His long career as a lawyer and financier was winding down, but he had a large family of ten children by Anna Maria Murray of Annapolis, Maryland. Several of Fitz's siblings were born at Clermont over the next 13 years, but after his Grandfather Mason's death on March 19, 1849, the estate was sold. Fitzhugh Lee had to find another Clermont.[24]

Fitz Lee became a cavalry officer, starting a career in a well-trodden family path. After attending educational academies in Maryland and Alexandria, Lee entered West Point. He was an able cavalry officer in the Army of Northern Virginia, earning a glorious reputation in the same vein as Confederate Generals James Ewell Brown (J.E.B.) Stuart, Thomas Rosser, and Joseph Wheeler. Fitz Lee distinguished himself during the Virginia raids around Richmond in the Spring of 1862 and the Battle of Spotsylvania two years later, where he held his position until Confederate reinforcements arrived. Despite an injury at the Third Battle of Winchester that autumn, Fitz Lee's war record was generally favorable-his reputation was only slightly marred by allowing a surprise attack by Union General Philip Sheridan's force at Five Forks in early 1865.[25]

Following the war, Fitz Lee searched for a new homestead, at last, finding another Clermont in Stafford County. The Fitzhugh family owned a 2,000 acre estate called Richland near the Potomac River tributary known as Aquia Creek. The plantation was originally owned by the Brent family before its purchase by William Henry Fitzhugh in 1821. Richland was known as "the racetrack field" due to the Brent penchant for horse racing, and the plantation boasted a wharf, flour mills, thirty-five dependencies, and well-cultivated fields. The main house was an attractive structure with a square covered porch and two symmetrical chimneys. Smith Lee lived at the estate with his son's family from 1865 until his death four years later; however, his soldier son was restless. Although Fitz inherited the estate upon Anna Fitzhugh's death in April 1874, the young man stayed a mere 12 years.[26]

Fitzhugh Lee married Alexandrian Ellen Bernard Fowle in April 1871. Nellie, as she was known in her family, was born on January 26, 1853. There was almost an 18-year age difference between Nellie and Fitz. The Fowles were a successful merchant family in Alexandria, owning an extravagant Federalist-style home on Prince Street. Nellie's father was George Dashiell Fowle, a businessman with little political experience. Despite the age difference, the marriage turned out to be a success for the former soldier. Eventually, the Fitzhugh Lees boasted seven children. He turned to farming for a short time, but later moved to business concerns in Lexington. Even in the presence of his cousins, he grew restless again and returned to Alexandria. In late 1883, he wrote his financier, "my intention is to sell out [my real estate] there and buy up here [Alexandria]-My only wonder is that I should not have seen it to be a wise thing earlier."[27]

Although occupationally unsettled, Fitzhugh Lee participated as a famous representative in numerous ceremonial events of the period. He was vice-president of the Lee Monument Association of the Army of Northern Virginia. He traveled to Richmond to addresses and meetings, and he gathered support for the statues of Robert E. Lee,

J.E.B. Stuart, and Thomas J. "Stonewall" Jackson. Never neglecting his important family ties, Fitz Lee gave a rousing speech in Boston, conjuring the memory of his grandfather, "Light-Horse Harry." By consistently invoking his legacy and heritage, Fitz Lee launched his political career.[28]

Unlike many other relatives, Fitzhugh Lee embraced politics. In fact, it was a natural progression for the ambitious former cavalry officer. In the fall of 1885, after almost a decade of gathering support for a run for office of Virginia's governor, he campaigned. The time was appropriate, as Democrats held power both statewide and nationally. A wave of nostalgic sentiment swept throughout the state and brought him victory. A great torchlight parade through the streets of Richmond marked the occasion. He began his term on January 1, 1886 after an inaugural ball was held in the First Regimental Armory. In doing so, Governor Fitzhugh Lee embraced a national unity. One Richmond resident wrote that the invitation to the ball pictured a likeness of Lee between two shields: one symbolizing Virginia, the other the United States. The newspapers reported the events boasted patriotic symbols, such as gilded eagles and victory palms.[29]

Even while Governor of Virginia, Lee engaged in risky business ventures. Like other former Confederate officers, he purchased stock in burgeoning mining and railroad interests. In November 1889 he purchased fifty shares in the Pittsburgh and Virginia Railroad. The following July he purchased one hundred shares in the South Boston Improvement Company. These speculative purchases represented the biggest mistake Fitz Lee ever made in the course of business. A state land craze developed in the late 1880s and well-to-do Virginians cross-invested among their ventures. One development company of interest to Fitzhugh Lee was formed about the mining operations and town of Glasgow, Virginia. The concern was located in the Shenandoah Valley, about 25 miles from Lexington. The desire for quick wealth resulted in Fitzhugh Lee's acceptance as the company president. However, his term as president of the Rockbridge Company cost him heavily. He was far from alone in the venture, as Fitz Lee's friends in the company included Lexington lawyer William A. Anderson as vice-president and fellow resident Greenlee D. Letcher as secretary. In addition, Fitz convinced his brother Robert C. Lee to invest early in the venture. After selling some lots in May 1890 his younger brother balked at an extra charge for "lot priviligc." As some of the money belonged to their mother, Robert C. Lee urged that Fitzhugh "sell a lot & give Mama $50 for the back taxes."[30]

The progress of building the town of Glasgow slowed by 1892. Other companies branched from the Glasgow investment, such as the Chicago Land Company of Virginia. Fitz was noted as company president on its letterhead. This enterprise handled promotional activity for another proposed town at Chicago, Virginia in February 1892. Its offices were in New York, Richmond, and Washington, D.C. From the company's financial offices in New York, Director W.J. Madden explained to Lee that "detail work" slowed development. However, Fitz was convinced the stock capitalization of $200,000 was too large an investment. In the meantime, the New York office moved off fashionable Wall Street to Broadway.[31]

Although the investment was shaky, enthusiasm for the Glasgow project and its new officers was evident. The company letterhead from the Rockbridge Company contained a seal with the motto, "Let Glasgow Flourish." The Rockbridge Company building was a lavish structure, even containing a grand stairway to horse-drawn carriages on Fitz Lee Street. The Hotel Brockenborough, a gargantuan inn, was a stone's throw from Lee's business office. On September 17, 1892, the hotel held a grand opening with many dignitaries. Fitzhugh Lee greeted all his special guests at the bottom of the great staircase. Unfortunately, it was indeed a "singular" event. Investment funds ran out by Christmas. As the financial Panic of 1893 descended upon the nation, Glasgow's investors were wiped out. Suffering with the other primary investors, Fitz Lee turned to other pursuits after his own situation turned for the worse. In 1894, Fitz became president of a Staunton insurance company and began writing a book.[32]

Always considering his family heritage, Lee began to write one of the first definitive biographies of his Uncle Robert in 1894. His book was one of the most complete works on the Confederate commander, and it was the first written by a close Lee relative (Robert E. Lee, Jr.'s book came a decade later).[33] Careful to keep his biography within the family's taste, Fitz Lee wrote much of the text on General Lee's military campaigns. Even so, the publication was not above family criticism. Custis Lee wrote his brother Robert in March 1896,

> I would caution you against giving any anecdote which might be used by immiral [sic] critics to belittle our father's name. For instance, Fitz Lee mentions that he rode through Washington City with Genl. Joe Johnston behind him on his horse. This may, or may not, be true, and is innocent enough; but should not have been put in the book, I think. Fitz also says that Genl Henry Lee ("Light Horse Harry") threw a boot at the head of an old negro mammy, who was waiting on him. I very much doubt whether this anecdote has any foundation in fact; but if it be true, I don't think Fitz should have published it.[34]

Whether or not it was intended, a piece of the Lee literary legacy had fallen to Fitz. He capitalized on the book's success, but his political life faltered. Lee met political defeat at the hands of younger men such as Thomas Staples Martin, a U.S. Senator from Virginia, in 1893. Using his business connections in the railroad industry, Martin clouded Lee's chances for furthering power. Fortunately for Lee, he was a friend of President Grover Cleveland. While finishing *General Lee,* President Cleveland offered him the post of Ambassador to Sweden, which he promptly refused. In April 1895, he accepted Cleveland's offer of District Collector of Internal Revenue in Western Virginia. The job provided Fitz Lee financial stability and repaired his tarnished image. However, the duties were difficult, as his district contained 52 counties. In April 1896, when Fitz Lee resigned his position, he was mindful of Cleveland's sacrifice in appointing his successor.[35]

> ...You know, as I do, that the President will be besieged, as soon as it is known-that the office of Collector of this District is vacant-Otey-Swanson-Martin-Daniel & Co will make a great effort to get the appointment of a man who responds, when they touch the button.[36]

For Lee, vacating the position of district collector was a move upward. President Cleveland appointed him Consul General of the United States with an immediate mission to Havana, Cuba. Although they initially liked each other, Lee's relationship with the President soured over time. Eventually, President Cleveland confided to his closest associates that he mistrusted Lee. As a Southerner, Lee believed Cuba was ripe for annexation to the United States. For years the island toiled under Spanish rule, a history Lee researched when writing a definitive and voluminous account of the struggles of Cuba.[37]

While Lee prepared for the tour south, he understood the value of his participation in Cuban events to his personal legacy. In a letter to the Commissioner of Internal Revenue, he stated,

> You can readily see that I do not care to land at Havana with a newspaper man, who being with me and about would get the credit of reflecting my views on the difficult public questions I shall have to consider; in addition, it will seem to the other correspondents as if I was giving greater facilities to Mr. Ryan [the requestor/correspondent] than to them, though of course I would act impartially to all...But his going at the same time I do might look as if I was taking a special correspondent, to give through him my opinions of the [crossed] matters in the "Queen of the Antilles."[38]

Lee entered Havana in June 1896. Although he served admirably by all accounts, the cool reception by Spanish authorities and President Cleveland's suspicions proved impossible to overcome. Both reasons forced his return to the United States in April 1898. This was evident in a response to one of Lee's first dispatches in July 1896, when Cleveland wrote Secretary of State Richard Olney of his suspicions.

> I am a little surprised at Consul-General Lee's dispatch. He seems to have fallen into the style of rolling intervention like a sweet morsel under his tongue. I do not think the purchase plan would

suit at all, though it is perhaps worth thinking of. Many of the fairest talkers in favor of intervening (Sherman, for instance) are opposed to incorporating the country into the United States system and I am afraid it would be entering upon dangerous ground...According to my remembrance, Lee's reference to Jackson's recognition of Texas is not fortunate.[39]

    Cleveland's odd relationship with Fitzhugh Lee ended with the former's advice to President-Elect William McKinley at his inauguration. He advised McKinley to mistrust the old officer. However, he also warned that Lee's removal was out of the question due to the unstable nature of politics in Cuba. The newly-elected President McKinley viewed intervention as positive, and that outright removal of Lee as Consul-General undermined the national position. The President circumvented the problem by surrounding Lee with other military officers of stature.[40]

Regardless of the political environment in Washington, Lee's cool demeanor under pressure of Spanish colonial rule was admired by his adversaries. However, outward appearances were deceiving. Lee was uncertain of the direction of politics in Havana, as the Spanish had a tenuous hold on Cuba. In October 1896 Fitz wrote his wife Nellie that he worried about his own safety, and for the need of direct political intervention. To supplement his fears, he gave a graphic account of a Cuban woman's death and the subsequent funeral rites. The description of the harrowing events took almost two pages of a letter.[41]

In February 1897 the Cuban situation climaxed following the death of an imprisoned American dentist named Ricardo Ruiz. On February 4, the 46-year-old man was arrested at his home a few miles outside Havana. He was falsely charged with an attack on a railroad train the previous month. Ruiz was thrown into a dark, squalid cell without proper ventilation. Under these conditions, the dentist went mad. The Acting Spanish Governor was informed that Ruiz was an American citizen, yet he waited ten days to refer the matter to a civil court. Three days later Ruiz died in his dank cell with contusions found on his head. Lee sent frequent dispatches to Secretary of State John Sherman and expressed his outrage, even suggesting that the United

States officially "demand from Spanish Government the release of all Americans imprisoned" in Cuba.[42]

Despite deteriorating relations between the United States and the militaristic Spanish authorities, Lee remained in Havana. The following February he witnessed the explosion of the battleship *Maine* in harbor of Havana, but remained fair-minded despite a growing emotional outcry for war. Anti-American sentiment grew among the Spanish, and Lee found himself followed by detectives. Finally deciding the situation was beyond his control, he moved back to Florida.[43]

Upon his return to the United States, Fitz Lee found he was a hero. Hundreds of telegrams beckoned him to visit Jasper, Florida. Once he appeared, large crowds greeted him. One telegram dated March 21, 1898 from the *Chicago Tribune* to a Richmond friend asked, "Would people of your state vote for Consul General Lee for Vice-President on republican ticket?"[44] In Waycross, Georgia, Lee received a hero's gun salute. One paper announced him as a presidential nominee in the next election. He arrived in Richmond to ovations. In Washington he was greeted with band music and fireworks. Fitzhugh Lee was followed in the press, and he became a symbol of the "New South."[45]

Of course, other heroes emerged from the conflicts of 1898. In the Philippine Islands in the Pacific Ocean, an American fleet headed by Commodore George Dewey defeated the Spanish at Manila Bay. The New York papers caught hold of the victory and within a week military wives, including Mrs. Nellie Lee, designed a special flag as a souvenir of the American victory. Among the letters that accompanied the flag to the newly-promoted Admiral Dewey in mid-May was one from Nellie Lee. She wrote, "It always gives me pleasure to know that the services of our brave men are appreciated and recognized."[46]

President William McKinley, a former Union soldier, gave Fitzhugh Lee further military opportunity. In the presence of the Secretary of War, McKinley gave Lee command of the main expeditionary force to Havana. It was uncertain why he did so, but military duty did lessen Lee's political ambition and thus McKinley's competition. Much of the fighting had subsided, so the objective of Lee's expedition was to stabilize Cuba.[47]

While Lee prepared for his return to Cuba, his personal prestige among the American people reached a crescendo. He was commissioned a Major General, and he was accompanied to Cuba by his son Fitzhugh Lee, Jr. Twenty-six ladies, wearing white with interspersed symbols of the Confederacy, Cuba, and the United States, boarded his southbound train in Danville, leaving his personal car adorned with flowers.[48]

Events in Cuba assured Fitz Lee lasting fame. Fitzhugh Jr. later wrote historian Douglas Southall Freeman that the fighting had stopped, and that Fitz Lee's 7th Army Corps occupied Havana and the province of Pinar del Rio. In "Camp Cuba Libre" near Jacksonville, Florida, Lee made his way to Cuba in triumphant style. He rode a fine horse named "Choctaw," borrowed from an admirer in North Carolina. On January 1, 1899, Lee made his entrance in Havana. Many photographs were taken of the old gentleman among the crowds. Fitz Lee was pictured on Choctaw as if greeting old friends instead of a conquered enemy. Several of the images were mass-produced for an appreciative public. His face was on the cover of *Leslie's Magazine,* and he was the subject of political cartoons in *Harper's Weekly.*[49]

The publicity following the events in Cuba elevated Fitzhugh Lee's image, and he appeared on buttons, ashtrays, fans, and sewing kits in full uniform. Companies cashed in on the patriotic theme--one advertising card featured laundry soap and another featured a "specially created hat" in honor of Lee. There was no effort to disguise his advanced age or girth. Although other heroes of the war such as Admiral Thomas Dewey received the same commercial popularity, Fitz Lee captured the public's imagination as a result of his uncle's legacy in 1898. The patriotic images had the Stars and Stripes included on most items. This was the Lee image the public wanted to see. It rejoined the old Confederacy with the Union, and it signified a common patriotism that transcended regional ties.[50]

The reality of maintaining that image following the war was a challenge. Fitz Lee's aged mother was dying in March 1899. Anna Maria Lee was almost completely blind, but moved independently until she broke her hip in a fall. Her condition deteriorated and she died before Fitzhugh could return home. Between personal and professional stresses, the events of 1898 and 1899 wore on Fitz, and he asked to be relieved from his Cuban command. Unfortunately, the Boxer Rebellion in China delayed his successor's arrival. Once relieved in Cuba, Fitz was ordered to Nebraska for a year. Although he wanted to lead troops again, he longed for more civic responsibilities. He decided to retire, and turned in his papers on March 3, 1901, returning to Virginia and a new home in Charlottesville. While many expected him to enjoy a well-deserved retirement, Fitz again became restless. Beginning in April 1902, he assisted plans on the memorial access road to President Thomas Jefferson's grave. In the short term, this local project satisfied him.[51]

In addition to his work on the Jefferson Memorial Road, Fitz Lee busied himself with the marriages of his children. His daughter Ellen married 1st Lieutenant James Cooper Rhea of Texas, one of her brother Fitzhugh, Jr.'s fellow officers from the 7th United States Cavalry. They preferred a military-style wedding, opting for a smaller ceremony at the "Little Church Around the Corner" in New York City. The ushers dressed in full military uniform. Fitz Lee escorted his daughter down the aisle in her gown made of Philippine hoosi cloth. Among those attending were Mrs. Jefferson Davis and General Joseph Wheeler, former Confederate cavalryman and U.S. officer in Cuba. In April 1904, Lieutenant George D. Lee married Kathre Larabee Burton in a similar wedding. The second event took place at the Highlands Apartment House ballroom in Washington, D.C. An entire army contingent attended, many to greet General Fitzhugh Lee and his wife. George Lee left afterward to his military post at Fort Riley, Kansas.[52]

The retired Fitzhugh Lee traveled more frequently with a new position as President of the Jamestown Exposition in September 1902. Without his assistance and high profile, there might have been no celebration. Having almost five years to prepare for the festivities planned in 1907, Lee shouldered great responsibility. The charter necessitated one million dollars in popular subscriptions due by January 1, 1904. He used his name and personal persuasion to get $200,000 from the Virginia Assembly and an additional $250,000 out of Congress. Lee embarked on a lobbying tour with legislators from each state to make up the shortfall. As a result of his efforts, twenty-two states participated or subscribed to the Exposition. However, by the closing months of 1904 it was clear that cash subscriptions remained short.[53] In addition to personal visits, Lee spent tireless hours signing business letters to state representatives on behalf of the

Exposition. One typical request read, in part:

> On behalf of the Commonwealth of Virginia
> and the Jamestown Exposition Company,
> we shall extend through your General assembly,
> an invitation to your state to make an exhibit at
> the Jamestown Tercentennial and Naval-Marine
> Exhibition in keeping with its dignity and
> resources...[54]

Lee signed each letter. As if he challenged Fitz Lee's fellow southerners, President Theodore Roosevelt queried, "Can not the colored people be given a show in connection with the Jamestown Exposition? They ought to have some chance to show what they have done in three hundred years."[55]

Lee's impending death solidified his legacy in the annals of American history. As if he realized his time was short, the old general pushed himself hard. He told his son George that "twenty-two thousand was oweing him and would come to [Mrs. Lee] in the event of his death..."[56] The words proved prophetic. Nellie Lee underestimated the severity of her husband's health during those last months. She wrote her husband's old friend and business partner William A. Anderson,

> I learned after his death that he had nearly died
> in two attacks he had in Washington during the
> winter--but he would not tell me. I begged him
> to give up the trip to Boston and wire the
> Exposition Co to send some one else...He would
> not consent to do it."[57]

There were many signs during Fitzhugh Lee's final journey to Boston in relation to his physical decline. He dashed off a brief letter to his wife on the evening of April 25, 1905, and the note was uncharacteristically written in almost unreadable scribble. Lee delivered a rousing speech on behalf of the exposition, but had to be physically assisted. A gentleman told the dying Fitz Lee his picture was beside three more of his other heroes. The old man modestly quipped that the other three were "all right," but he should "scratch out" the image of himself.[58]

On April 28, 1905, Lee boarded a train for Washington when he suffered a fatal stroke. Even accompanied by his brother Dan, the stress still proved too much. Once stricken, he apologized to his brother for speaking too softly. Fitzhugh Lee was buried in Richmond's Hollywood Cemetery in a huge procession. His unlucky business ventures eventually killed him--by overwork.[59]

Nellie Lee never forgave the Jamestown Company for her husband's death. In turn, the loss of the Company's biggest fundraiser hurt the enterprise. The settlement of its obligations to him became a bitter situation. In a long letter to the company's board of directors in March 1906, Mrs. Lee wrote,

> He entered upon the active discharge of his duties as your President on the 1st day of January, 1903, and from that time until the date of his death, he devoted himself actively and assiduously to the interests of your Company, and spent his means, his time, and himself in your service...I think that there can be little question but that his death was occasioned by exposure, loss of rest, and the strain to which he was subjected by his efforts, and his successful efforts in advancing the interests of your Company...I had hoped your Board would voluntarily, and without any suggestion from me, make provision for the settlement of this just obligation, but I have to confess, to some disappointment, that nothing has been done, though more than ten months have elapsed since General Lee's death.[60]

Nellie Lee authorized lawyer Anderson and her son Fitzhugh Lee, Jr. to act on her behalf to settle the Jamestown Exposition Company dispute. After this designation, she retreated with her daughter's family to Catoosa Springs, Georgia. The lawsuit took almost eight years to settle.[61]

Fitz the Younger

Fitzhugh Lee, Jr. had an impressive military career, although it existed in the shadow of his famous father. Less ambitious than his father, Fitz Jr. attained the rank of captain while still in his thirties. He inherited his love of horsemanship from his father and great-grandfather, "Light Horse Harry" Lee.

In his mother's estimation to lawyer Anderson in May 1905, "Fitzhugh is a very level headed young man with most excellent Judgement and fine business qualities."[62] This statement, true as it was, understated Fitzhugh Lee Jr.'s full talents. After the death of his father, the family's military legacy faded in a mire of a changed America.

Fitz Lee, Jr. was born in Alexandria on January 6, 1875, one of four children. Ellen had preceded him and George Dashiell, Nannie, and Virginia followed. Fitz, Jr. followed the military traditions of his father by attending the Virginia Military Institute. However, instead of immediately entering the Army, he worked as a shop laborer on the Pennsylvania Railroad. Lee insisted on starting at the bottom of the career ladder in Altoona rather than capitalize on his heritage. President William McKinley called Fitz, Jr. to Washington upon the outbreak of the Spanish-American War. He was commissioned in the army as a second lieutenant.[63] The local newspapers reported that "the palms of his hands bore evidence of the hard labor...and the President made note of this as a sign of that stamina which would make him a good soldier."[64] Fitz Jr. served alongside his father, and he witnessed the rebirth of the Lee legacy. His contribution to it, the raising of the American flag at Santiago, proved to be his military highlight. The young man shied away from further grandeur, despite good service in the Phillippines during the height of agitations there. He won praise, but loneliness was a losing battle in the Philippines. In February 1901, he wrote his mother a detailed letter on his spartan surroundings and complained of the "lonesome hole" that lacked American female company. Shortly after, he secured a transfer to the 7th United States Cavalry, General George A. Custer's old unit.[65]

In 1904, President Theodore Roosevelt chose Fitz Lee, Jr. as one of his military aides (He served alongside another famous descendant, Lieutenant Ulysses S. Grant III). His duties primarily revolved around his skill in horsemanship. Lee gained President Roosevelt's admiration by instructing his sons in handling "jumper" horses. He did not play polo like his brothers, but this was due to the fact that it would affect his "jumping hands." President Roosevelt called Lee the "castor of the horse," a great compliment for the young man. He shipped some of the training horses to the President's home at Oyster Bay.[66]

Roosevelt's admiration of Fitzhugh Lee was characteristic of the rough-hewn President. Shortly after forming the "Rough Riders," Theodore Roosevelt wrote to General Fitzhugh Lee expressing his hope to join his force, incorrectly believing that the old officer was leading the first thrust of the military operation into Cuba. Roosevelt sought Robert E. Lee's autograph as one of the great military leaders of the nation, and he was not ashamed to ask young Fitz for his assistance in obtaining one. The Roosevelt genealogy gave an additional reason for his close ties to the Lees. President Roosevelt's mother was a Georgian by birth who was brought up under the pre-Civil War conditions of plantation life. Political cartoons lampooned Roosevelt courting the Southern vote, yet it did not dominate newspaper headlines.[67]

Fitz, Jr.'s rides with the President were legendary. In April 1906, the President wrote his son Kermit,

> Yesterday I took my first ride on the new horse, Roswell, Captain Lee going along on Rusty as a kind of a nurse. Roswell is not yet four and he really is a green colt...if I can arrange to have Lee handle him a couple of months here, and if Ted and I can regularly ride him down at Oyster Bay, I think he will turn out all right."[68]

Fitz's participation in Roosevelt's exercise was not limited to horseback riding; in November 1907 he participated in a party of four going to Rock Creek to do some climbing and swimming. In December he hunted bear, while the following month Fitz became a hardened veteran in the President's "scramble walks" down Rock Creek.[69] Later President Roosevelt wrote to Kermit,

> On Monday Mother and I with Ethel, Postmaster
> General Meyer and Captain Fitz Lee rode down
> to Mount Vernon...We had a lovely time;
> tho the weather would not have suited some
> riders...We were glad to ride up to it by
> the route which Washington himself general took."[70]

While service with the President was pleasant, other issues haunted Fitz. The Jamestown Exposition settlement deeply disturbed him, as he was protective of his mother's interests. Fitz was primarily involved in the legal proceedings between 1905 and 1907, when the Exposition was in its final preparations. A number of letters were exchanged between the young man and his lawyer Anderson. In all honesty, Anderson defended the Lees out of loyalty to the General's memory. Trying to raise money for his family expenses, Fitz Jr. sold his parent's Charlottesville residence and wrote Anderson that "I have not heard from the Jamestown people."[71]

The Lees presented a statement of claim that coincided with the presentation of the Jamestown Bill, requesting funds for the coming festivities, in Congress. Fitz Jr. sent a copy of the claim statement to his father's successor in the Jamestown Company, Henry St. George Tucker. After some months passed, Anderson and Fitz Jr. looked into the matter of the bill. In the summer of 1906 Mr. Barton Myers, representing the Jamestown Exposition Company, communicated with the family. Little was accomplished through the ensuing negotiations, and Fitz Jr. became irate when settlement stalled yet again. Although he was physically stationed in Washington, Nellie Lee lived in the Philippine Islands with her daughter's family. She planned a return in the spring of 1907, and money was needed for her transport.[72]

> Mother has not been very well lately & I am
> trying now to get her started home in January
> on a transport that leaves Manila for New York
> via the Suez...I shall have to borrow the money
> to get them home so it would mean a great deal
> to me if our Jamestown business could be fixed
> up.[73]

The "Jamestown business" remained. Anderson pushed officials for a final payment, but Fitz, Jr.'s active participation in any collection effort ceased following the Spring of 1907. Nellie Lee arrived in Washington, D.C., but almost immediately suffered a severe asthma attack. Further delays resulted. Finally, a voucher for payment of $1,000, far below the requested settlement of what was owed General Fitzhugh Lee, was submitted in October.[74]

The reason for Fitz Jr.'s declining involvement in the Jamestown issue was a change in vocation. The U.S. War Department sent all three of the President's military aides to new posts in July 1907. Lee, Jr. occasionally visited Washington, yet was in various posts throughout the United States. He constructed railroad bridges as an engineer in Iowa. Like his brother George and brother-in-law James Rhea, he identified with life in the cavalry.[75]

During the autumn of 1908, Fitz, Jr. attended cavalry school in Saumur, France. He wrote President Roosevelt about his exciting European experiences. A keen observer of horsemen, Fitz Jr. was in an equestrian paradise. He informed Roosevelt that the "officers and better class dislike their President and are continuously drawing comparisons between yours ours and theirs..."[76] He had difficulty speaking French, but the school had thirteen foreign officers from different countries. One was a Russian Prince, who Fitz remarked had "large decorations & many gorgeous uniforms."[77] He called them "picked" men, but their presence pressured Fitz Jr. to excel. The sores from days of hard riding were relieved by cotton bandages and alcohol baths.[78]

A typical day at the French Cavalry School began with the practice of a "stand," which meant rifle shooting at a target from 20 feet. The afternoons were devoted to training the horses. The thoroughbreds and colts went to a riding facility, followed by a stint in open fields. An hour was devoted to the "jumpers" or "carriere." This was potentially painful because the officers used flat saddles without the use of stirrups. The end of the day was devoted to "Service en Campagne," a staff practice to lead officers into an organized patrol. Fencing and mounted drilling came on alternate days. At night, there might be French language lessons. Fitz Jr. admitted the experience was invaluable to him, but he was disappointed with the slow pace of life.[79]

Once Fitz, Jr. returned to America, his life became more frenetic. In December 1910 the Jamestown settlement issue reemerged. At the suggestion of Nellie Lee, Anderson retained Judge Theodore S. Garnett of Norfolk as a second lawyer. He forwarded Garnett a statement of claim that amounted close to $7,400. The judge requested a special master to look into the Lee claim and the decomposing Jamestown Exposition Company. The exhibition was a financial failure, likely the primary reason for the long delays of settlement. Garnett succeeded in having the special master appointed, but the resulting examination of the company's financial state was disappointing. The land and exhibit buildings were sold at a great loss. The company settled with the Lees in March 1913, when forced to pay a paltry $750.88 to Mrs. Lee. Once a newspaper reported that payment was rendered, a creditor asked for payment from a 1905 purchase Mrs. Lee made for her daughter's wedding. General Lee's family suffered for his unwise business ventures almost a decade after his death.[80]

Fitz Jr. was out west during the final days of the Jamestown debacle. Tensions heightened with Mexico, as a revolutionary named Pancho Villa raided towns along the American border. The slaughter of Americans in Columbus, New Mexico confirmed the need for military action, and President Woodrow Wilson mobilized the military. Former President Roosevelt wrote Fitz Jr. that he was interested in raising a new cavalry division reminiscent of his "Rough Riders" 17 years before. He planned for Lee to be one of his officers. The younger man suggested a mixed national guard and regular unit for the ideal command. Roosevelt's personal plans were delayed until May 1917, when he wrote Secretary of State Newton Baker to raise the regiment. Roosevelt's idea, and Fitz, Jr.'s hopes, faded when the new unit was dismissed by President Woodrow Wilson.[81]

Although Fitz, Jr. waited for a promotion that never materialized, his old military unit saw action against the Mexicans. In March 1916, the 7th U.S. Cavalry rode to the Mexican town of Minaca, a distance of 310 miles from their Arizona encampment. Colonel George A. Dodd, the elderly leader of the unit, saw the men chase Pancho Villa down the Santa Maria Valley and engaged in a sporadic series of firefights. Following the Mexican campaign, Fitz Jr. moved to various places throughout the west. In the spring of 1917, he was stationed at

Camp Stewart in El Paso, Texas. In one letter, he revealed that the military situation along the border was "muzzled." Fitz Jr. wrote Roosevelt that military preparations against Mexico were becoming necessary, and he pointed to the another revolution in Czarist Russia as a chilling example. Fitz Jr. focused on the need for cavalry schools, and indicated that the Mexican incursions made them necessary.[82]

> If we could only start this Mexican business going, it would prove fine schooling for something...Our Patrols and Border Detachments are now allowed to return fire, and I am confidently looking for this to "Start Something." Its really a great opportunity and very possibly will bring results, especially when Villa, Caranza, Zapata & Co. find out its about all up with them. Three Patrols of the outfit stationed here, the 10th. Cavalry, have been fired upon in the last five days, on returning the fire the Mexicans in every case fled to the hills![83]

President Roosevelt's affection for Fitz, Jr. was reflected in letters between the two men. It revealed a largely paternal relationship. In November 1908, the President responded in a letter to the young man, "Indeed, Fitz, as you know, we are just as fond of you as if you were one of the family."[84] Lee sent a saddle bag as a gift to the President that he took on his African trek in 1909. Of the President's sons, Kermit was closest to Fitz Lee Jr. President Roosevelt noted that "Kermit is looking forward to his week with you" in horse riding.[85] The bond between the two never abated. Shortly after he left his position as an aide to President Roosevelt, Fitz thanked Kermit for the gift of a pin.

> ...I want to tell you now Kermit that both the pin and the thought pleased me more than anything I have ever had happen & I shall treasure it all my life, it was perfectly beautiful & just the kind of pin I love to wear--you give me too credit for my small share in helping you to become a

proficient jumper.[86]

It appeared that Kermit Roosevelt viewed Fitzhugh Lee, Jr. as an older brother or father figure. Evidence of the close relationship to Kermit's sister Ethel became evident in a 1932 letter.

> I was awfully glad to have Ethel's address and shall send her a little note in a few days. As you know, I have always been very devoted to her and feel that I had a hand in bringing her up as a child. She is certainly a little wonder and strangely coincident, we have been within a few miles of each other several times in recent years, but fate seems to have intervened each time...[87]

While the social connections appeared lasting, Fitz, Jr.'s post-Washington career wound down in the 1930s. Later in his military career, he was stationed at the Headquarters of the Fourth Corps at Fort McPherson, Georgia. Eventually he received a command at Fort Bliss, Texas. In January 1933, Fitz, Jr. sent Kermit Roosevelt a photo of his home in Georgia, a house reminiscent of Arlington House with its long white columns.[88]

His frequent moves and family changes ensured a quiet life for Fitzhugh Lee, Jr. as he aged. In the late spring of 1933, his mother Nellie died in Alexandria at the age of 80. In 1939, Fitz, Jr. retired with 41 years of military experience. He moved with his wife to Tucson, Arizona, and died there in November 1954 at the age of 79.[89]

In his youth, Fitz, Jr. carried the devotion and legacy of the Lee family. Like his father and grandfather, he emulated the ideal horseman. His ties to the Roosevelt family made him the "torch bearer" of the military legacy of Robert E. Lee for a limited number of years. Ironically, Fitz Jr. was almost forgotten by the time of his death. In an ever changing society of suburban neighborhoods and military machines, where horses were replaced by tanks, he knew society moved on, and his reputation paled in the shadow of his famous father.

Alexandria to West Virginia and Beyond: Edmund Jennings Lee and his Descendants

Edmund Jennings Lee and his descendants remained in Alexandria for generations until their "Arlington" was found in the Virginia mountains. Born in 1772, the younger brother of General "Light-Horse Harry" Lee was a successful businessman and the mayor of Alexandria from 1814 to 1818. Edmund Lee married wisely, as his wife Sally was not only his cousin, but the daughter of the famed Richard Henry Lee of Westmoreland County. In January 1801, the young businessman acquired a fine residence on North Washington Street in Alexandria. Several of their nine children, particularly Cassius Francis Lee and his sister Anne, were close to their cousin Robert E. Lee. Several other Lees lived nearby, including Robert and his mother Ann Carter Lee. Edmund's sister, Mrs. Mary Fendall, resided a short walk away on Orinoco Street.[90]

In addition to a neighborhood, the family shared a certain religious fervor. Through Sally Lee, the children valued the local Episcopal institutions from an early age. Her obituary described some of her notable practices in matters of faith.

> A consistent profession of religion by females in the circumstances in which she was placed, is at all times attended by trials of no ordinary magnitude...she prayed not only *for* her children, but *with* them; and if, one of them had been betrayed into the commission of a sinful act, she took the child alone before God, endeavored to impress upon its mind a sense of the guilt incurred, and of the displeasure of God, more than her own, and supplicated on her knees, with the offender, the pardoning mercy of the Most High.[91]

The family sponsored the Virginia Theological Seminary and attended Christ Church in Alexandria. In addition to his duties as mayor of Alexandria, Edmund Lee served as one of the wardens of Christ Church. The church was known for its connections with George Washington, and the position of warden carried much responsibility.

As early as 1833, Edmund's children held positions of responsibility in Christ Church, and they served on numerous church councils for successive terms.[92]

A new generation of prominent Lee family members emerged in the 1830s. Edmund's second son, William Fitzhugh Lee, joined the order of deacons in Loudoun County, Virginia in 1825. Although living some distance from Alexandria and only 21 years of age, he proved equal to the task. In Loudoun he married Mary Catherine Simms Chilton. The young man became an ordained preacher three years later, and he took charge of two historic Richmond churches. It became common the young man to preach in the farm country west of the city, and he became quite popular. He was recognized by an Episcopal bishop for "his zeal in the discharge of his sacred duties" and "possessing a mind of the most vigorous character."[93]

Unfortunately, William Fitzhugh Lee's health was greatly affected by his work. The Episcopal bishop indicated William Lee's zeal was the very cause of his bad constitution. His health was characterized as "naturally feeble," but his overwork ensured illness.

> He would sometimes preach three times on the Lord's day, and frequently in the week, by means of which unusual effort his lungs became affected, and the disease, which terminated his life, obtained such a firm hold on his system, that he was obliged to relinquish his pastoral charge, and to bid adieu to the congregation he had formed, and to which he was most ardently and affectionately attached.[94]

William Lee's religious endeavors lasted beyond retirement. He founded a major religious publication, *The Southern Churchman,* in January 1835. He directed the magazine until the winter of 1836-37, when the retired preacher became so gravely ill that his wife rightly feared for his life. In his dying days, William moved to Alexandria to live with his brother Cassius. May 1837 proved a tragic month for the family of William Fitzhugh Lee. On May 6, his 14-month-old son Arthur died. Only two days later, his mother Sally Lee passed. Having lived through these grievous events, William lingered in deteriorating condition until May 19, yet cognizant to his last obligations. *The Southern Churchman* published a long account of his passing after a private conversation with an Episcopal bishop. At the age of 33, William Fitzhugh Lee accomplished more than some people in a normal life span. The family's suffering did not end with William's death, however; on May 24, Edmund Jennings Lee's sister Lucy died suddenly.[95]

Edmund Jennings Lee had lost four members of his family, and fell on financially hard times after the Panic of 1837. He sold his Washington Street home in Alexandria and moved to a more modest residence on Orinoco Street. Until his death six years later, Edmund Jennings Lee and his son Cassius were the key members of the family residing in Alexandria. Before his death, the aging Edmund recouped enough of his losses to buy back the Washington Street home with Cassius. In his 1843 will, Edmund Jennings Lee left his son,

> Cassius F. Lee the House and Lot on Washington Street at the bottom of his garden, under condition that he discharges my Estate from a debt of about Five hundred dollars, besides interest, for which he holds my note."[96]

A different path was in store for Edmund Jennings Lee's eldest son and namesake. He graduated from Princeton and practiced law in Virginia. In his desire to find new pastures, Edmund moved west to the Jefferson County settlement of Shepherdstown, situated on the Potomac River. His first visit to the hamlet was at the invitation of Captain Abraham Shepherd, a landowner who met the young Edmund Lee at a church convention. There he met Captain Shepherd's daughter Eliza, and married her in 1823. The "Lower Farm," a twenty-five acre property of Captain Shepherd, became the couple's home, called "Leeland."[97]

The location of Leeland was a mixed blessing. The house was noted for its wide circular path in front of its large frame main house. A spacious hall occupied most of the first floor, although adequate space allowed for a bedroom. Outside the mansion was a detached law office and kitchen outbuildings. Leeland's importance was in its proximity to other famous Virginia families in the area, such as the

Washingtons. It ensured the reestablishment of Lee family prominence further west, and ensured the perpetuation of legacy. However, the down side was also the estate's location. While Shepherdstown was a trade center with an opening to the west, and the need for interior trade routes encouraged transportation improvements along the Potomac River, the terrain contributed to a sweltering summer heat that turned the environment unhealthy. In 1833, cholera spread from the workers on the Chesapeake & Ohio Canal, which ran alongside town, to the Lee family. Of the five children born to Edmund and Eliza Lee, three of them died. Eliza fell victim to the epidemic in August.[98]

In spite of the tragedy, young Edmund remained in Shepherdstown. He practiced law and espoused Whig politics. According to local rumor, he viewed his beautiful neighbor, Henrietta Bedinger, through his spy glass. After a courtship, she became Edmund Lee's second wife in September 1835. In addition to his two surviving children from his first marriage, the couple raised five more. The eldest son of the second marriage was Edwin Gray Lee, followed by Ida, Henrietta, Edmund III, and Henry. Edmund's wife, often called by her nickname "Netta," ran the estate with customary efficiency. Her surviving letters focused on family life at Shepherdstown. She kept careful watch over her relations and reported their movements enthusiastically.[99]

> Edmund is in Charles Town. How I do wish he had a clog to his foot in the shape of a nice suitable wife to keep him at home, age and religion agreeing. He expects to go next week or the week after again to Baltimore-courting, I have no doubt...William, I hear, is not at all pleased with Alice's marriage. I suppose he thinks they are both too poor.[100]

Henrietta Bedinger Lee knew the value of the family's legacy through her old home, known as Bedford. Her father, Daniel Bedinger, purchased the dismantled masts of the legendary ship *Constitution*, in Alexandria. He removed the mast beams of the vessel for his home, installing them as columns. Her social standing and sense of family history only increased when she married Edmund Lee.[101]

Some members of the family visited or settled near Edmund Lee. Several of his brothers lived nearby and practiced law. However, Cassius Lee wrote his brother from Alexandria that water transport to the western part of the state was hard to attain. This was a convenient excuse, but it highlighted the difficulties of periodic travel between the two family seats.

> I have repeatedly been to --- to inquire for a boat to Shephardstown. Molly Harper has always promised me to let me know when opportunity offered. I did hear on the day of the election (accidently) that a boat was here, but it was raining with great violence, & the boatman, I was told, was in a hurry & would not wait.[102]

Like Ravensworth, Leeland was endangered by fire several times. By far the most serious occurred on April 12, 1856. *The Shepherdstown Register* reported that,

> citizens hastened to the scene of conflagration, but the wind was blowing a perfect hurricane at the time, which urged the progress of the destroying element, consequently nothing could be rescued of any great value with the exception of a desk which contained a quantity of Mr. Lee's valuable papers, everything else, including a quantity of valuable furniture, a large amount of silver-ware, a splendid piano, and clothing of every description were consumed in a few moments with the dwelling.[103]

Unlike Ravensworth, the fire's origin was less suspicious. The chimney contained a structural defect which increased the risk of fire. The flames consumed the mansion, and a strong wind blew hot ashes for miles, causing a number of fires around Shepherdstown that day. Edmund and his family moved over to Bedford. The Hartford

Insurance Company covered $2,000 worth of damage, but Edmund's personal losses were far beyond this monetary amount.[104]

The Civil War ensured additional grief for the Leeland branch of the family. Edmund's younger brother, Richard Henry Lee, practiced law with his brother for some years. Prior to the outbreak of hostilities between North and South, he became the Commonwealth's Attorney for Jefferson County. Although this was a great opportunity, the outbreak of war forced the family to choose sides. Arguably the emergence of their cousin Robert as a major figure in the Confederacy put considerable pressure on the other Lees, and Edmund's family was no exception. Richard Henry Lee became a lieutenant in Thomas "Stonewall" Jackson's brigade of Virginians, the 2nd Virginia Regiment. In leading his men in a heated skirmish in the Shenandoah Valley, he fell seriously wounded.[105]

One of the most mysterious Civil War careers in the family belonged to Edwin Gray Lee. Before the Civil War, he attended school in Alexandria and later at the College of William & Mary. At the time of the war, he practiced law in Lexington. Like his Uncle Richard Henry, Edwin served in the Stonewall Brigade. He was commissioned a lieutenant by May 1861, and found promotion as a personal aide to General Jackson. As the war dragged on, Edwin Lee ranked as the Colonel of the 33rd Virginia Regiment. However, sickness removed him from active field duty. In the Civil War's final year, the Confederate Government assigned him to Canada.[106] At the end of 1864, Confederate Secretary of State Judah Benjamin needed an able replacement for returning Commissioners Jacob Thompson and Clement Clay. Author Alexandra Lee Levin described the work as largely secretive.

> [Edmund Lee was] the Lee family pamphleteer of the Civil War, just as Arthur Lee was of the Revolution. He wrote from Canada a long open letter urging Britain and France to come in on the side of the Confederacy..Edwin's pamphlet was sent to Paris where it was translated by Louisiana-born Pierre Paul Joseph Pecquet, Count du Bellet, a publisher who had aided the Confederacy all through the war. M. Pecquet

managed to get a copy of Edwin's pamphlet into the hand of the Emperor Louis Napoleon, but too late--Kirby Smith's trans-Mississippi Army had just surrendered.[107]

Levin points out a curious link between Edwin Gray Lee and President Abraham Lincoln's assassins, describing a meeting between an agent named "Harrison" and Edwin Lee on April 6, 1865. This was an alias for conspirator John H. Surratt, later tried for complicity in Lincoln's death. It was possible Surratt stayed in Canada for months before fleeing to Europe.[108]

Edwin Lee's Uncle Cassius resided in Hamilton, Canada doing similar work for the Confederates. While Edwin met with dignitaries, his uncle left for home on July 6, 1865. As he could not receive an immediate pardon, Edwin was stranded in Canada until March 1866. In effect, he was in exile.[109]

Even while Edwin was far away, the war came to his childhood home. On July 19, 1864, Union cavalry troops burned Bedford. As conflicting loyalties were common in western Virginia, the fire was set because of local rumors. The occupying New York regiment heard that Edmund Jennings Lee was secretly working for the Confederate forces. Although this was true of Edmund's family, the surname was likely the necessary motivation. The aged Edmund Lee wisely removed himself to a relative's home in Clarke County, Virginia. As part of Union General David Hunter's policy to damage property usable by enemies, the 1st New York Cavalry set Bedford aflame after turning out a sick Henrietta and her two teenaged children. Hunter's men burned the outbuildings as well, accumulating damage that amounted to $25,000.[110]

The Civil War never left Edwin Gray Lee. After his return from Canada, his wartime sickness worsened. John Surratt was caught and tried in Washington, D.C. in the summer of 1867, and Lee was summoned to testify. He took the occasion to visit relatives for several weeks until his testimony on July 15. Edwin wrote in his own diary that "walked down from the witness stand & shook hands with Surratt. Poor boy, how badly he looks."[111] He felt the former fugitive should be acquitted, but despaired of the judicial process. The charges against Surratt were later dropped.[112]

Edwin Gray Lee's health deteriorated rapidly. He was in excruciating pain when he gave his testimony, and it worsened despite working on sedentary literary pursuits. Most of these related tales of the Civil War, including pieces on "Stonewall" Jackson and Confederate President Jefferson Davis' capture. In a desperate attempt to improve his health, Edwin went south to a warmer climate. In November 1869, he wrote his father from Mobile, Alabama, that he felt better. When he returned to Virginia, his self-analysis proved premature. Edwin and his wife stayed at Lexington, where he died in August 1870.[113]

Leeland was rebuilt after the war, but the new manor house lacked its predecessor's preeminence. One reason was the death of Edmund Jennings Lee II on September 10, 1877 at the age of 80. The old lawyer's family dispersed, as most of his children moved from Shepherdstown. Edwin died and his brother Henry left to attend the Virginia Theological Seminary. Of Edmund's children, only his namesake and a married sister represented the Lees in Shepherdstown. A former Confederate cavalryman in his early twenties, Edmund Lee III took to farming the hilly plain of Jefferson County. He married twice, the first time to Rebecca Rust of Loudoun County in 1875. Following her death, Edmund married Bessie Read Neilson. Each owner of Leeland traditionally added to the house, so the young man built one of the first bathtubs in the area, complete with an onsite water tank and pump. Tragically, he died in the summer of 1896 following surgery. Four years later, one of his sons died attempting to rescue a drowning friend. The remaining legatees had little interest in the house, so it was purchased by a cousin.[114]

Of all the family members wandering from home, Edmund Jennings Lee IV outdid them all, serving as an overseas missionary in Anking, China, in the spring of 1902. He remained as a minister for 25 years. His wife Lucy later wrote a book, *An American Sojourn in China*. She penned that Edmund decided on the post to the Far East, stating, "Anything I may do at home will be done by someone else if I do not do it; but anything of value which I may be able to do in China will probably not be done unless I do it."[115] In April 1902 Edmund IV and his family reached Anking, in the Chinese province of Anhwei. The Lees frequently visited the rented quarters of many other missionary families in Shanghai, clustered together in an area known as "All Saints Row." When war between the Russians and Japanese was imminent in 1904-05, and again during Chinese tensions in 1911, Edmund took the ladies to the relative safety of Shanghai. In calmer times, he worked with youthful Chinese Christians. One day he planned to turn the mission over to them.[116]

The missionary family life included disease and danger. The lack of plumbing and inadequate cleanliness bred illness. Servants assisted with cooking and as messengers between missionary establishments. In turn, the missionaries trained the local populace in the clothing trade and organized businesses. Although they had good intentions, it was precisely the resulting businesses that caused problems with the Chinese authorities. After 16 successful years in Central China, the Lees faced another internal political squabble. In March 1927, Chinese authorities under the young nationalist Chiang Kai Shek ordered their evacuation. The Communist opposition detested the infiltration by religious missionaries, and killed an American in Nanking. As before, the Lees found refuge in Shanghai for what they believed to be a temporary period. However, American companies began closing. Armistead Lee wrote that he saw the body of an executed man floating in Shanghai's Soochow Creek. In May, Edmund's family left for the United States while he battled dysentery in Shanghai. The missionary returned to Washington early the following year.[117]

Upon his return to America, Edmund worked with former missionaries in fomenting Christian sentiment and assistance to the Chinese from afar. He formed an organization, "Friends of the Chinese," to raise money for students in America. According to Armistead, his father was saddened by the Communist takeover of mainland China in 1948. He passed away in 1962 with the hope someday that evangelism would again take hold in China.[118]

The Poet and His Traveling Brood

Charles Carter Lee was the oldest full brother of Robert E. Lee, and his contributions to the family legacy were minimized because of his role as caretaker. In his youth, he assumed control of his father's estate-or what was left of it after his father "Light-Horse Harry," drove the family into financial turmoil. After the settlement of his father's estate, Carter Lee forged a life of his own making. That life was unsettled, and he resembled "Light-Horse Harry" in this respect. Although he trained for law, Carter Lee wrote scads of poetry. His poetic writings consumed a large portion of two storage trunks. Historian Paul Nagel wrote that Carter was something of a bohemian spendthrift while studying law at Harvard. In his youth, he maintained the closest contact with his eldest half-brother Henry "Black-Horse Harry" Lee, who had lost Stratford Hall, then lived abroad after a sex scandal involving his sister-in-law. Carter held the family legacy together as best he could under these circumstances, but damage control continued until "Black-Horse Harry" died in Paris in 1837. Taking his half-brother's financial trouble to heart, Carter frequently left his law office in Washington, D.C. to his own inherited and purchased lands in Capon Springs and Hardy County in the western portion of Virginia. In the early 1840s, Carter Lee settled near Richmond. Then in his fifties, he married Lucy Penn Taylor, a granddaughter of agricultural philosopher John Taylor of Caroline, on May 13, 1847; they eventually had seven children. At Fine Creek Mills, located in agricultural Powhatan County, Charles Carter Lee purchased a home named Windsor Forest. Rather than building or inheriting Windsor, the mansion was acquired as a converted residence.[119]

Charles Carter Lee's ideology was deeply rooted in heritage and culture. He inherited early Federalist influences from his father, and adhered to a Washingtonian nationalism found in southerners such as Chief Supreme Court Justice John Marshall. Much of his boyhood was in the urban environment of Alexandria. Carter wrote another strong unionist, Edward Everett, of Massachusetts, a long diatribe on the common ties between that state and Virginia. He used a letter from his relative and patriot, Richard Henry Lee, whom Carter believed contributed to a larger American legacy by his devotion to sectional harmony. Carter Lee attempted to write his own memoir, which he started during the last few years of his long life. While beginning with a clear focus, Carter soon lost himself in his own recollections. The result was confusing to the reader, with frequent stops and starts in the subject matter. Essentially the memoir consisted of a disorganized manuscript of poetry, religious teachings, and flashes of autobiography. As the work progressed, religious issues dominated later writings. Eventually, the project was scrapped and left in the same trunks containing the papers of his father and half-brother Henry.[120]

Not all of Charles Carter Lee's projects went unfinished. He completed a notable book of antebellum poetry, called *Virginia Georgics,* which was published in 1858. In the lines of the book, Carter Lee consistently reflected on his family. Historian Ethel Armes wrote of his fixation with the family loss of Stratford Hall. He described the estate in great detail, even pining over the fruit in its gardens. Armes included a long passage of the memoir in her own book on Stratford Hall in 1936.[121]

> I think there was a mile of solid wall
> Surrounding offices, garden, stables, and all;
> And on the eastern side of the garden one,
> Pomegranates ripened in the morning sun;
> And farther off, yet sheltered by it, grew
> Figs, such as those Alcinous' garden knew,
> And owned, when they increased my childhood's blisses,
> By him who was called the American Ulysses.[122]

Symbolic passages in *Virginia Georgics* made Carter Lee one of the first to promote the family legacy through his own writing. Other aspiring poets asked his opinion on matters of rhyme.[123]

Charles Carter Lee did little in the last decade of his life. He was 61 at the outbreak of the Civil War, and played no major role, but sifted through his memoirs and worried about the value of his western Virginia lands. He was not lacking for guests, as relatives frequently visited him at Windsor. The deaths of his younger brothers Smith and Robert, in 1869 and 1870 respectively, left Carter as the lone Lee representative of his generation. However, he survived Robert by only six months. He died on March 21, 1871, passing the torch of legacy to a new generation of Lees.[124]

Ravensworth in its prime
Alexandria Library, Special Collections

After the fire, August 1926
Alexandria Library, Special Collections

George Taylor Lee
Alexandria Library, Special Collections

Graves of Cazenove and Marguerite DuPont Lee
Congressional Cemetery
Author's Collections

Mrs. Oscar Wood in her forties
Author's Collections
Courtesy: Wood Family

Former Ravensworth employee Russell Wood in the 1980s
Author's Collections
Courtesy: Carolyn Oliver

Fitzhugh Lee, Jr. readies a mount during
the Mexican Intervention, ca. 1916
Author's Collections

Mr. and Mrs. Fitzhugh Lee, Jr. on Vacation, ca. 1930
Author's Collections

Handbill for concert honoring Mrs. Fitzhugh Lee
Author's Collections

Campaign card for Edward Campbell "Cam" Sheads,
amiable neighbor to the Lees at Ravensworth
Author's Collections. Courtesy: Bill Sheads

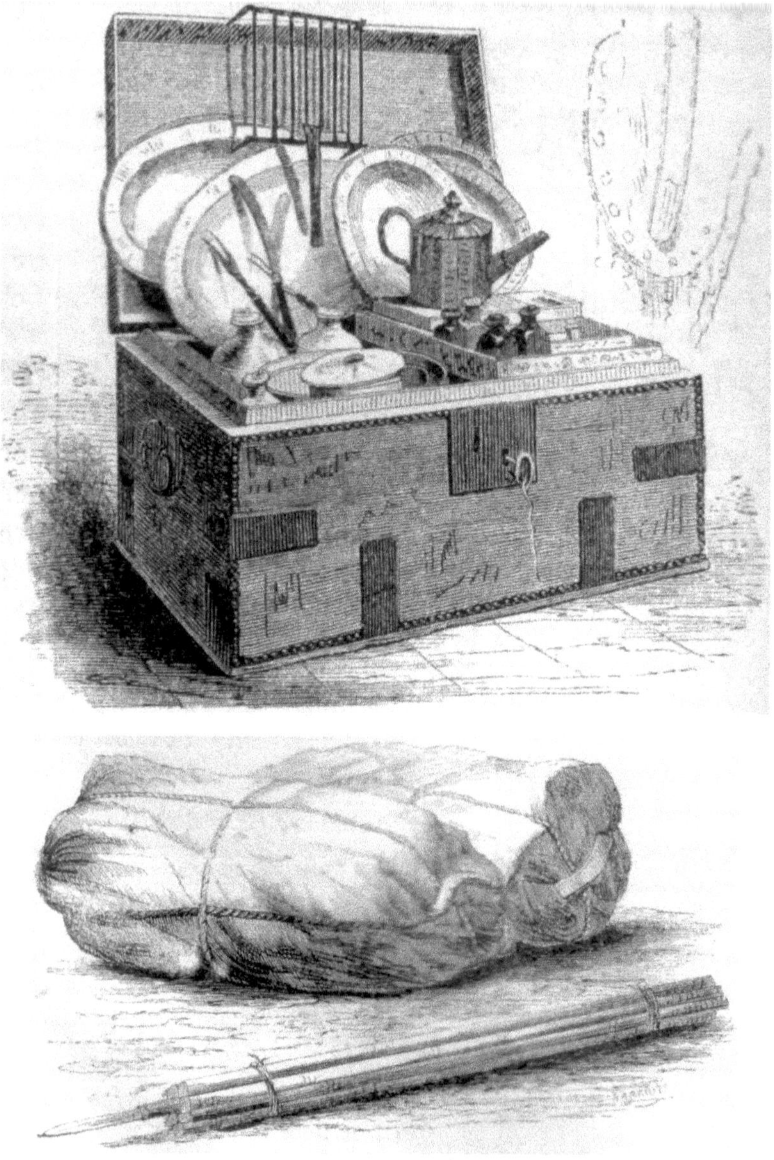

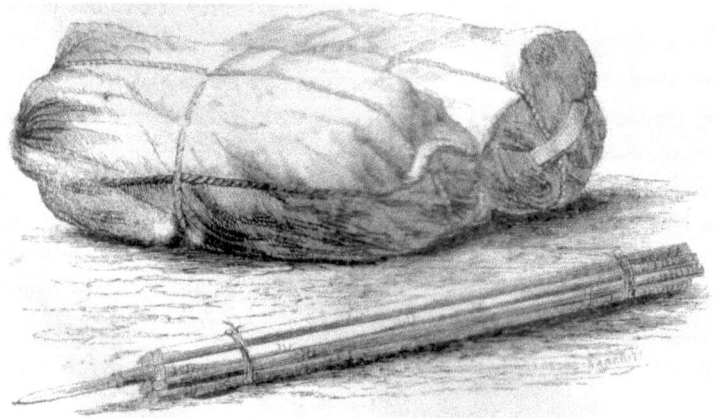

Some family legacies held by Mary Middleton Lee:
Washington's famous camp chest with his
tent from the Revolutionary War
Harper's New Monthly Magazine

The Unknown Man: George Taylor Lee

George Taylor Lee was named for his maternal grandfather. He was the eldest son of the poet lawyer Charles Carter Lee and his wife Lucy Penn Taylor. In his lifestyle, George often copied his father. He wandered outside Virginia for many years, aspired to scholarly endeavors, and he believed in the idea of a strong central government. George Lee preferred life in the western parts of the country, either among the hardscrabble farmers in mountainous Tennessee or Arkansas. His collective interests were not anti-Southern, but he counseled national patriotism in postwar America. His travels, his decision to leave Virginia, and his outspoken political pleas for sectional reconciliation all contributed to George Taylor Lee's largely unknown contributions to the family legacy.[125]

Alongside his famous Lee cousins, George represented a reconstructed Confederate soldier. At age 16, he participated in one of the Civil War's most legendary moments--the charge of the Virginia Military Institute cadets at the Battle of New Market in May 1864. However, it was only in the 1920s when George Lee's recollections of New Market gained popularity. He shunned personal glory, writing on the subject as the surviving member of a unit rather than a Lee. George practiced a self-effacement notable in General Robert E. Lee himself.[126]

George infrequently corresponded with his Lee cousins, but their exchanges indicated mutual respect and admiration. Upon his May 1888 marriage to Arkansan Ella Goodrum Fletcher, George Washington Custis Lee sent a present and wrote his cousin, "I am very glad to have been able to do something to give you a start in the world, although I can not take to myself all the credit you give me."[127] Robert E. Lee knew George better than Carter's other children, who were still quite young; they met on General Lee's final retreat to Appomattox Courthouse, and stayed with the Lee's in Lexington.[128]

George Taylor Lee "appreciated" or "understood" the family legacy more than most members of his generation. He was gracious enough to converse when questioned on the subject. His cousin Cazenove Lee requested an article for the Society of the Lees of Virginia in July 1929; the group wanted George's input because he was one of the last of an older generation of Lees. Publically, he refused to acknowledge his own contributions. In response to Cazenove Lee's request for the article, he wrote, "I cannot say just now what I can do about writing something for your magazine. There is little or nothing concerning my life that is worth telling."[129]

In fact, George's contribution to the family legacy was indeed worth telling. In a letter to Cazenove Lee two months after his request for an article, the old man wrote a voluminous account of his actions at New Market, interpreting the details of the charge to a family member. His grasp of details at the advanced age of 81 was impressive, even recalling his starting day at the Virginia Military Institution "on December 10th, 1863, at which time I was 15 years, 9 months and 2 days old."[130] On the express orders of General John C. Breckinridge, George Lee marched with the cadets to Staunton, Virginia on May 10, 1864. The next day the cadets marched along muddy roads. He wrote Cazenove,

> ...imagine a seventeen year old boy (some
> younger), loaded with an old Belgian musket,
> a muzzle-loader, a haver-sack with some rations
> in it, a canteen of water and a blanket, and you
> will easily realize that that boy had a heavy load
> to bear...[131]

George's shoes were roughly made and "did not fit very well. Besides, the leather in them had not been sufficiently tanned and was a little better than raw-hide."[132] He delayed by visiting the ladies, therefore foregoing entire meals. When the cadets reached New Market, they dodged exploding shells from the Union artillery positioned close to the town. George recalled the cadets formed ranks in double file for the line of battle. As they did, fire rained down on the cadets.[133]

> A circumstance which impressed this on my mind
> is this: shortly before reaching the [Bushong]
> house, Woodlief was struck and fell out of ranks.
> He was close to me, and, as he fell to the ground,
> seeming in much pain, I asked Capt. Preston if
> I had not better go to him; but he ordered me to

stay in ranks.[134]

One shell sent fragments and debris into George Lee's face, causing him minor cuts. He momentarily recovered and followed the other cadets through a thickening cloud of gunpowder and rain. After a heavy round of fire, he drifted from the center of the cadet line. Unable to keep pace, George found cover behind a tree. He dropped to one knee and fired at the shiny federal belt buckles through the thick smoke and pouring rain. However, the heavy Belgian musket George carried limited him to a scant eight shots.[135]

George's more creative military writings caused consternation from other veterans of the battle. In May 1909, in a fit of nostalgia, George wrote "a little ballad with the battle as my subject." He combined a romantic ballad with the reality of war. After sending the piece to a colleague in Lexington, it came back with scathing remarks highlighting his factual errors on the course of the battle. He admitted that the ballad was not intended for publication, but "something by which my children might hereafter have an idea of the impressions made on me at that time."[136]

In addition to his military contribution, he added literary ones. He wrote several books after 1900 and marketed them efficiently to publishers. In 1904, the Broadway Publishing Company released a book of prose called *The Puritan Maid*. George often reflected the family ideology in his writings; an explanatory note in the preface of *The Puritan Maid* referred to the sectional problems in postwar times. He claimed the prose was a continuation of his father's work with some editorial changes. When he published *The Puritan Maid,* George reminded his readers of Charles Carter Lee's leanings towards a national outlook. George Taylor Lee thus fulfilled his father's goals, which mirrored his own. He wrote in the preface that his express purpose was to "remind our people that they are of common parentage."[137]

Until his writings appeared, George Taylor Lee's contribution to the family legacy was little known. Generally, he practiced law and drifted west to Lonoke, Arkansas. He set up a practice and married the widowed Ella Fletcher on May 15, 1888. Lonoke was considered frontier country, and therefore it was hard to gather literary works. He wrote his younger brother John Penn Lee to send him some "good reading matter" he left in Virginia, including books on Greek and Roman history, an atlas, and not surprisingly, "Taylor's Enquiry" and the "Letters of Thos. Jefferson."[138]

In 1891, George Taylor Lee moved east to the mountain town of Johnson City, Tennessee. He resided there most of his adult life. George and Ella were content in the community, where they raised three children. He viewed himself as "a lawyer in a country town, who finds difficulty in both making ends meet in his effort to provide for the wants of himself, a wife, and three children..."[139]

George Taylor Lee's writings made a little money, but left an impression on the reading public. By World War I, he was the "literary Lee" of his generation. Even in advanced age, George wrote a patriotic composition based on the "Great War." However, his final writing was his most lasting. In 1927, *South Atlantic Quarterly* magazine published his account of the Lee family. His article, entitled "Reminiscences of General Robert E. Lee, 1865-68," was an intimate view of historic events from a first-person standpoint. He recalled little-known events from the closing days of the Civil War. In one account, George Lee attended a dinner in March 1865 at his Uncle Robert's house at Richmond's Franklin Street. He described General Robert E. Lee as troubled over the fate of the Confederate Congress. George wrote that General Lee said, "...they do not seem to be able to do anything except to eat peanuts and chew tobacco, while my army is starving."[140]

George reconstructed his accounts from distant memory and qualified them by stating he did not use exact words; however, the insights were invaluable, as the account humanized General Lee by expressing his growing unease and concern over the outcome of war, the capture of his son Custis, and his tired and hungry army. Only weeks after their March meeting, George relates, he marched west from Richmond to rural Farmville, Virginia. There he again unexpectedly met his uncle. General Lee was bewildered at George's presence, to which the young man responded that in Richmond he faced certain imprisonment. General Lee understood the dire situation, and shared a breakfast of fried chicken and bread with his nephew. As the Confederate army surrendered at Appomattox, George Lee fled into the Blue Ridge Mountains near Roanoke. After a month in hiding, he voluntarily surrendered in Richmond. A kindly

Federal officer, himself an admirer of Robert E. Lee, treated him well.[141]

George Taylor's assessment of Robert E. Lee's life after the Civil War was lasting. He debunked the myth that his uncle's post-war life was melancholy due to the "Lost Cause." In fact, George wrote Robert E. Lee was generally happy and "did not have the manner of a man borne down by disappointment and grief. It is true that he was generally grave and reserved, but this was natural with him."[142] George Taylor humanized General Lee, acknowledging the person instead of the image of a soldier. While retaining the reputation of the man, he wrote examples of Robert E. Lee's mortal nature, such as when the religious man fell asleep during a church service. George Lee concluded his article by describing himself as patriotic "by inheritance from a long line of patriotic ancestors and taught him by his father's words, Virginia was his country..."[143] He restated his Uncle Robert's allegiance to the Union after the Civil War, and urged that his fellow southerners be patriotic. To his nephew, Robert E. Lee "was not a sort of demigod, sitting on a pedestal far removed from other men, cold, gloomy and unapproachable..."[144]

In matters of money, he left the primary care of the West Virginia lands to his brother John. Unfortunately neither George's real estate nor his writing brought him wealth. Ella Lee fell gravely ill in 1929, and he faced an embarrassing financial realization. Luxuries such as his membership in the Society of the Lees could not be paid. He offered a statement of withdrawal, but Cazenove Lee would not hear of it. He wrote George that,

> This Society looks upon you, Sir, as the head of our family and our most distinguished member... It therefore gives me pleasure to advise you that in the future you will be relieved of the payment of the dues to this organization, and that your membership will continue as in the past.[145]

The old man took this as an "honorary" membership, and he wanted to repay the Society in some fashion for their good deed. Although doctors advised George Lee to stop writing articles and letters in 1929, he continued on with a detailed study of his ancestor John Taylor of

Caroline. Furthermore, he rallied against the 18th Amendment to the United States Constitution, thinking the idea of Prohibition absurd.[146]

George Taylor Lee's passing in 1933 removed a valuable and wise family scholar. Following his death, the role passed to Cazenove Lee, who held it until his own death in 1945. The man who died in 1933 hardly resembled the martial image of an eager cadet at New Market. During most of his life, George Taylor Lee was a true advocate of "self-denial," preferring the military legacy to fall to others. During his last decades of life, he realized he did not want to be forgotten, despite his protestations, and his writings ensured his place in academic history.[147]

The Poet's Other Children

George Taylor Lee was one of the seven children of Charles Carter and Lucy Penn Lee. Although he appeared the most willing to carry the family standard, several others contributed significantly. The second son, Henry, and the third son, Robert Randolph, led quiet and conventional lives, the latter living on his father's Windsor estate. The two daughters married doctors, and the elder, Mildred, moved to Norfolk to start her family. The two younger sons, Williams Carter and John Penn Lee, prospered in Virginia.[148]

Williams Carter Lee, born September 8, 1852, was a promising young man. He often accompanied his father on his frequent travels.[149] Williams had a head for business, calculating the monetary value in the construction of a rail depot in a letter to his brother George. He was an advocate of temperance, and consulted his brother on its importance.

> ...if you will attend closely to your business, a thing which I have no fear of you not doing from idleness and indifference. But any excessive drinking would be ruiness [sic] to an employee in such a business..to resist the first drink given him that makes me an advocate of temperance societies. We all have temptations to be vicious in one way or another, and I have always found it the case with me that the resolution to abstain altogether is

the only one that bears any fruits...[150]

His life pursuits were education and law. After entering college life at 16, Williams taught in a Charlestown, West Virginia high school from 1877 to 1879. The following year he practiced law in the town of Rocky Mount, a country town south of Roanoke, Virginia. He worked on further academic studies at Washington & Lee. There he became a polished orator and debater in the Washington Literary Society. In the summer of 1881, he returned to Rocky Mount as a potential law partner.[151]

Tragedy struck Williams Carter Lee on the eve of his law partnership in Rocky Mount. On October 25, 1881, the young man was returning from the Yorktown Centennial by train. While passing Charlottesville, another train collided with his. The caboose caught fire and collapsed under the weight of the second train. Two men were caught beneath the wreckage--one was Williams Carter Lee. Although quickly rescued, the young man was gravely injured. His sister Catherine Randolph Lee wrote her brother George Taylor Lee about his harrowing injuries caused by the accident.[152]

> It was soon discovered that his leg was mashed above the knee, the chest and other parts of the body being also much injured. His leg was hurt too badly to be set, and too high up to be taken off even if he could have stood the operation, and he was never again able to walk without crutches.[153]

Williams Carter Lee never recovered. At Windsor there was some early signs of hope, but his injuries caused him constant agony. He died on June 26, 1882 and was buried at St. Luke's Church in Powhatan County. The man who might have carried the Lee legacy honorably died horribly.[154]

The youngest son of Charles Carter and Lucy Penn Lee emerged as quiet family caretaker. John Penn Lee was close to his Uncle Robert's family, as evidenced by a bequest in the will of his cousin Mary Custis Lee upon her death in 1918. However, by the time of his own death on September 24, 1928, John Penn Lee was primarily remembered for his own accomplishments as lawyer, judge and father. He was born at the family home at Windsor, but was attracted to western Virginia. However, he "stayed put" in Virginia, attending Washington & Lee, where he often saw his cousin Custis Lee.[155]

John Penn Lee knew mortality from his youth. His father died when he was three years old, and he was often surrounded by surrogate "parents" in the form of elder siblings. George Taylor Lee was a full 19 years his senior, and much of the existing correspondence between them reads like a father advising his playful son. Their mother Lucy was protective of John, regularly recording his activities in letters to friends and relatives. In June 1884, when John began his studies at Washington & Lee, brother George found that John wrote their mother on the subject of his [George's] romantic activities! Lucy teased her son.

> So they say, you are in love with Miss Bruce. There are two sisters. Is it the oldest, or the youngest. John seems not to believe you are in such trouble.[156]

As Lucy traveled little, she stayed in Virginia on the occasion of George's wedding in Arkansas. She suggested that the newlyweds visit her in Virginia. Lucy politely refused the invitation on the account of "...so many months still before John will leave us, that I cannot tell yet what combination of circumstances may keep me here."[157]

At the time of the 1888 wedding, John Penn Lee had graduated from Washington & Lee. His excellent grasp of academics gained him a early reputation for legal skill. Cousin Robert E. Lee, Jr. wrote George Taylor Lee in May 1888 that "John I see whenever I go to Lex--& I call him 'Lord High Chancellor'-the rest of your people I never see & hear of very rarely."[158] Later the two family branches rarely saw each other. One reason was the constant wanderlust displayed by Carter Lee. Custis Lee saw a bit of it in John Penn Lee. He wrote George in Arkansas that "John is well, and will doubtless be graduated in Law next June; he is talking of trying his luck in Texas..."[159] Instead, John Penn Lee moved to Rocky Mount, where he set up a law practice with Judge P.H. Dillard. The partnership lasted until 1914, when Dillard moved on to the Circuit Court.[160]

Although John Penn Lee was a legal scholar, he was still young and pursued romantic interests. He wrote his sister-in-law Ella about his flirtations in Rocky Mount. In the letter, John thanked Ella for a gift of a winter muffler.

> ...we had a big dance, and I walked in the room with my overcoat & muffler on--just to speak to some of the girls before I took my wraps off--and the girls all said that my muffler made me look fine..."[161]

John settled down eight years later when, on December 2, 1896, he married Isabella Gilman Walker of Lynchburg. Seven children followed, and five survived infancy. Catherine Dabney Walker Lee was followed by brothers Richard, Chiswell, Charles Carter, and Henry. John Penn Lee became judge of the Franklin County Court from 1898 to 1904, then served as a Virginia delegate. During World War I, he served on several county boards. Finally in 1918, John became Commonwealth's attorney in Franklin County, a position he kept until his death in 1928.[162]

John Penn Lee was the caretaker of legacy through his stewardship of the family papers. The large number of papers from his wandering father and paternal grandfather were kept in two trunks which he maintained. However, the disposition of the Lee papers fell to his children.

Spreading Branches, Spreading Legacy

The family legacy was distributed among the many branches of the Lees. The current image is the collective handiwork of Robert E. Lee children, nephews, nieces, and cousins, who controlled and preserved the reputation of the family as its personal representatives. Once Robert E. Lee died, his descendants proved an extension of the man himself. They possessed the inherited traits of self-denial, humor, religious fervor, and love of nation. The members of the family followed different aspects of the tradition, Robert E. Lee Jr. became scholarly after bursts of youthful activity, while Fitzhugh Lee carried on the family martial image. His son Fitzhugh Lee Jr. was a quiet horseman with early promise. The Edmund Jennings Lee family went west to farther frontiers, carrying the religious legacy of the family. Charles Carter Lee was the consummate Federalist holdover, but it was the oldest son, George Taylor Lee, who carried the closest image of the citizen-soldier that was Robert E. Lee. He combined the traits of warrior, poet, and scholar.

Each of the Lees carried a piece of a wide spreading legacy. As the lines became longer and members less aware of their common bonds, the Lees were still well aware of their fascination among the American people. They are, and were, human beings with a purpose and image to fascinate future generations of those intrigued with our heritage. The mid-Twentieth Century was no different.

Legacy IV: Transition

A Legacy Dispersed

The demise of stately homes such as Ravensworth, the family's societal position, and the changing nature of stewardship of the traditional family possessions caused the Lee legacy to fall into disarray. Older generations of the family passed on. New influences, especially those outside the family, gradually overshadowed the Lee legacy. Ravensworth became a casualty to suburbia, replaced by a shopping center and segmented into housing plots. Society looked to new role models in a modern world. In World War II, cavalry meant armored tanks, not horses. The Lees welcomed the lack of notoriety, seeking honorable professions as businessmen, churchmen, and doctors. They literally disappeared into the general population of the mid-Twentieth Century. Interests such as memorial foundations and societies replaced the departed family members. The Robert E. Lee Foundation at Stratford and the Lee Chapel at Washington & Lee University became the primary representatives of the family's legacy.

After years of indifference, there was renewed historical interest in the family during the Civil War's Centennial in the 1960s. The newspapers sparked a flurry of newly-published research studies on the Lees. Workers on the old family estates became news. Thousands of people visit Arlington House, still a centerpiece of Lee history within the boundaries of the famous cemetery. Visitors pass through the home's restored grandeur and view its precious artifacts.

Post-Mansion Ravensworth

Starting in the 1920s, the old estates disappeared and many of the old families moved away. Automobiles outpaced the old horse-drawn wagons. His dairy became the focal point of Ravensworth. However, leisure sport gradually overshadowed any occupational purpose.

In the early 1900s, the breeding of horses was one of George Bolling Lee's favorite hobbies. His horses remained on the Ravensworth property for decades after the fire. Retired Virginia State Senator Omer Hirst specifically recalled one of his prize stallions was "Dress Parade," a foal sired by the great race horse "Man O'War."

Born in 1923 and dammed by a mare named "Thrasher," the exceptional horse chewed the grass of Ravensworth upon his acquisition by Doctor Lee.[1]

Despite Doctor Lee's absence, the Ravensworth farm remained a working dairy. After the departure of dairy manager Roscoe Allen, Doctor Lee hired a local farmer named R.J. Sprague to the position. Shortly after, his supply of prize-winning Holstein cows increased. In November 1930 the dairy's production reached "an average of 312,532 pounds of milk and 405.8 pounds of butter fat."[2] Worker Douglas Dove recalled, "We were milking 10 or 12 cows then, I guess. Dr. Lee bought ten heifers from up North somewhere. He paid $500 apiece for 'em, Holsteins."[3] The Fairfax County Herd Association report for 1931 noted that six cows from Ravensworth were on its honor roll. In the same year, Dr. Lee won second prize for milk production. Longtime resident Mayo Stuntz recalled that Sprague's success led to his later employment as a Fairfax County milk inspector. With the departure of Sprague, the dairy's production slowed.[4]

The long-term servants largely remained in the area when Doctor Lee arrived for periodic visits. He returned with his family every summer for a few weeks. While there, Doctor Lee often visited his old companions and neighbors. Cam Sheads remembered a casual visit long after Ravensworth burned. Douglas Dove recalled that he picked up Doctor Lee in a new 1927 Dodge at Union Station, as the old train station stop fell into disuse. Sam Ayres stayed on for another 20 years. Dove recalled, "they had a 30-acre garden there that had been neglected for 10 or 20 years, and Dr. Lee told me that he'd give me $15 a month to stay there..."[5] The prized garden was tended for years by Samuel's father Jonah Ayres, yielding "corn and wheat, sugar beets."[6]

After its conversion from a dairy concern to a summer cottage, Ravensworth became a revered place for hunters. Douglas Dove noted a number of wild animals, including "...foxes and crows and hawks and owls. I never heard anything about peacocks. I used to hunt rabbits and squirrels all over the place..."[7] Cam Sheads went fox hunting on horseback with other local families. All the surrounding families kept dogs used for the hunt. He carried the signal horn to hail the hunters at the designated meeting place. Sheads recalled, "the dogs would come running, and the men would soon follow."[8]

Prohibition had a big impact on the area around Ravensworth. Illegal stills had always existed in the neighborhood, primarily in the back creeks and hidden coves in the southern portion of Fairfax County, and, most people were sympathetic to distillers and their customers. In the case of Russell Wood, where alcohol was at least a secondary factor in the destruction of a life, and possibly two homes, the authorities reacted only after some serious detriment to society. One of the investigators of the Ravensworth fire, Virgil Williams, became familiar with gun-slinging characters in rooting out Prohibition activity. In January 1922 bootleggers in a car sped through Fairfax by way of Little River Turnpike. Williams heard of the bootleggers' route and tried to stop them. The *Fairfax Herald* reported that the men inside the car drew their weapons on the lawman. Williams received no support, and the car careened past him.[9]

Law enforcement support for Agent Virgil Williams arrived as police from other jurisdictions assisted the Fairfax County Prohibition agents in their periodic raids on local stills and bootleg shanties. Much of the new support was due to the actions of a new Commonwealth's Attorney, Wilson M. Farr. For the next 14 years, Farr was a vigorous prosecutor who won the respect of local citizens. After high profile raids on mash stills and his work on the Ravensworth fire, Williams ran for Fairfax County sheriff in 1927. A late scandal allegedly fomented by political rivals prevented his candidacy for that office, but he continued his detective duties. When Prohibition ended in 1933, Williams served in the Navy and later worked as a building contractor. He retired at 75 years of age, and he died only 11 months later, in November 1968. Wilson Farr returned to private practice after a term as Commonwealth's Attorney and died in 1959. For both, the Ravensworth fire investigation was a highlight in their careers.[10]

In addition to changing mores, suburbanization was an effective catalyst for community change. As early as 1950, suburbs cropped up in a steady westward creep. The suburban lifestyle brought new homes, diverse classes of families, stores, and modern appliances. Houses became individual neighborhood centers to themselves. Civic associations took over the influential roles traditionally held by respectable estates. However much history revered the name of Lee, especially in Northern Virginia. By the 1930s, the family had dispersed throughout the country. Dr. George Bolling Lee tended his medical practice in New York.

The Missing Lees

Increasing numbers of the Lee family moved away from Virginia, and Ravensworth had become a vacation home. As a result, their former neighbors saw them infrequently. Douglas Dove remembered,

> Dr. Lee had an office in the Plaza Hotel in New York City. He was a surgeon. He would visit Ravensworth once or twice a month. It was recreation for him...they'd have emergency cases up in New York and he'd have to go back in a hurry.[11]

Despite career demands, Doctor Bolling Lee represented the family at many honorary functions. In April 1928 he and his young son Robert E. Lee IV visited Stone Mountain, Georgia to introduce the public to the equestrian statue of his grandfather carved into the side of the mountain. In 1934, Doctor Lee received an honorary degree from Gettysburg College, alongside Ulysses S. Grant III. The two shook hands in a gesture of national reconciliation. Additionally, Doctor Lee served as honorary president of the Robert E. Lee Memorial Foundation, and assisted its primary mission in acquiring the old Lee homestead of Stratford Hall.[12]

Commemorative events concerning the Lees and Ravensworth continued well into the 1930s. On April 30, 1932, Burke resident Hazel Davis planted a memorial tree in honor of the Lees. Doctor Lee wrote her a letter of appreciation, and acknowledged his love of community. Additionally, he credited his deceased brother, Robert E. Lee III, for much of the honor.

> My brother, whom you all know, lived here for more than twenty years and represented this county (Fairfax) in the Legislature. He was

devoted to his friends and neighbors, and was active in all local enterprises, and interested in everything pertaining to the county and its people. He loved Ravensworth, and knew no other home until very near the end of his life. He would have preferred to have spent his remaining days there, but unfortunately circumstances were such that it was impossible...I, too, entertain great love and affection for this dear old place and its neighbors.[13]

In October 1936, *The Fairfax Herald* suggested a historical highway marker for the old estate. However, the marker was to be placed on the well-traveled Little River Turnpike, almost two miles north of the estate. The report stated that "Fairfax County should be proud to proclaim that she has within her borders the spot which was to Robert E. Lee as a second home."[14] It took almost another 50 years until the marker was finally placed at the site of Ravensworth and dedicated.

Memorials to the Lee family appeared in burgeoning literary efforts, in the many biographies that appeared during the 1930s and 1940s. Douglas Southall Freeman's four volume tribute, *R.E. Lee, A Biography*, was published by Scribners in 1934 and 1935. In 1940, an elderly friend of Custis Lee, Greenlee D. Letcher, wrote friends and relatives in assisting Dr. James Lewis Howe's research on Washington & Lee University.[15] After he was asked for any memory of Custis Lee, a gentleman named L.M. Harris wrote Letcher two special memories involving a precious Lee artifact.

> The General [Custis Lee] brought over to the College as a gift the Prayerbook of Martha Washington. He said: "I had to get it when Mildred was not at home. It's as hard to get blood out a beet as to get anything out of Mildred...I suppose that you remember that at Genl. Custis's receptions the liquor was distributed from Gen'l Washington's

punch-bowl.[16]

Following the death of Doctor Lee on July 13, 1948, he left his estate to his two children, Robert E. IV and Mary Walker Lee. Mary wed Fairfax County businessman A. Smith Bowman. Robert E. Lee IV married and a fifth of that name survives. He was president of the Fairfax County Historical Society in the 1970s.[17]

Like their relatives at Ravensworth, other branches of the Lee family collected the heirlooms and attended occasional ceremonies. However, press coverage lessened as the decades passed, so their appearances and life events are more difficult to trace. The descendants of Charles Carter Lee, the brother of Robert E. Lee, were periodically mentioned in newspapers and journals. In June 1901, Carter Lee's son Henry died in Macon, Georgia. The *Macon Telegraph* gave the obituary a respectable half a column. Fitzhugh Lee's younger brother Major John Mason Lee, who had served in the Confederacy, received considerable news coverage upon his death in March 1924. Carter's descendant George Taylor Lee III presented the original certificate of membership for "Light Horse" Harry Lee in the Society of the Cincinnati to a museum in October 1977.[18]

Some Lee descendants received their press due to misfortune. Doctor Charles Henry Lee was the grandson of Edmund Jennings Lee of Alexandria. Born in 1866, he attended the Alexandria Theological Seminary. Charles was ordained a priest in 1894, and he served as pastor in Culpeper County, Virginia and Macon, Georgia. His wife Susan, the daughter of Virginia author John Esten Cooke, shared his religious devotion. In February 1938, Charles Henry Lee was 71 years old, and in his eleventh year of service at Episcopal Christ Church on St. Simon's Island, Georgia.[19]

Doctor Lee's charge mixed traditional southern values in a changing environment. St. Simon's Island was a budding resort with a thriving business in development. Lee had a personal attachment to the area; a short distance south was Cumberland Island, a second oasis that served as the deathbed of his ancestor, "Light Horse Harry" Lee, in 1818. His attraction to St. Simon's was understandable, as Episcopalian founder Charles Wesley had purportedly preached under its surrounding oak trees trimmed with Spanish moss.[20]

Unfortunately, the resort environment of St. Simon's Island

disturbed Charles Lee's charge as rector of the Christ Church when development and gambling moved into the area in the late 1930s. The 6'2" Lee was known for his religious zeal against the onset of any vice. The appearance of the new pastime of gambling affected his congregation, and Doctor Lee became increasingly troubled. He was not alone in opposing the development of a resort by two brothers, Henry J. and W.H. Cofer. Although the formation of resorts was not new in Glynn County, a new causeway linking neighboring Sea Island anticipated greater traffic and unexpected plans. The St. Simon's Island residents did not realize that the new development included gambling shanties that multiplied in large numbers. Instead of a tasteful resort that enhanced the island's traditional roots, Lee and other county officials faced greater uncontrolled criminal activity. In his usual zeal, Lee was outspoken about the problems. In opposing the gambling shanties, he allied himself with the headmaster of the Sea Island School, G.C. Durand. Lee knew there was risk, stating to his wife that "some great tragedy will have to occur before Glynn County will have law and order."[21]

Reverend Lee's statement about tragedy proved prophetic. On the night of February 5, 1938, he and his wife Susan were in the church rectory, a building several hundred yards from the church. Lee was composing a sermon for his Sunday service, when they heard a loud noise close to the church. Both the reverend and his wife looked up, but neither could discern its identity or direction; they assumed that a car had backfired on the road. They never saw the shattered window of their quarters. Someone had fired a shot at them and, being both a bit hard of hearing, they never noticed. Mrs. Lee retired for the night while the doctor resumed working on his sermon. A few minutes before midnight, his wife heard another backfiring noise. Looking outside the bedroom window, she spied the shape of an automobile on the road moving towards the pier. Deciding to look in on her husband's progress, Mrs. Lee found Doctor Lee sitting upright on the sofa and facing the fully-shattered window. Upon closer inspection, she noticed he was shot in the right temple. Mrs. Lee immediately summoned Durand and Doctor E.H. Egbert, but nothing could be done for Charles Lee. The local police arrived at the rectory, and later questioned a servant on the property. They found the .38-caliber bullet slugs, one of which was copper-jacketed. Both slugs were found in the house after having passed through two walls.²²

Officials began the search for Reverend Lee's murderer. Glynn County Police Chief L.O. Godwin began his search with the motive. Durand and Egbert were unequivocal in their own opinions of the guilty party, and coroner J.D. Baldwin opened a full investigation on their theory. The coroner made a determined effort to find the killer. After eight months of intense investigation, two African-American island residents were arrested as hired killers. One of them, George Cleyborn, confessed his employment by the Cofer brothers to kill Reverend Lee. The Cofers were arrested and, in late January 1939, Cleyborn was convicted of first-degree murder. Interestingly, the press barely noted the victim's connection to Robert E. Lee.[23]

The press largely localized coverage of the Lee family in politics. In the 20th century, most of the Lees avoided political campaigns. When they did, the name no longer assured a victory. One example of the changing public perception of the Lee name was found in Alexandria resident Fitzhugh Lee Opie's unsuccessful mayoral campaign in 1967. The Lee name was revered in Alexandria, and Opie was the great-grandson of General Fitzhugh Lee through his daughter Ellen. At 37, he was a businessman with little political experience. Despite this disadvantage, Opie waded into an already crowded mayoral contest. As a Democrat, Opie was dissatisfied with the selection of his party, Alexandria City Councilman Charles E. Beatley, Jr. He entered the race in mid-April 1967, only two months before the election, as an independent candidate. Opie was assisted by local Republicans seeking a political foothold in Alexandria. When the two candidates spoke in May rallies, Opie questioned Beatley's position on the slow construction of public housing. Within days, rumors circulated that the Lee descendant attended a local Nazi rally. When an audience questioned Opie on the subject, he became defensive. A spate of unfounded rumors followed, including one that Opie beat his wife, another that tied his loyalties to high-rise developers, and a third calling him the captive of "Jewish merchants on King Street." Opie attempted to control the damage to his campaign. The *Alexandria Gazette* reported that Fitzhugh Lee Opie responded to the Nazi connection as "so patently silly that it barely needs challenging." In the end, it was the short time frame that proved detrimental to Opie's campaign. He lost the election to Beatley.[24]

The Societies

After 1920, the largest collective strength behind the Lee name was in the form of family or memorial societies. Although many family societies and foundations started earlier, their increased use as a device of legacy became dominant at this time. The desire for a large memorial to Robert E. Lee inspired the initiation of one foundation in his name. Private donations and public associations funded many statues of General Lee.

The Lee family organized themselves into a society in1922. Genealogists within the family built upon the work of Edmund Jennings Lee's grandson, Cassius Lee, Jr., who had collected information in the 1870s. His voluminous studies sparked an interest in a compilation after Cassius' early death in September 1892 at the age of 48.[25]

The formation of the Society of Lees of Virginia grew out of the collective interest in the studies of Cassius and his brothers, who had tried to complete his work. Between December 1921 and April 1922, 72 members of the family joined the organization. Among the first members were John Penn Lee, Mildred Washington Lee, and George Taylor Lee. Although Cassius' brother Edmund Jennings Lee resided in Philadelphia, he pulled together the collections of letters and complicated nerational relationships. He died in late 1922, leaving Cazenove Lee as the pivotal force in the organization until his own death in 1945.[26]

Other memorial groups were founded in the interest of the family. The core of membership of the Robert E. Lee Memorial Foundation, incorporated in 1929, reached well beyond the family goals of remembrance and preservation. Its membership extended to interested persons and businesses in completing its mission. The acquisition process lasted six years and an aggressive fund raising campaign, which was largely accomplished through the efforts of two women. Mrs. Charles D. Lanier resided in Connecticut, but had status in the south as the daughter-in-law of the famous Southern poet, Sidney Lanier. She found an unpublished paper among her father-in-law's belongings, pleading for the establishment of a permanent memorial to General Robert E. Lee. In 1916, May Lanier expressed the idea in a letter to the United Daughters of the Confederacy. However, historical researcher Ethel Armes provided the momentum for the cause. Her painstaking research and writing convinced a wide national audience that Stratford Hall was the perfect memorial to General Lee.[27]

The greatest efforts of May Lanier and Ethel Armes occurred between 1928 and 1930. Miss Armes labored over an historical account purchasing Stratford Hall in the summer of 1928. Her research was intended for the audience at the well-attended November meeting of the United Daughters of the Confederacy in Houston, Texas. Mrs. Lanier paid for 10,000 copies of a booklet called "Old Stratford Hall," to explain the cause. Unfortunately, the Houston meeting proved disappointing; while the Daughters of the Confederacy approved of May and Ethel's efforts, they did not assist. Mrs. Lanier's mother graciously allowed her daughter to post seven Liberty bonds as collateral for a loan. Mrs. Lanier raised a cash payment of $5,000, and shortly afterward, formalized the organization with the assistance of Georgian Eugene Stetson, President of the Guaranty Trust of New York. The Robert E. Lee Memorial Foundation became incorporated February 11, 1929. The first Board of Directors included Dr. George Bolling Lee, Mrs. Charles Dana Gibson, and Stetson. When its membership dedicated Stratford Hall on October 12, 1935, the organization met that goal. Doctor Douglas Southall Freeman gave a spirited address and equated the purchase of the Lee home with the restoration of Williamsburg. As a result of the efforts, Mrs. Lanier was appointed "President" for her natural life.[28]

Lanier and Armes were successful in other fund raising efforts to restore Stratford. In 1936, Armes wrote a book of almost 600 pages, titled *Stratford Hall, the Great House of the Lees* through Richmond's Garrett and Massie publishing firm. The giant work was divided into four sections. The foreword of the limited edition was penned by President Franklin Delano Roosevelt. Armes, in her new position as Executive Secretary of the Robert E. Lee Memorial Foundation, remained its creative element. Through the book's success, prominent American learned of the Foundation's efforts, and donor dollars financed the restoration of the estate stables and gate house. Automobile magnate Henry Ford donated a truck for the work crew. Two of the most important monetary gains arrived in the form of a non-interest bearing loan and a gift of $50,000 from the United

Daughters of the Confederacy. The Foundation paid the property mortgage in full within six years.²⁹

Both the Robert E. Lee Foundation and the Society for the Lees of Virginia had a large slice of the legacy pie. For the most part, the Foundation was formed of people outside of the family. The Society of the Lees of Virginia had mixed emotions on the nature of the Stratford Hall acquisition. A Foundation official wrote a retrospective account on the early struggles of Mrs. Lanier. The account mistakenly named May Field Lanier as the sole force in the acquisition, neglecting earlier attempts by Cazenove Lee and others. The complaints came to the Society's Eleanor Lee Templeman, who had the awkward duty of keeping peace between the Foundation and Society.³⁰ She politely wrote the author of the paper, Mrs. Frank Griffin, that it was a mistake to ignore prior efforts by the Lee family.

> The real credit to which that group is entitled is that, in these circumstances, they swallowed their own disappointment and misgivings and magnanimously pitched in to do what they could to redeem Stratford on Mrs. Lanier's terms... I would not have brought it up now if others had not, but, in the circumstances, think it desirable to put the matter in proper context and perspective.³¹

The Robert E. Lee Foundation and the Society of the Lees in Virginia were two examples of the transformation of legacy from family to an organized group structure. No one person carried the entire Lee standard in 1930, although there appeared many descendants who claimed to be the bearer. Both institutions found collective power in common goals.

Change

The third and final element of a lessened predominance was the advent of social change in a new neighborhood structure. Modernization turned large estates into broader suburbs. In the 1950s many of the old residents around the former estate of Ravensworth were gone. Development businesses carved out new neighborhoods of single family homes. As part of President Dwight D. Eisenhower's highway initiatives, the Capitol Beltway circled the city. One of its interchanges was Braddock Road, crossing the old Ravensworth estate at the cloverleaf exit. Faced with fresh traffic near their lands, the Lees sold the estate. Developers purchased Ravensworth for a new industrial park complex, single family homes, and a shopping center in 1957.[32]

At the time of the sale, there were still vestiges of the old estate of Ravensworth. The four family graves, William Fitzhugh, Ann Fitzhugh, William Henry Fitzhugh, and Anna Maria Sarah Fitzhugh, remained on the property. Shortly after, the family moved them to the historic Pohick Episcopal Church south of Alexandria. The beautiful old structure made a suitable burial place for the Fitzhughs, whose monuments were placed near the east wall of the church.[33] The *Alexandria Journal* announced the sale of the remaining Lee land in April 1959. Developers reported that a subdivision, preserving the old outbuildings, was in the plans. Unfortunately, the structures were destroyed when construction began in the spring of 1960. Shortly afterwards Ravensworth Shopping Center appeared, with a grocery, pharmacy, and post office. The gray buildings of an industrial park rose behind the market. Finally, the remaining grounds became a housing development called Ravensworth Farms. Some of the brick of the estate was recycled as material in the new houses.[34] In early 1973, a newspaper article proudly proclaimed a Lee connection as "the new 88 acre Springfield Mall Regional Shopping Center is situated on a portion of what was once the plantation of a famous American family."[35]

The same motivations that finished Ravensworth also applied to neighboring Ossian Hall. When Senator Bristow died in 1944, his will stipulated the sale of the house. His son, Joseph, was interested in preserving the house.[36] In May 1957, he wrote Eleanor Lee Templeman to raise concerns about vandalism at Ossian Hall.

> I was told the other day that someone drove a
> truck up at night and took the mantels, the
> stairway, and the colonial ironwork off the doors
> at Ossian Hall near Annandale. The realtors
> holding this property have been attempting to sell

it to several historical societies...You cannot leave a house empty, historical or otherwise, without danger of extensive damage from vandals. You cannot blame these recent incidents on the damn Yankees.[37]

In August 1957, Joseph Bristow wrote Eleanor Lee Templeman that "a number of individuals tell me they will contribute small amounts to preserve this remaining Colonial Mansion if some association that will last and not fold up..."[38] The granddaughter of Francis Asbury Dickins expressed her sadness at the "desecration of the old place."[39] However, preservation efforts made little headway. The price of restoration was high, even if the land was inexpensive. A local preservationist stated the land was available for $30,000, but the conditioning of the property was considerably more. Finally, in 1959, developers purchased the boarded shell of what was Ossian Hall. That September, Fairfax County volunteer firemen razed the damaged house to the ground.[40]

Despite the sad moments accompanying the decline of Ravensworth and Ossian Hall, there were a few positive changes. After months of sorting through piles of unfiled papers at the National Archives in 1970, a diligent researcher found Robert E. Lee's Oath of Allegiance to the United States. President Gerald Ford officially pardoned Lee later in the decade, with numerous members of the family in attendance. The Lee family decided to relocate the remains of Robert E. Lee's daughter Annie in 1993 following vandalism at her Warrenton, North Carolina grave. Although not disturbed since her death from typhoid fever in October 1862, the concern among scholars, residents, and families led to her joining her relatives at the Lee Family Crypt on the campus of Washington & Lee University.[41]

On September 11, 1993, a number of older residents came back to the Ravensworth site for the dedication of a new historical marker. The efforts of Dan Cragg of the Fairfax County Historical Commission brought old residents and young politicians together. Fairfax County Supervisor Sharon Bulova represented the district. Several of the Dove family represented the workers of the old estate. Marker T-42 marks the spot alongside the Ravensworth shopping center on Port Royal Road, stating:

RAVENSWORTH

Near here stood Ravensworth, a Fitzhugh and Lee family home. Build about 1796 by William Fitzhugh, the mansion stood on the largest single land grant in Fairfax County, the 21,966 acres acquired by Fitzhugh's great-grandfather in 1685. During the Civil War the house was not molested by either side. After the war Ravensworth came into the possession of Robert E. Lee's second son, Maj. Gen. W.H.F. ("Rooney") Lee. Ravensworth, a frame Palladian-style mansion, was one of the most imposing residences in Fairfax County until it burned in 1926.[42]

Legacy Today

As the historical marker at Ravensworth indicated, the real legacy of the Lee family passed through its institutions, artifacts, and societies to the care of the American people. The ghosts of Generals Washington and Lee, along with their long-passed descendants, told us their story through these varying legacies. Generations recorded their thoughts through books and postcards. Arlington House and Lee Chapel receive thousands of visitors each year, and all who come are seeking a small piece of the Lee legacy. The honor of carrying that piece of the American past enlightens all of us. It is sad that there is no more Ravensworth or Ossian Hall to visit, but their descendants remain. They understand, as much as anyone, that the name of Lee still commands attention and reverence. As Americans, we carry that responsibility today.

Appendix: Lee Family Charts

A. "Light Horse Harry" and Partial List of Children

Henry ("Light Horse Harry")   (1756-1818)
m. (1) Matilda Lee
        Henry ("Dark Horse Harry)
        (1787-1837)
m. (2) Anne Hill Carter
    (d. 1829)
        Charles Carter
        (1798-1871)
        Sidney Smith
        (1802-1869)
        Robert Edward
        (1807-1870)

B. Three Brothers and List of Children

Robert E. Lee
(1807-70)
m.   Mary Anna R. Custis
        (1808-73)

George W. Custis ("Custis")
(1832-1913)
Mary Custis
(1835-1918)
William Henry Fitzhugh ("Rooney")
(1837-91)
Annie
(1839-62)
Agnes
(1841-73)
Robert E. Lee, Jr.
(1843-1916)
Matilda Childe
(1846-1905)

Charles Carter Lee
(1799-1871)
m.   Lucy Penn Taylor
George Taylor
(1847-1933)
Henry
(1849-1901)
Williams Carter
(1852-82)
Robert Randolph
(1853-1926)
Mildred
(d. 1857)
Catherine Randolph
(d. 1865)
John Penn
(1867-1928)

Sidney Smith Lee
(1802-69)
m.   Anna Maria Mason
    (1811-98)

Fitzhugh
(1835-1905)
Sidney Smith
(1837-1888)
John Mason
(1839-1924)
Henry Carter
(1842-89)
Daniel Murray
(1843-1916)
Robert Carter
(1848-1903)
Elizabeth Mason
(1853)

C. Line of Succession at Ravensworth

William Fitzhugh
(1741-1809)
m   Ann Randolph
      (ca. 1747-1805)

William Henry Fitzhugh	Mary Lee Fitzhugh
(1792-1830)	(1788-1853)
m Anna Maria Goldsborough (1792-1874)	m George Washington Parke Custis (1781-1857)

Mary Anna Randolph Custis
(1808-1873)
m   Robert Edward Lee
      (1807-1870)

William Henry Fitzhugh Lee
(1837-1891)
m (2)   Mary Tabb Bolling
      (1846-1924)

Robert E. Lee III	George Bolling Lee
(1869-1922)	(1872-1948)
m Mary M. Pinckney (d. 1959)	m Helen Keeney
Robert E. Lee IV	Mary Walker Lee

D. Partial Tree of Edmund Jennings Lee Family
From the Papers of the Lee Society of Virginia

Edmund Jennings Lee
(1772-1843)
m   Sarah Lee

    Edmund Jennings
    (1797-1877)
    m (1) Eliza Shepherd (d. 1833)
       (2) Henrietta "Netta" Bedinger (1810-98)

        Edwin Gray
        (1835-70)

        Edmund Jennings III
        (1845-96)
        m   (1) Rebecca Laurence Rust (d. 1882)

            Edmund Jennings Lee IV

William Fitzhugh
(1804-37)
m   Mary Catherine Simms Chilton
    (1806-84)

Cassius Francis
(1808-90)
m   (1) Hannah Hopkins (1811-44)

        Cassius Francis Jr.
        (1844-92)

    (2) Anne Eliza Collins (1819-85)

        Edmund Jennings
        (1853-1922)

    Cazenove Gardner
    (1850-1945)
    m Marguerite DuPont

Richard Henry
(1821-1902)
m Evelyn Byrd (1823-89)

    Charles Henry
    (1866-1938)
    m Susan Randolph Cooke

ENDNOTES

Legacy I: Homes

1. Omer L. Hirst, Telephone Interview with Author, June 15, 1999.

2. Hirst Telephone Interview with author, June 15, 1999; Dan Cragg, comp., *Memories of Ravensworth-An Interview with Mr. Douglas Dove*, Typescript, September 1993.

3. Hirst Interview, June 15, 1999.

4. Cragg, Comp., *Memories of Ravensworth*. The gentleman described by Douglas Dove was Frederick Segessenman, a Swiss gardener who lived adjacent to the estate.

5. *Fairfax Herald*, August 6, 1926.

6. Cragg, *Memories of Ravensworth*.

7. *Fairfax Herald*, August 6, 1926.

8. *Fairfax Herald*, August 20, 1926.

9. *Fairfax Herald*, August 6, 1926; Cragg, *Memories of Ravensworth*.

10. *Fairfax Herald*, August 6, 1926.

11. Ibid.

12. *Fairfax Herald*, August 6, 1926; Angela Lindsey, Kristin Oliver, and Eileen Corrigan, *The Lees of Ravensworth "The Forgotten Generation,"* in Historical Society of Fairfax County, Virginia, Inc., Essay Awards, 1991, Volume 1, No. 4. This study, which evolved from a school project, was among the first to look into the 1926 Ravensworth fire from a historical view.

13. *Fairfax Herald*, August 6, 1926; Audrey B. Capone, "Ravensworth: A Short History of Annandale, Virginia," *Annandale Community Directory*, 12th Edition (Annandale,VA: Annandale Chamber of Commerce, 1998), 35.

14. Exerpt from Chuck Green, "The History Corner," *The Ravensworth Farmer*, Vol. XVIII, Issue 8, 5.

15. Exerpt from Chuck Green, "The History Corner," *The Ravensworth Farmer*, Vol. XVIII, Issue 8, 5-6; Capone, "Ravensworth," 36.

16. "Early Economics at Ravensworth," *Ravensworth Farmer*, Volume XVIII, Issue 9, 12; Henry Fitzhugh Account Book, Leaves 88 and 120, Virginia Historical Society.

17. "Early Economics at Ravensworth," *Ravensworth Farmer*, Volume XVIII, Issue 9, 12; Capone, "Ravensworth," 36.

18. Eleanor Lee Templeman, "Ravensworth," in *Historical Society of Fairfax County, Inc., Vol. 7, 1960-61*, 46; Capone, "Ravensworth," 36.

19. Templeman, "Ravensworth," in *Historical Society, Vol. 7, 1960-61*, 47.

20. Douglas H. Thomas to Editor, January 23, 1897, in *Virginia Magazine of History and Biography, Volume 4*, 1897, 467-468; Elizabeth Pugh Lawrence, *Genealogical Chart of the Fitzhugh-Grymes Family at "Eagle's Nest," King George County, Virginia 1674-1940*, April 1971.

21. Mary P. Coulling, *The Lee Girls* (Winston-Salem, NC: John F. Blair, Publisher, 1987), 5.

22. R.E. Calvert to Isabelle Van Havre, 5 May 1808, in Margaret Law Calcott, ed., *Mistress of Riversdale: The Plantation Letters of Rosalie Stier Calvert, 1795-1821* (Baltimore, MD: John Hopkins University Press, 1991), 188.

23. Handwritten Obituary in George Bolling Lee Papers, Virginia Historical Society. "Bath" is referring to Berkeley Springs, which

was famous for its aquatic healing properties since George Washington's day.

24. R.E. Calvert to Isabelle Van Havre, May 5, 1808, in Calcott, ed., *Mistress of Riversdale*, 188; Lawrence, *Genealogical Chart*; Fairfax County Minute Book 1807-08, May Court 1807, 81, Fairfax County Archives.

25. "Early Economics at Ravensworth," *Ravensworth Farmer*, Volume XVIII, Issue 9, 12; Fitzhugh Family Cemetery, Cemetery FX143, *Cemeteries of Fairfax County, Virginia*, Fairfax County Public Library; Fairfax County Will Book J, 244-48, Fairfax County Archives.

26. William Henry Fitzhugh to Mary Lee Custis, July 29, 1813, Virginia Historical Society.

27. Lawrence, *Genealogical Chart*; Nellie M. Marshall, comp., *Tombstone Records of Dorchester County, Maryland 1678-1964, Vol. I* (Cambridge, MD: Dorchester County Historical Society, Inc., 1993), 112; "Early Economics at Ravensworth," *Ravensworth Farmer*, XVIII, Issue 9, 12; Coulling, *The Lee Girls*, 6.

28. "Early Economics at Ravensworth," *Ravensworth Farmer*, XVIII, Issue 9, 12.

29. Marguerite Vance, *The Lees of Arlington: The Story of Mary and Robert E. Lee* (E.P. Dutton & Company, Inc., 1949), 39.

30. "The Loss of Ravensworth," *Alexandria Gazette*, August 4, 1926; "Original Members of the Society," in *Memorial of the Semi-Centennial Anniversary of the American Colonization Society January 15, 1867* (Washington, D.C., Colonization Society Building); Ibid., 16-17; P.J. Staudenraus, *The African Colonization Movement 1816-1865* (New York: Columbia University Press, 1961), 114; John C. Calhoun to V[irgil] Maxcy, January 8, 1828, in Clyde N. Wilson and Edwin Hemphill, ed., *The Papers of John C. Calhoun* (University of South Carolina, 1972), 332; "Early Economics at Ravensworth," *Ravensworth Farmer*, XVIII, Issue 9, 12; "A History Lesson," *Ravensworth Farmer*, Vol XVIII, Issue 4, 7; 1860 Slave

Schedules, Fairfax County, 544; C. Goldsborough to Doctor Vans M. Sulivane, August 28, 1834, as typed in Dorchester County Historical Society Notebook, Dorchester County, Maryland Library.

31. C. Goldsborough to Doctor Vans M. Sulivane, August 28, 1834, as typed in Dorchester County Historical Society Notebook.

32. R.E. Lee, Jr., *My Father General Lee* (New York, NY: Doubleday and Co., 1960), 363.

33. Poem to William H. Fitzhugh, dated 1829, Charles Carter Lee Collection, Library of Virginia, Reel 12.

34. Templeman, "Ravensworth," in *Historical Society, Vol. 7, 1960-61*, 47; John W. Wayland, *Historic Homes of Northern Virginia and the Eastern Panhandle of West Virginia* (Staunton, VA: McClure Company, Inc., 1937), 556; Charles Goldsborough to C.C. Lee, May 25, 1830, Charles Carter Lee Papers, Library of Virginia, Reel 3.

35. Goldsborough to C.C. Lee, May 25, 1830, Charles Carter Lee Papers, Library of Virginia, Reel 3.

36. Templeman, "Ravensworth," in *Historical Society, Vol. 7*, 47; Goldsborough to Lee, May 25, 1830; Marshall, comp., *Tombstone Records of Dorchester County*, 112.

37. *Alexandria Gazette*, August 4, 1926; Frederick Warren Alexander, comp., *Stratford Hall and the Lees Connected with Its History-Biographical, Genealogical, and Historical* (Oak Grove, VA: 1912), 311; Ibid., 277.

38. Entry of August 6, 1853 in Mary Custis Lee DeButts, ed., *Growing Up in the 1850's-The Journal of Agnes Lee* (Chapel Hill, NC: University of North Carolina Press for the Robert E. Lee Association, Inc., 1984), 20. Used by Permission of the Publisher.

39. Anna Maria Fitzhugh to Mrs. Dickins, October 2, 1843, Francis A. Dickins Papers, University of North Carolina at Chapel Hill, Southern History Collections, Folder 7.

40. Ibid.

41. Fitzhugh to Dickins, October 2, 1843; Bill Sheads Interview, Fairfax Station, VA, September 22, 1999.

42. Lawrence, *Genealogical Chart*; Coulling, *Lee Girls*, 86; Ibid., 88-89.

43. Alexander, comp., *Stratford Hall*, 312; Ibid., 320; Ibid., 315; Ibid., 327; Notes of H.T. Wickham, January 22, 1925, Address of same for occasion of presentation of portrait of General W.H.F. Lee to Lee Camp, Virginia Historical Society.

44. Notes of Wickham, January 22, 1925, Virginia Historical Society; "Address of Mr. Wise, of Virginia," in *Memorial Addresses on the Life and Character of William H.F. Lee (A Representative from Virginia) Delivered in the House of Representatives and in the Senate, Fifty-Second Congress, First Session* (Washington, D.C.: Government Printing Office, 1892), 35-36; Hu Maxwell, *The History of Randolph County, West Virginia-From Its Earliest Settlement to the Present* (Morgantown, WV: The Acme Publishing Company, 1898), 140.

45. Coulling, *The Lee Girls*, 104; Ibid., 132-133.

46. Coulling, *The Lee Girls*, 87-88; Ibid., 95; Ibid., 134; James A. Ramage, *Gray Ghost-The Life of Col. John Singleton Mosby* (Lexington, KY: University Press of Kentucky, 1999), 209-212.

47. M.C. Lee to Mary Macon, June 1870, Personal Papers, Acc. 23689, Library of Virginia.

48. Deposition of Anna Maria Fitzhugh in Original Claim #14013, Case Files for Congressional Cases 1884-1952, in Records of the U.S. Court of Claims, Record Group 123, National Archives and Records Administration.

49. "A History Lesson," *Ravensworth Farmer*, Vol. XVIII, Issue 4, 7.

50. Depositions of Daniel W. Lewis and Alfred Bayless in Anna Maria Fitzhugh, Original Claim #14013, Case Files, RG 123, National Archives.

51. Alexander, comp., *Stratford Hall and the Lees*, 325.

52. M.C. Lee to Mary Macon, June 1870, Personal Papers, Acc. 23689, Library of Virginia.

53. Lee, Jr., *My Father, General Lee*, 350.

54. Alexander, comp., *Stratford Hall and the Lees*, 328; "*The Cocke Family of Virginia-(Henrico.)-Fourth Generation Continued*" in *Proceedings of the Virginia Historical Society at its Annual Meeting Held in the Society's Building, December 19th, 1896, with the List of Officers and Members of the Society* (Richmond, Va: Wm. Ellis Jones, Book and Job Printer, 1896), 331-332. For more information on George W. Bolling, see Alexander H.H. Stuart, *A Narrative of the Leading Incidents of the Organization of the First Popular Movement in Virginia in 1865 to Re-Establish Peaceful Relations Between the Northern and Southern States, and of the Subsequent Efforts of the "Committee of Nine," in 1869, to Secure the Restoration of Virginia to the Union* (Richmond, Va: Wm. Ellis Jones, Book and Job Printer, 1888), 27; Ibid., 34; R.E. Lee to (W.H. F.) Fitzhugh Lee, June 8, 1867, Virginia Historical Society.

55. Alexander, comp., *Stratford Hall*, 328.

56. Lee, Jr., *My Father, General Lee*, 325-326; Lawrence, *Genealogical Chart;* Coulling, *The Lee Girls*, 175-176; Ibid., 178-180.

57. Robert E. Lee to Mary Lee, July 20, 1870 in Lee, Jr., *My Father, General Lee*, 418.

58. Chuck Green, "The History Corner," *Ravensworth Farmer*, Volume XIV, Issue 2, 4; Testimony of Francis E. Barrier, March 28, 1889 in Case Files for Congressional Cases, Original Claim 14013, No. 20, Ann M. Fitzhugh's Exr., vs. The United States, Copy in Fairfax County Archives. Original in Record Group 123, National Archives, Washington, D.C.

59. "Will of Mrs. A.M. Fitzhugh," in William H. Fitzhugh, Personal Papers. Box 240A, Alexandria Library Special Collections.

60. Court of Claims, Executors of Anna Maria Fitzhugh vs. the United States, Petition, Congressional Case, No. 20, Record Group 123, National Archives, Washington, D.C.

61. W.H.F. Lee to Mary Tabb Lee, November 17, 1874, George Bolling Lee Papers, Virginia Historical Society.

62. "For Harriet," Notes dated October 1883, from Margaret Dickins, Francis Asbury Dickins Papers, Southern History Collections, University of North Carolina at Chapel Hill, Folder 18.

63. Ibid.

64. Battaile, trustee vs. Fitzhugh Admr., 877, CFF #6L, Liber R, No. 4, Fairfax County Archives.

65. Ibid.; Deposition of Edwin C. Fitzhugh, in Southern Claims Commission Case File 14,896, 1877-1883, Record Group 233, National Archives; Jean Geddes, *Fairfax County-Historical Highlights From 1607* (Middleburg, VA: Denlinger's Publishers, Ltd. 1967), 78.

66. Sue Battaile to Mrs. Watts, July 17, 1875, Virginia Historical Society.

67. Edwin C. Fitzhugh, Southern Claims Commission Case File 14,896, RG 233, National Archives.

68. Dollie Fitzhugh to T.R. Love Esq., March 21, 1878, Virginia Historical Society.

69. Ibid.

70. Thomas R. Love to Miss Dolly Fitzhugh, March 26, 1878, Virginia Historical Society.

71. Omer Hirst Interview, June 15, 1999.

72. R.E. Lee (III) to Mary Tabb Lee, February 9, 1880, George Bolling Lee Papers, Virginia Historical Society. Bolly is brother George Bolling Lee as he was eight at the time.

73. R.E. Lee (III) to Mary Tabb Lee, March 30, 1881, George Bolling Lee Papers, Virginia Historical Society.

74. R.E. Lee [III] to Mary Tabb Lee, February 9, 1880, George Bolling Lee Papers, Virginia Historical Society.

75. William Henry Fitzhugh Lee to Mary Tabb Lee, March 26, 1881, George Bolling Lee Papers, Virginia Historical Society.

76. William Henry Fitzhugh Lee to Mary Tabb Lee, March 28 & 29, 1881, George Bolling Lee Papers, Virginia Historical Society.

77. William Henry Fitzhugh Lee to Mary Tabb Lee, March 28 & 29, 1881, George Bolling Lee Papers, Virginia Historical Society; Omer Hirst Interview, June 15, 1999.

78. 1900 Census, Fairfax County, T623, Roll 1707, 375/376, National Archives and Records Administration; 1900 Census, Fairfax County, T623, Roll 1707, 372/373; 1900 Census, Fairfax County, T623, Roll 1707, 387/388; Mary Tabb Lee to Mrs. Watt, Undated Letter, Watt Papers, Virginia Historical Society.

79. Presentation W.H.F. Lee to Mrs. Courtenay and Lady Friends of the W.L.I. in General W.H.F. Lee of Virginia, *The Curious Story of a Tapestry Portrait of WASHINGTON Ceremonies Attending the Presentation of the COURTENAY FLAG* (Walhalla, SC: The Keowee Courier Presses, 1903), 21.

80. Mildred Lee to Mrs. Hay, July 15, 1879, Lee Family Papers, Special Collections, Leyburn Library, Washington & Lee University.

81. General Register, Annandale Precinct, 1902-03, Fairfax County Archives; Mary Lee's Scrapbook, in George Bolling Lee Papers, Section 23, Virginia Historical Society.

82. W.H.F. Lee to Mary Tabb Lee, 21 Dec 1875, in George Bolling Lee Papers, Virginia Historical Society.

83. "Address of Mr. O'Ferrall, of Virginia, on the Life and Character of William H.F. Lee, in *Memorial Addresses on the Life and Character of William H.F. Lee, (A Representative From Virginia Delivered in the House of Representatives and in the Senate, Fifty-Second Congress, First Session* (Washington, D.C.: Government Printing Office, 1892), 27-29.

84. Alexander, *Stratford Hall*, 326; "Address of Mr. Herbert, of Alabama," in *Memorial Addresses*, 43; "Address of Mr. Washington, of Tennessee," in *Memorial Addresses,* 50.

85. Alexander, *Stratford Hall and the Lees*, 315; Ibid., 326.

86. *Fairfax Herald*, April 19, 1929.

87. Sargent, ed., *A History of an Expedition Against Fort Duquesne in 1755; Under Major-General Edward Braddock* (Arno Press, 1971). The original issue of this book was printed by Philadelphia, Pennsylvania publisher Lippincott, Grambo & Co. in 1854. The cites are on pages 232 and 283.

88. "Mr. William Watt," *Fairfax Herald*, April 7, 1911; Geddes, *Fairfax County Highlights*, 78; Bill Sheads Interview, September 22, 1999.

89. Geddes, *Fairfax County Highlights*, 78.

90. R.E. Lee III to R.W. Burch, September 18, 1895, Letter Press Book, R.E. Lee Papers, Duke University, Box 1-B.

91. 1900 Census, Fairfax County, T623, Roll 1707, 386; William Henry Fitzhugh Lee to Mary Tabb Lee, January 15, 1884, Lee Papers, Virginia Historical Society; William Henry Fitzhugh Lee to Mary Tabb Lee, April 8, 1884, Lee Papers, Virginia Historical Society.

92. Fairfax County Deeds, Book 958, 429; Fairfax County Law Book 38, 45; Bill Sheads Interview, September 22, 1999; 1910 Census, Fairfax County, Virginia, Falls Church District, 370/377.

93. R.E. Lee III to Lilly Newman, November 26, 1894, Letter Press Book, R.E. Lee Papers, Duke University. Box 1-B.

94. Indenture, G.W.C. Lee, Mildred C. Lee, W.H.F. Lee, M.T. Lee, Robert E. Lee to John S. Barbour, Receiver of the Washington City, Virginia Midland & Great Southern Rail Road, December 24, 1877, Liber W-4, 135, Fairfax County Archives; E.R. Conner, III, *Railroading on the Washington Division* (Manassas, VA: REF Publishing, 1986), 23; Exerpt of letter from Southern resident Samuel Spencer, July 29, 1901, in Connor, III, *Railroading*, 25; Indenture, G.W.C. Lee to Southern Railway Company, September 6, 1901, Liber I-6, 460, Fairfax County Archives; Sketches Showing Right of Way-thro' lands of Custis Lee, Fairfax Co., Va. Grade Reduction-Virginia Midland Railroad, August 27, 1901, Liber I-6, 460-B, Fairfax County Archives; Bill Sheads Interview, Fairfax Station, VA, September 22, 1999; G.W.C. Lee to Miss Lloyd, April 9, 1902, Special Collections, Leyburn Library, Washington & Lee University.

95. G.W.C. Lee to Miss Lloyd, July 16, 1903, G.W.C. Lee Papers, Special Collections, Leyburn Library, Washington & Lee University.

96. James Lewis Howe, "George Washington Custis Lee," *Virginia Historical Magazine*, Vol. XLVIII, October 1940, No. 4.

97. G.W.C. Lee to Captain R.E. Lee [Jr.], January 4, 1900, Lee Family Papers, Virginia Historical Society; G.W.C. Lee to Jno. L. Campbell, July 17, 1901, G.W.C. Lee Papers, Special Collections, Leyburn Library, Washington and Lee University.

98. Mary Tabb Lee to N.W. Bowe, Undated, George B. Lee v Mary M. Lee, File C, Fairfax County Archives.

99. Ibid.

100. G.W.C. Lee to Captain R.E. Lee [Jr.], January 4, 1900, Lee Family Papers, Virginia Historical Society.

101. G.W.C. Lee to Jno. L. Campbell, July 16, 1902, G.W.C. Lee Papers, Special Collections, Leyburn Library, Washington and Lee University.

102. Howe, "George Washington Custis Lee," *Virginia Historical Magazine*, 326-327.

103. Deposition of George Bolling Lee, Appendix "C," Lee v. Lee, Fairfax County Archives.

104. Alexander, *Stratford Hall*, 328.

105. D'Anne A. Evans, *Wakefield Chapel* (Fairfax, VA: Fairfax County Office of Comprehensive Planning, 1977), 57-58.

106. Ibid.

107. Evans, *Wakefield Chapel*, 57-58; Cragg, *Memories of Ravensworth*.

108. Coulling, *Lee Girls*, 193-194; *Fairfax Herald*, October 11, 1912; James Lewis Howe, "George Washington Custis Lee," *Virginia Magazine of History & Biography*, Vol. XLVIII, No. 4, October 1940, 326-327.

109. Mary Custis Lee to Mim and Jen, February 24, 1913, Lee Family Papers, Special Collections, Leyburn Library, Washington and Lee University.

110. R.E. Lee to Edmund R. Cocke, March 17, 1913, Lee-Jackson Foundation Papers, Special Collections, Leyburn Library, Washington and Lee University.

111. 1860 Slave Schedules, Fairfax County, Virginia, M653, Roll 1389, 544; *Alexandria Gazette*, April 11, 1944; Bill Sheads Interview, Fairfax Station, VA, September 22, 1999.

112. 1900 Census, Fairfax County, T623, Roll 1707; Death Register, South District, Fairfax County, 1881, Fairfax County Archives; Death Register, 1897, Fairfax County; Death Register, South District, 1895.

113. Geddes, *Fairfax County*, 79.

114. Cragg, *Memories of Ravensworth*; Cam Sheads Interview, Fairfax County Public Library.

115. A. Bower Segeser, *Joseph L. Bristow: Kansas Progressive* (Lawrence, KS: University Press of Kansas, 1968), 157; John F. Jerman to Joseph Bristow, Telegram, January 9, 1918, Bristow Papers, Kansas State Historical Society, Reel 118.

116. "J.L. Bristow Dies; Former U.S. Senator," *Washington Post*, July 15, 1944.

117. Segesser, *Joseph L. Bristow*, 157.

118. Virginia Moore Phone Interview, Rockville, MD, May 12, 2000.

119. Virginia Moore Interview, May 12, 2000; "Arneita Sullivan, 74, Dies; Companion of Mrs. Lee," *Washington Star-News*, January 12, 1974.

120. Ibid.

121. *Fairfax Herald*, June 5, 1908; Bill Sheads Interview; "Mr. William Watt," *Fairfax Herald*, April 7, 1911; Mary Tabb Lee to Mrs. Elizabeth Watt, Undated, Watt Papers, Virginia Historical Society; Cragg, *Memories of Ravensworth*.

122. "Col. R.E. Lee Weds," *Fairfax Herald*, July 4, 1919; "Dr. George B. Lee, Gynecologist, 75," *New York Times*, July 14, 1948; Cragg, *Memories of Ravensworth*.

123. Cragg, *Memories of Ravensworth;* John W. Wayland, *Historic Homes of Northern Virginia*, 558; Bathurst Brown Bagby, M.D., *"Recollections,"* (West Point, VA: The Tidewater Review, 1950), 55.

124. Will of Robert E. Lee III, Appendix "E," Lee v Lee, File "C," Fairfax County Archives; Will of Mary Tabb Lee, Type Copy, Fairfax County Archives.

125. Ibid.

126. Ernest Dove Telephone Interview, May 30, 1999; Deposition of Andrew Nelson, February 5, 1901, Higgins v Botts, CFF 48E, Fairfax County Archives; *Fairfax Herald*, April 30, 1926.

127. Ernest Dove Phone Interview, May 30, 1999; Lee Hubbard Telephone Interview, May 18, 1999.

128. Tombstone from National Memorial Park, Block I, 750; Hugh and Ethel Wood Interview, Waynesboro, VA, August 22, 1999.

129. Service Discharge Records, Berkeley County, WV, No. 674884, National Archives and Records Administration; Hugh and Ethel Wood Interview, August 22, 1999.

130. Criminal Court Docket Book, Fairfax County Archives; Hugh and Ethel Wood Interview, Waynesboro, VA, August 22, 1999.

131. *Fairfax Herald*, April 30, 1926; *Herndon News Observer*, July 29, 1926; Bill Sheads Interview, Fairfax Station, VA, September 22, 1999.

132. *Fairfax Herald*, August 6, 1926.

133. "Fire Destroys Ravensworth," *Alexandria Gazette*, August 2, 1926.

134. Lee v. Lee, #10, 484-485, Fairfax County Archives; *Fairfax Herald*, August 6, 1926.

135. *Alexandria Gazette*, August 4, 1926. Statement was taken from the *Richmond News-Leader*.

136. Dr. George Bolling Lee to Greenlee D. Letcher, March 28, 1940, Copy of Letter, Leyburn Library, Special Collections, Washington and Lee University.

137. *Fairfax Herald*, August 6, 1926.

138. Ibid.; "V. Williams of Fairfax Dies at 75," *Northern Virginia Sun*, November 16, 1968; R.E. Lee IV Phone Interview, June 8, 1999.

139. *Fairfax Herald*, August 13, 1926.

140. Ibid.

141. Lindsey, Oliver, and Corrigan, *Lees of Ravensworth - "The Forgotten Generation,"* in Historical Society of Fairfax County, Virginia, Inc., *Essay Awards 1991 Volume 1,* 4; Fairfax County Minute Book 12, Page 288, Fairfax Court House; Criminal Court Docket Book, Fairfax County Archives.

142. Hugh and Ethel Wood Interview, Waynesboro, VA, August 22, 1999; G.B. Lee v. Mary M. Lee, Chancery Case, November 1926 Term, Release, Mary M. Lee to George Bolling Lee. More on the suit appears later in the book.

143. Lucy Walsh Phinney, *A History of a Name and a Place-The Story of the Mount Vernon Unitarian Church and Hollin Hall* (n.p.: Evergreen Historical Associates, Fall 1994), 8-9; "Hollin Hall by Mrs. Winfield Scott Macgill," *Historical Society of Fairfax County, Virginia, Volume 9, 1964-65*, 39.

144. Phinney, *A History of a Name and a Place*, 25; "Hollin Hall," *Historical Society of Fairfax County, Virginia, Volume 9*, 39; John Stephens, Phone Interview, September 9, 1999.

145. John Stephens, Phone Interview, September 9, 1999; Phinney, *A History of a Name and a Place,* 25.

146. Fairfax County Minute Book 13, 274; "Charged with Arson-Young Man Accused of Having Caused Fire at Hollen [sic] Hall," *Fairfax Herald*, November 9, 1928.

147. "Charged with Arson," *Fairfax Herald*, November 9, 1928.

148. "Plead Guilty. Wood Sent to Penitentiary for Ten Years for Hollin Hall Fire," *Fairfax Herald*, November 23, 1928.

149. Fairfax County Minute Book 13, 274.

150. Index Cards to Penitentiary Inmates, Virginia State Penitentiary, Card 23831 R642, Virginia State Archives; Hugh and Ethel Wood Interview, Waynesboro, VA, August 22, 1999; Carolyn Oliver Phone Interview, August 25, 1999; Carolyn Oliver Phone Interview, August 29, 1999; "Russell F. Wood," *Evening Journal*, November 12, 1986; Berkeley County Register of Deaths, Page W-6.

151. Will of Grace E. Wood, Will Book 138, 116, Fairfax County Courthouse; National Memorial Park, Cemetery Plat Block I, 750, 1&2; Judith A Campbell, comp., *Page County Virginia-Death Notices Volume 6* (Rileyville, VA: Judith A. Campbell, October 1995), 126; Hugh & Ethel Wood Interview, Waynesboro, VA, August 22, 1999.

Legacy II: Artifacts and Keepsakes

1. Ruth Preston Rose, "Mrs. General Lee's Attempts to Regain Her Possessions After the Civil War," *The Arlington Historical Magazine, Volume 6*, October 1978, No. 2, 29.

2. Ibid.; Mary C[ustis] Lee to Philip Fendall, Sept 11 [1866], Lee Family Papers, Special Collections, Leyburn Library, Washington and Lee University.

3. List One in M.C. Lee to Philip Fendall, September 12, 1866, Lee Family Papers, Special Collections, Leyburn Library, Washington and Lee University.

4. List Two in M.C. Lee to Philip Fendall, September 12, 1866, Lee Family Papers, Special Collections, Leyburn Library, Washington and Lee University.

5. List Three in M.C. Lee to Philip Fendall, September 12, 1866, Lee Family Papers, Special Collections, Leyburn Library, Washington and Lee University.

6. Mary Lee to Philip Fendall, September 12, 1866, Lee Family Papers, Special Collections, Leyburn Library, Washington and Lee University; Mary Lee to Philip Fendall, October 12 [1866], Lee Family Papers, Special Collections, Leyburn Library, Washington and

Lee University.

7. Lee to Fendall, October 12 [1866], Lee Family Papers, Special Collections, Leyburn Library, Washington and Lee University.

8. Rose, "Mrs. General Lee's Attempts," *Arlington Historical Magazine*, Volume 6, Number 2, 32-34.

9. G.W.C. Custis to Capt. R.E. Lee, January 4, 1900, Lee Family Papers, Virginia Historical Society.

10. Mildred C. Lee Death Record in John W. Wayland, *Robert E. Lee and His Family* (Staunton, VA: McClure Printing Company, 1951), 63.

11. "Lee-Washington Bible--Its True History Given in an Interesting Story by General G.W.C. Lee, Its Rightful Owner," *Richmond Times-Dispatch*, March 10, 1904.

12. Copy of letter, Gen G.W.C. Lee to Mrs. Howard, February 5, 1907, G.W.C. Lee Papers, Special Collections, Leyburn Library, Washington & Lee University; G.W.C. Lee to John L. Campbell, April 5, 1907, G.W.C. Lee Papers, Special Collections, Leyburn Library, Washington & Lee University.

13. Custis Lee's Handwritten Notes from *Catalogue of the G.W. Custis Lee Collection of Oil Paintings--Washington and Lee University--Lexington, Virginia*, Attachment of Letter Copy, G.W.C. Lee to Mrs. Howard, February 5, 1907, Special Collections, Leyburn Library, Washington & Lee University.

14. G.W.C. Lee to Capt. R.E. Lee, October 20, 1909, Lee Family Papers, Virginia Historical Society.

15. Will of General G.W.C. Lee, as stated in Wayland, *Robert E. Lee and His Family*, 44-45. Robert, Jr. was known as "Rob." In the will, Robert E. Lee III was known as "Robert Edward Lee, Jr."

16. Ibid.

17. Exerpt of letter, George Bolling Lee to John W. Wayland as printed in Wayland, *Robert E. Lee and His Family*, 46.

18. Will of Mary Custis Lee, February 9, 1918, District of Columbia Archives.

19. Ibid.

20. Ibid.

21. "Col. R.E. Lee Weds," *Fairfax Herald*, July 4, 1919.

22. George Bolling Lee to Mary Tabb Lee, January 28, 1920, George Bolling Lee Papers, Virginia Historical Society.

23. Lindsey, Oliver, and Corrigan, *"The Lees of Ravensworth"* in *Essay Awards 1991*, 4; "Wants Lee Relics," *Fairfax Herald*, October 12, 1923.

24. Magnolia Cemetery, Charleston, South Carolina; "Mrs. Robert E. Lee 3D," *New York Times*, May 20, 1959; *South Carolina Historical and Genealogical Magazine*, Volume Number 3, July 1900, 257-258; Sandie Smithers Patton, *Flat Rock-Little Charleston of the Mountains* (Asheville, NC: Church Printing Co., n.d.), 57.

25. Magnolia Cemetery, Charleston, South Carolina; *South Carolina Historical and Genealogical Magazine*, Volume XXXIX, 1938, 32.

26. "Colonel Robert E. Lee Buried in Lexington Saturday," *Lexington Gazette*, September 19, 1922.

27. Ibid.

28. Lindsey, Oliver, and Corrigan, "The Lees of Ravensworth," *Essay Awards*, 4-5; "Mrs. Mary Tabb Lee Dead," *Fairfax Herald*, May 29, 1924.

29. Lindsey, Oliver, and Corrigan, "The Lees of Ravensworth," *Essay Awards*, 5; Will of Robert E. Lee [III], Appendix "C," Lee v. Lee,

Fairfax County Archives.

30. Will of Robert E. Lee [III], Appendix "C," Lee v. Lee, Fairfax County Archives.

31. Ibid.

32. Appraisal of Estate of Robert E. Lee III dated February 9, 1923, Appendix "C," Lee v. Lee, Fairfax County Archives.

33. Ibid. Daniel Parke was Martha Washington's grandfather. Serving under the Duke of Marlborough at the Battle of Blenheim (1705), Parke carried the victorious message to the Queen Anne Stuart of England (1665-1714). Parke later settled in Virginia.

34. Ibid.

35. "Wants Lee Relics," *Fairfax Herald*, October 12, 1923.

36. Ibid.

37. Appraisal of Estate of Robert E. Lee III, Appendix "C," Lee v. Lee, Fairfax County Archives.

38. *Fairfax Herald*, July 4, 1924.

39. Deposition of James M. Love, Lee v. Lee, File "C," Fairfax County Archives.

40. Ibid. The other two witnesses to the will were Captain Robert E. Lee III and Rooney's sister Mildred Lee.

41. "Mrs. Mary Tabb Lee Dead," *Fairfax Herald,* May 29, 1924; Cragg, *Memories of Ravensworth.*

42. "Lee Suit Angle," *Fairfax Herald*, May 5, 1925; Will of Mary Tabb Lee, February 3, 1923, District of Columbia Archives, Box 799, 326-327.

43. Will of Mary Tabb Lee, February 3, 1923, District of Columbia Archives.

44. "Mrs. Mary Tabb Lee Dead," *Fairfax Herald*, May 29, 1924; Lindsey, Oliver, and Corrigan, "The Lees of Ravensworth," *Essay Awards*, 6; "Lee Suit Angle," *Fairfax Herald*, May 5, 1925.

45. Appraisal, Lee v. Lee, #10, 484.

46. Ibid., 484-486.

47. Lindsey, Oliver, and Corrigan, "The Lees of Ravensworth," *Essay Awards*, 7-8.

48. "Lee Case," *Fairfax Herald*, June 19, 1925; Lindsey, Oliver, and Corrigan, "The Lees of Ravensworth," *Essay Awards*, 8.

49. "Lee Case Settled," *Fairfax Herald*, November 5, 1926; Lindsey, Oliver, and Corrigan, "The Lees of Ravensworth," *Essay Awards,* 8.

50. "Portrait Presentation," *Fairfax Herald*, May 13, 1927; "Portrait Unveiled," *Fairfax Herald*, May 27, 1927; Advertisement, *Fairfax Herald*, December 3, 1926.

51. "Tax Removed," *Fairfax Herald*, February 3, 1928.

52. "Antiques of Lee Family Recovered," *Alexandria Gazette*, February 12, 1929.

53. Ibid.; "Relic Recovered," *Fairfax Herald*, February 15, 1929.

54. "Six Will Face Jury in Theft of Lee Relics," *Alexandria Gazette*, February 25, 1929; 1910 Census, Charlottesville, T-624, Reel 268; 1920 Census, Alexandria, T625, Reel 297; Death Record of Russell L. Garland, Death Records, Alexandria, Virginia, Works Progress Administration, Statewide Public Records Project, Official Project 165-1-31-85; *Hill's 1938 Alexandria City Directory* (Richmond, VA: Hill Directory Co., Inc., Publishers, 1938), 283; *Boyd's Directory of the District of Columbia, 1928* (Washington, D.C.: R.L. Polk & Co., Publishers), 532.

55. *Alexandria Gazette*, February 25, 1929; Newman v Newman, Fairfax County Courthouse.

56. Will of Mary Custis Lee, District of Columbia Archives, February 9, 1918.

57. "Case of Persons Charged with Stealing Antiques from Ravensworth Now Underway," *Alexandria Gazette*, February 23, 1929; "Plead Guilty-Three Convicted in Ravensworth Robbing Get Suspended Sentences," *Fairfax Herald*, March 29, 1929.

58. "Case of Persons Charged with Stealing Antiques from Ravensworth Now Underway," *Alexandria Gazette*, February 23, 1929.

59. "Antiques of Lee Family Recovered," *Alexandria Gazette*, February 12, 1929.

60. Ibid.

61. "Court Disposes of Five Out of Six Cases Charged with Larceny of Lee Relics," *Alexandria Gazette*, March 30, 1929; "Plead Guilty," *Fairfax Herald*, March 29, 1929.

62. "Not Guilty Verdict in Case of Man Charged with Theft of Lee Relics," *Alexandria Gazette*, March 30, 1929; "Plead Guilty," *Fairfax Herald*, March 29, 1929; Ernest Dove Interview, May 30, 1999; Registers, Sharon Cemetery, Alexandria, Virginia.

63. "Loss of Washington Relics Brings $14,500 Insurance Suit," *Washington Evening Star*, July 7, 1932; Mary Tyre Phone Interview, December 23, 2001, Flat Rock, North Carolina.

64. "Chauffeur-Heir Seeks Job With 'Nice Family,' *Washington Post*, June 7, 1959.

65. "Count de Blackmere," *New York Times*, January 22, 1941; Mary Tyre Phone Interview, December 23, 2001, Flat Rock, North Carolina.

66. "Loss of Washington Relics Brings $14,500 Insurance Suit," *Washington Evening Star*, July 7, 1932.

67. Ibid.

68. Jean Eliot, "Mrs. Robert E. Lee Receives Guests in Gown of Romance," *Washington Evening Star*, June 6, 1935.

69. Ibid.

70. Ibid.

71. "Count De Blackmere," *New York Times*, January 22, 1941; Carolyn Hagner Shaw, pub., *The Social List of Washington and Social Precedence in Washington. 1948 Edition* (Washington, D.C.: Carolyn Hagner Shaw, 1948), 226; "Dr. George B. Lee, Gynecologist, 76," *New York Times*, July 14, 1948.

72. Kermit Edney, *Kermit Edney Remembers-Where Fitz Left Off* (Alexander, NC: Worldcomm, 1979), 90.

73. Records of Magnolia Cemetery, Magnolia Cemetery Trust, Charleston, South Carolina; Captain Robert C. Peniston to R.W. Harris, October 30, 1979, Lee Chapel Files, Washington and Lee University.

74. "Chauffeur-Heir Seeks Job With 'Nice Family,'" *Washington Post*, June 7, 1959; "Mrs. Robert E. Lee III, Widow of General's Kin," *Washington Post*, May 21, 1959.

75. "Mrs. Robert E. Lee III, Widow of General's Kin," *Washington Post*, May 21, 1959.

76. Last Will and Testament of Mary M. Lee, June 23, 1950, District of Columbia Archives; Last Will and Testament of Mary M. Lee., April 15, 1953, District of Columbia Archives; Last Will and Testament of Mary M. Lee., February 5, 1959, District of Columbia Archives.

77. Last Will and Testament of Mary M. Lee, April 15, 1953, District of Columbia Archives; Last Will and Testament of Mary M. Lee, February 5, 1959, District of Columbia Archives. Edney, *Kermit Edney Remembers*, 90; "Returned Heirlooms Highlight Tour," *Washington Star*, October 13, 1963.

78. "Retired Heirlooms Highlight Tour," *Washington Star*, October 13, 1963.

79. Edney, *Kermit Edney Remembers*, 91.

80. Notes of Edwin Hemphill, "Memorandum on the Status of the Lee Manuscripts in Rocky Mounts," August 19, 1936, in Society of the Lees of Virginia Papers, Box 264-M, Folder M-10, Alexandria Library Special Collections.

81. Notes of Hemphill, "Memorandum on the Status," August 19, 1936, Society of the Lees of Virginia Papers, Alexandria Library Special Collections; "John Penn Lee," in *History of Virginia, Volume VI-Virginia Biography* (Chicago, IL: The American Historical Society, 1924), 343.

82. Notes of Hemphill, "Memorandum on the Status," August 19, 1936, Society of the Lees of Virginia Papers, Alexandria Library Special Collections; C.G. Lee, Jr. to Mr. C. Carter Lee, February 26, 1933, Society of the Lees of Virginia Papers, Box 264M, Folder M-10, Alexandria Library Special Collections.

83. Lee, Jr. to C. Carter Lee, February 26, 1933, Society of the Lees of Virginia Papers, Alexandria Library Special Collections.

84. C. Carter Lee to Mrs. Charles D. Lanier, February 20, 1933, Society of the Lees of Virginia Papers, Box 264-M, M-10, Alexandria Library Special Collections.

85. C.G. Lee, Jr. to Miss Ethel Armes, February 27, 1933, Society of the Lees of Virginia Papers, Box 264-M, M-10, Alexandria Library Special Collections; C. Carter Lee to Cazenove G. Lee, February 28, 1933, Society of the Lees of Virginia Papers, Box 264-M, M-10, Alexandria Library Special Collections.

86. Mrs. Charles D. Lanier to Dr. Henry Lee, July 25, 1933, Society of the Lees of Virginia Papers, Box 264-M, M-10, Alexandria Library Special Collections; Mrs. Charles D. Lanier to Mr. Charles Carter Lee, July 24, 1933, Society of the Lees of Virginia Papers, Box 264-M, M-10, Alexandria Library Special Collections; "Memorandum on the Status," Society of the Lees of Virginia Papers, Alexandria Library Special Collections.

87. Cazenove G. Lee, Jr. to Dr. Burton Hendrick, January 17, 1935, Society of the Lees of Virginia Papers, Box 264-M, X-20, Alexandria Library Special Collections.

88. C.G. Lee, Jr. to Mrs. Charles D. Lanier, February 11, 1935, Society of the Lees of Virginia Papers, Box 264-M, X-20, Alexandria Library Special Collections; Cazenove G. Lee to Elise, February 11, 1935, Society of the Lees of Virginia, Box 264: X: 20, Alexandria Library Special Collections.

89. C.G. Lee to Mrs. Charles D. Lanier, February 11, 1935, Society of the Lees of Virginia Papers, Box 264-M, X-20, Alexandria Library Special Collections; C.G. Lee to Mrs. Emerson Root Newell, February 11, 1935, Society of the Lees of Virginia Papers, Box 264: X: 20, Alexandria Library Special Collections; C.G. Lee to Elise, February 11, 1935, Society of the Lees of Virginia Papers, Box 264: X: 20, Alexandria Library Special Collections.

90. Douglas Southall Freeman, *The Cornerstones of Stratford-Address at the Dedication of Stratford, October 12, 1935, by the Robert E. Lee Memorial Foundation* (Richmond, VA: 1935), 5; Description and Collection Summary, Charles Carter Lee Papers, Reel 11, Virginia State Archives; "Charles Carter Lee 1906-1958," in *Proceedings of the Sixty-Eighth Annual Meeting of the Virginia State Bar Association* (Richmond, VA: Virginia State Bar Association, 1959), 182.

91. Eleanor Lee Templeman, *Arlington Heritage-Vignettes of a Virginia County* (Privately Published, 1959), Introduction; Eleanor Templeman to John Melville Jennings, February 7, 1971, in Society of the Lees in Virginia Collection, Box 264: B: 1, Alexandria Library Special Collections.

92. "Line of Inheritance 6 Generations," Chart in Society of the Lees of Virginia Collections, Artifacts, Box 264: B: 1, Alexandria Library Special Collections.

93. Templeman to Jennings, February 7, 1971, in Society of the Lees of Virginia Collection, Alexandria Library Special Collections, Box 264: B: 1; Copy of Motion for Judgment, Templeman v Marie W. Weitzel and Torrey T. McKenny, Law and Equity Court of the City of Richmond, in Society of the Lees of Virginia Collection, Alexandria Library Special Collections, Box 264: B: 1.

94. Copy of Motion for Judgment, Templeman v Weitzel and McKenny, Law and Equity Court of the City of Richmond, in Society of the Lees of Virginia Collection, Alexandria Library Special Collections, Box 264: B: 1; Templeman to Jennings, February 7, 1971, in the Society of the Lees of Virginia Collection, Alexandria Library Special Collections, Box 264: B: 1; Eleanor Templeman to Mr. Anderson [written in pencil above type copy is "Richmond Atty.], September 10, 1952, in Society of the Lees of Virginia Collection, Alexandria Library Special Collections, Box 264: B: 1.

95. Templeman to Jennings, February 7, 1971, in Society of the Lees of Virginia Collection, Alexandria Library Special Collections; Templeman to Anderson, September 10, 1952, Society of the Lees of Virginia Special Collections, Alexandria Library Special Collections; "Line of Inheritance 6 Generations," in Society of the Lees of Virginia Collection, Alexandria Library Special Collections, Box 264: B: 1; "List of Articles Which Alice Reading Sold," in Society of the Lees of Virginia Collection, Alexandria Library Special Collections, Box 264: B: 1, Unstapled.

96. Templeman to Jennings, February 7, 1971, in Society of the Lees of Virginia Collection, Alexandria Library Special Collections.

97. Ibid.; Eleanor Templeman to Frances Shively, July 8, 1977, in Society of the Lees of Virginia Collection, Alexandria Library Special Collections, Box 264: B: 3.

98. Templeman to Shively, July 8, 1977, in Society of the Lees of Virginia Collection, Alexandria Library Special Collections.

Legacy III: Family and Military Reputation

1. Edmund Jennings Lee, M.D., edit., *Lee of Virginia 1642-1892 Biographical and Genealogical Sketches of The Descendants of Colonel Richard Lee with Brief Notices of the Related Families of Allerton, Armistead, Ashton, Aylett, Bedinger, Beverley, Bland, Bolling, Carroll, Carter, Chambers, Corbin, Custis, Digges, Fairfax, Fitzhugh, Gardner, Grymes, Hanson, Jenings, Jones, Ludwell, Marshall, Mason, Page, Randolph, Shepherd, Shippen, Tabb, Taylor, Turberville, Washington, and Others* (Baltimore, MD: Genealogical Publishing Co., Inc., 1974), 507; Bagby, M.D., "Recollections," 54; Wayland, *Robert E. Lee and His Family*, 56-57.

2. R.E. Lee [Jr.] to Whit, May 8, 1898, Lee Family Papers, Special Collections, Leyburn Library, Washington And Lee University.

3. Fitzhugh Lee, *General Lee* (New York, NY: D. Appleton and Company, 1894), Preface; "Fitz, Jr., Private Secretary Remembers Fitz, Sr., Consul-General," in Ardyce Kinsley, Comp., *The Fitzhugh Lee Sampler* (Lively, VA: Brandylane Publishers, 1992), 136.

4. "Col. Fitzhugh Lee Dies," *New York Times*, November 14, 1954.

5. Lee, *Lee of Virginia*, 404-405; Ibid., 472-475; "The Edmund Jennings Lee House (428 North Washington Street)," Society of the Lees of Virginia Papers, Leeland Collection, Box 264: Z: 26.

6. "Proceedings of the Virginia Historical Society in Annual Meeting Held February 25, 1915," in *Virginia Magazine of History and Biography*, Volume XXIII (New York, NY: Kraus Reprint Corporation, 1968), xliv-xlv; Joseph Davenport to Bar [tholomew] Dandridge, [1773 December], Lee Family Papers, Virginia Historical Society; Frederick S. Daniel, "A Visit to a Colonial Estate," *Harper's New Monthly*

Magazine, Volume LXXVI., December, 1887, 521; Lists, 1815-1818, Compiled by William Claiborne and Thomas E. Stuart of Negro slaves, stock, corn, and personal property on the estates of George Washington Parke Custis in New Kent and King William, Lee Family Papers, Virginia Historical Society.

7. "Proceedings of the Virginia Historical Society in Annual Meeting Held February 25, 1915," in *Virginia Magazine of History and Biography,* Volume XXIII (New York, NY: Kraus Reprint Corporation, 1968), xliv-xlv; Ibid., xlvii.

8. Lee, *Lee of Virginia,* 507; "Proceeding," *Virginia Magazine of History and Biography,* Volume XXIII, xlv.

9. "Proceedings," in *Virginia Historical Magazine,* xlvi; Bagby, M.D., *"Recollections,"* 54; Lee, *Lee of Virginia,* 507; G.W.C. Lee to Capt. R.E. Lee [Jr.], March 4, 1894, Lee Family Papers, Virginia Historical Society; "A Family Tree," in Coulling, *Lee Girls,* 201.

10. G.W.C. Lee to Capt. R.E. Lee, March 3, 1896, Lee Family Papers, Virginia Historical Society. Jones served in the Confederate Army and wrote *Personal Reminiscences, Anecdotes, and Letters of Robert E. Lee* in 1874. Doctor White's *Robert E. Lee* was published in 1897.

11. R.E. Lee [Jr.] to Mrs. Campbell, Nov 29, 1899, Lee Family Papers, Special Collections, Leyburn Library, Washington And Lee University.

12. Frank L. Farnell to R.E. Lee [Jr.], May 12, 1896, Lee Family Papers, Virginia Historical Society; Appendix with Chronology, in John W. Wayland, *Robert E. Lee & His Family,* 88; Robert E. Lee Jr. to Francis Bellamy Esq., October 8, 1896, Lee Family Papers, Virginia Historical Society.

13. Harper Brothers to Captain Robert E. Lee, October 20, 1899, Lee Family Papers, Virginia Historical Society; Walter H. Page to Captain R.E. Lee, January 22, 1900, Lee Family Papers, Virginia Historical Society; Henry Tyrrell to Captain Robert E. Lee, October 31, 1899, Lee Family Papers, Virginia Historical Society; Henry Tyrrell to Captain Robert E. Lee, January 30, 1900, Lee Family Papers, Virginia Historical Society.

14. Appendix, in Wayland, *Robert E. Lee and His Family*, 88; B.W. Green to Robert E. Lee [Jr], October 25, 1904, Lee Family Papers, Virginia Historical Society; W.J. DeRenne to Capt. Robert E. Lee, October 28, 1910, Lee Family Papers, Virginia Historical Society.

15. "Proceedings," in *Virginia Historical Magazine*, xlvii; G.W.C. Lee to Robert E. Lee, Jr., October 9, 1904, Lee Family Papers, Virginia Historical Society.

16. Bagby, "Recollections," 54-55.

17. Ibid.

18. R.E. Lee, Jr. to Belle Willard Roosevelt, January 16, 1914, Kermit Roosevelt Papers, Library of Congress.

19. R.E. Lee, Jr. to "Whittie," March 18, 1906, Lee Family Papers, Special Collections, Leyland Library, Washington and Lee University.

20. Ibid.; Bagby, "Recollections," 54-55; R.E. Lee, Jr. to "Whit," December 12, 1912, Lee Family Papers, Special Collections, Washington and Lee University.

21. Wayland, *Robert E. Lee And His Family*, 56-57; "A Family Tree," in Coulling, *Lee Girls*, 196; Program, *250th Anniversary of the founding of King William County Virginia*, April 1952, Circuit Court, King William County, 3; Ibid., 12.

22. Marietta Minnigerode Andrews, *Memoirs of a Poor Relation-Being the Story of a Post-War Southern Girl and her Battle With Destiny* (New York, NY: E.P. Dutton & Co., Inc., 1927), 26.

23. Published excerpt of account of Anna Maria Sarah Goldsborough Fitzhugh, "A Reluctant Scholar," in Kinsley, et al., *The Fitzhugh Lee Sampler*, 3-5.

24. Family Record in Bible, Marriage Records, Virginia Historical Society; Edith M. Sprouse, *Clermont: The Rest of the Story*, Typescript, Special Collections, Alexandria Public Library, 8; Anna Maria Goldsborough Fitzhugh, Bible Record, Virginia Historical Society;

Sprouse, *Clermont*, 11-12.

25. Ibid.; "Fitzhugh Lee," in Stewart Sifakis, *Who was Who in the Confederacy* (New York: Facts on File, 1988), 167; "Gen. Philip Sheridan, USA, Remembers the Shad Bake," in Kinsley, *Fitzhugh Lee Sampler*, 79-81.

26. Historical and Archaeological Committee Citizens to Serve Stafford, *Foundation Stones of Stafford County, Virginia Volume II* (Fredericksburg, VA: Fredericksburg Press, Inc., 1992), 86-88; Jerrilynn Eby, *They Called Stafford Home-The Development of Stafford County, Virginia from 1600 until 1865* (Bowie, MD: Heritage Books, Inc., 1997), 43-49.

27. Wesley E. Pippenger, *Alexandria, Virginia Life in 1850: The Diary of Ella Hooe Fowle (1832-1855)* (Arlington, VA: January 1999), vii-viii; "Brief History," 711 Prince Street, Sale Flyer, Special Collections, Alexandria Public Library; Fitzhugh Lee to Charlie, December 20, 1883, Special Collections, Leyburn Library, Washington & Lee University.

28. James L. Nichols, *Fitzhugh Lee: A biography* (Lynchburg, VA: H.E. Howard, Inc., ca. 1989), 116-117; Ibid., 119.

29. Robert Beverley Munford, Jr., *Richmond Homes and Memories* (Richmond, VA: Garrett and Massie Inc., 1936), 110-111.

30. Duplicate Copy of Stock Assignment, Pittsburgh and Virginia Railroad Company, November 23, 1889, Papers of Fitzhugh Lee, Collection 8494, Reel Two, University of Virginia Special Collections; Stock Certificate, South Boston Improvement Company, Papers of Fitzhugh Lee, Collection 8494, Reel Two, University of Virginia Special Collections; Nichols, *Fitzhugh Lee-A Biography*, 138-139; Lynda Mundy-Norris Miller, *Glasgow, Virginia: One-Hundred Years of Dreams* (Natural Bridge Station, VA: Rockbridge Publishing Company, 1992), 41-43; *Prospectus of the Rockbridge Company*, in Rockbridge Company Papers, Special Collections, Leyburn Library, Washington & Lee University; Subscription Certificate, Rockbridge Company, September 7, 1889, Papers of Fitzhugh Lee, Collection 8494, Reel Two, University of Virginia Special Collections; Robert C. Lee to Fitzhugh Lee, May 30, 1890, Papers of Fitzhugh Lee,

Collection 8494, Reel Two, University of Virginia Special Collections.

31. W.J. Madden to Fitzhugh Lee, February 27, 1892, Papers of Fitzhugh Lee, Collection 8494, Reel Two, University of Virginia Special Collections; Fitzhugh Lee to J. Preston Carson, March 22, 1892, Collection 8494, Reel Two, University of Virginia Special Collections, Reel Two, University of Virginia Special Collections.

32. Nichols, *Fitzhugh Lee-A Biography*, 138-139; Miller, *Glasgow, Virginia*, 41-43; "Sallie Sadler Cleveland's Diary," in Miller, *Glasgow, Virginia*, 153.

33. Appendix with Chronology, in Wayland, *Robert E. Lee & His Family*, 88.

34. G.W.C. Lee to Captain Robert E. Lee, Jr., March 3, 1896, Lee Family Papers, Virginia Historical Society.

35. Nichols, *Fitzhugh Lee-A Biography*, 144-145; "Gubernatorial Opponent John Wise Offers His Opinions on the Senate Defeat," in Kinsley, *Fitzhugh Lee Sampler*, 132-133; "Fitz, Jr., Private Secretary, Remembers Fitz, Sr., Consul-General," *Fitzhugh Lee Sampler*, 136.

36. Fitzhugh Lee to Joseph S. Miller, April 11, 1896, Fitzhugh Lee Letters, Personal Papers, Virginia State Archives.

37. President Grover Cleveland to Secretary Richard Olney, July 16, 1896, in Allan Nevins, ed., *Letters of Grover Cleveland 1850-1908* (New York, NY: DaCapo Press, 1970), 448. Lee's book was completed in 1899 with General Joseph Wheeler, and was entitled *Cuba's Struggle Against Spain with the Causes for American Intervention and a Full Account of the Spanish-American War, including Final Negotiations.*

38. Fitzhugh Lee to Jos. S. Miller, May 6, 1896, Fitzhugh Lee Letters, Personal Papers, Virginia State Archives.

39. Cleveland to Olney, July 16, 1896, in Nevins, ed., *Letters of Grover Cleveland*, 448.

40. Cleveland to Olney, February 16, 1898, in Nevins, ed., *Letters of Grover Cleveland*, 494-495; Lewis L. Gould, *The Spanish-American War and President McKinley* (Lawrence, KS: University Press of Kansas, 1982), 27-28.

41. Fitzhugh Lee to Mrs. Fitzhugh Lee, October 20, 1896, Papers of Fitzhugh Lee, Collection 8494, Reel Two, University of Virginia Special Collections.

42. Copy of Despatch to Secretary of State John Sherman, June 1, 1897, Papers of Fitzhugh Lee, Collection 8494, Reel Two, University of Virginia Special Collections; Copies of Telegrams to Assistant Secretary of State, February 4, 1897, February 18, 1897, February 19, 1897, Papers of Fitzhugh Lee, Collection 8494, Reel Two, University of Virginia Special Collections.

43. Nichols, *Fitzhugh Lee-A Biography*, 149; Ibid., 156-159.

44. Telegram forwarded to General Fitzhugh Lee, *Chicago Tribune* to P.R. Neel, March 21, 1898, Papers of Fitzhugh Lee, Collection 8494, Reel Two, University of Virginia Special Collections.

45. Robert L. Scribner, "Ex-Confederate in Blue," *Virginia Cavalcade*, V, No. 4, 18.

46. Adelbert M. Dewey, *The Life and Letters of Admiral Dewey From Montpelier to Manila-Containing Reproductions in Fac-simile of Hitherto Unpublished Letters of George Dewey during the Admiral's Naval Career and Extracts from his Log-Book* (New York: The Woolfall Company, 1898), 395; Ibid., 399.

47. Fitzhugh Lee (Jr.) to Dr. Douglas S. Freeman, November 24, 1931, Courtesy of Donna Lee Wilson, Alexandria, VA.

48. Scribner, "Ex-Confederate in Blue," *Virginia Cavalcade*, 19; Fitzhugh Lee to Eliot Danforth, April 14, 1898, Special Collections, Leyburn Library, Washington and Lee University.

49. Lee to Freeman, November 24, 1931, Courtesy of Donna Lee Wilson; Scribner, "Ex-Confederate in Blue," *Virginia Cavalcade*, Volume V,

Number 4, 19-20; Nichols, *General Fitzhugh Lee-A Biography*, 165; "Choctaw Returned to Col. Cameron," Clipping, from Papers of Fitzhugh Lee, Undated, Collection 8494, Reel Three, University of Virginia Special Collections; Scribner, "Ex-Confederate," 20.

50. The hat advertisement was located in Scribner, "Ex-Confederate," 21. The other items are from the author's collections.

51. "Mrs. Anna Maria Lee," Clipping, Undated, in the Papers of Fitzhugh Lee, Collection 8494, Reel Three, University of Virginia Special Collections; Typed letter copy of letter, Adjutant General H.C. Corbin to General Fitzhugh Lee, August 1, 1890, in the Papers of Fitzhugh Lee, Collection 8494, Reel Three, University of Virginia Special Collections; "Virginia Lee Remembers the Final Years," in Kinsley, *The Fitzhugh Lee Sampler*, 152-153; Nichols, *Fitzhugh Lee-A Biography*, 173; "Fitzhugh Lee: A Local Boy Who Made Good," *Fairfax Chronicles*, Volume IX, Number 4, 4.

52. "Mrs. Lee Has A Military Wedding," undated clipping, in Papers of Fitzhugh Lee, Collection 8494, Reel Three, University of Virginia Special Collections; "First Easter Wedding,"*Washington Post*, April 5, 1904, Clipping, in Papers of Fitzhugh Lee, Collection 8494, Reel Three, University of Virginia Special Collections.

53. "Virginia Lee Remembers the Final Years," in Kinsley, *The Fitzhugh Lee Sampler*, 153; Harry Warren Readnour, *General Fitzhugh Lee, 1835-1905: A Biographical Study* (Charlottesville, VA: 1971, from UMI, Ann Arbor, MI), 266-267.

54. Fitzhugh Lee to Unknown, July 27, 1904, Author's Collections.

55. President Theodore Roosevelt to General Fitzhugh Lee, December 1, 1904, Theodore Roosevelt Papers, Manuscript Division, Library of Congress, Reel 336.

56. Excerpt from Mrs. Ellen Barnard Lee to William A. Anderson, June 14, 1905, in William A. Anderson Papers, University of Virginia Special Collections.

57. Ibid.

58. Fitzhugh Lee to Mrs. Fitzhugh Lee, April 25, 1905, in Papers of Fitzhugh Lee, Collection 8494, Reel Three, University of Virginia Special Collections. This was noted as possibly "Fitzhugh Lee's last letter."; "Fitzhugh Lee's Last Address," ca. April 29, 1905, Clipping, in Papers of Fitzhugh Lee, Collection 8494, Reel Three, University of Virginia Special Collections. This clipping was undated and untitled, although it appears to be from a Boston newspaper. A subsequent search from April 29, the date Fitzhugh Lee's death appeared in the papers--to May 3, 1905 in four major Boston newspapers were negative.

59. "Virginia Lee Remembers the Final Years," in Kinsley, *The Fitzhugh Lee Sampler*, 153; Nichols, *Fitzhugh Lee-A Biography*, 175-177; "Death of General Fitzhugh Lee," *Fairfax Herald*, May 5, 1905; Readnour, *General Fitzhugh Lee*, 267.

60. Mrs. Ellen B. Lee to Board of the Jamestown Exposition Company, Typed Copy, Stamped March 1906, in William A. Anderson Papers, University of Virginia Special Collections.

61. Mrs. Ellen Barnard Lee to William A. Anderson, May 31, 1905, in Anderson Papers, University of Virginia Special Collections.

62. Ibid.

63. Works Progress Administration, *Alphabetical Index Birth Records, Alexandria, Virginia, Dates Included 1853-1911-Appendix Dates Prior to 1853, Official Project 165-1-31-85, W.P. 5822*; Lee, *Lee of Virginia 1642-1892*, 496; "Col. Fitzhugh Lee Dies," *New York Times*, November 14, 1954; "Young 'Fitz' Lee," *Fairfax Herald*, January 11, 1907.

64. "Young 'Fitz' Lee," *Fairfax Herald*, January 11, 1907.

65. Ibid.; Fitz Lee [Jr.] to Ellen Lee, February 15, 1901, Papers of Fitzhugh Lee, Collection 8494, Reel Three, University of Virginia Special Collections.

66. "Young 'Fitz' Lee," *Fairfax Herald*, January 11, 1907; "Col. Fitzhugh Lee Dies," *New York Times*, November 14, 1954; Donna Lee Wilson

to Author, E-Mail, May 3, 2000; Lee to Freeman, November 24, 1931, Courtesy Donna Lee Wilson; Theodore Roosevelt to Fitzhugh Lee, Jr., July 23, 1907, Theodore Roosevelt Papers, Reel 346, Manuscripts Division, Library of Congress; Fitzhugh Lee, Jr. to Kermit Roosevelt, Undated, Kermit Roosevelt Papers, Manuscripts Division, Library of Congress.

67. Peggy and Harold Samuels, *Teddy Roosevelt at San Juan: The Making of a President* (College Station, TX: Texas A&M University, 1997), 20; Theodore Roosevelt to General Fitzhugh Lee, February 2, 1905, Reel 337, Theodore Roosevelt Papers, Manuscript Division, Library of Congress; Carol Felsenthal, *Alice Roosevelt Longworth* (New York: G.P. Putnam's Sons, 1988), 14. Some political cartoons, at least three notable ones, appeared in 1904-05 era newspapers.

68. Theodore Roosevelt to Kermit Roosevelt, April 12, 1906, in Will Irwin, Ed., *Letters to Kermit from Theodore Roosevelt 1902-1908* (New York: Charles Scribner's Sons, 1946), 135-136.

69. Theodore Roosevelt to Kermit Roosevelt, November 3, 1907, in Irwin, Ed., *Letters to Kermit*, 220; Theodore Roosevelt to Kermit Roosevelt, December 8, 1907, in Irwin, Ed., *Letters to Kermit*, 226-227; Theodore Roosevelt to Kermit Roosevelt, January 15, 1908, in Irwin, Ed., *Letters to Kermit*, 227-228.

70. Theodore Roosevelt to Kermit Roosevelt, June 1, 1907. Reprinted by permission of the publisher from *The Letters of Theodore Roosevelt, Volume 5: The Big Stick, 1905-1907,* selected and edited by Elting E. Morrison (Cambridge, MA: Harvard University Press, Copyright @ 1952 by the President and Fellows of Harvard College, Copyright @ renewed 1980 by Elting E. Morrison, 675.

71. Fitzhugh Lee, Jr. to William A. Anderson, May 4, 1906, William A. Anderson Papers, University of Virginia Special Collections.

72. *IN THE MATTER OF THE INDEBTEDNESS OF THE JAMESTOWN EXPOSITION COMPANY TO GENERAL FITZHUGH LEE'S ESTATE,* Typed Copy, to C. Brooks Johnson, Esq., April 23, 1907, in William A. Anderson Papers, University of Virginia Special Collections; Fitzhugh Lee, Jr. to Anderson, May 22, 1906, in Anderson Papers, University of Virginia Special Collections;

Fitzhugh Lee, Jr. to Anderson, May 26, 1906, in Anderson Papers, University of Virginia Special Collections; Fitzhugh Lee, Jr. to Mr. Barton Myers, July 25, 1906, in Anderson Papers, University of Virginia Special Collections; Fitzhugh Lee, Jr. to Anderson, October 9, 1906, in Anderson Papers, University of Virginia Special Collections.

73. Fitzhugh Lee, Jr. to William A. Anderson, October 9, 1906, in Anderson Papers, University of Virginia Special Collections.

74. Fitzhugh Lee, Jr. to William A. Anderson, November 1907, in Anderson Papers, University of Virginia Special Collections; Anderson to Mrs. Ellen B. Lee, in Anderson Papers, University of Virginia Special Collections.

75. Col. Fitzhugh Lee to Dr. Douglas S. Freeman, November 24, 1931; *Fairfax Herald*, July 26, 1907.

76. Fitzhugh Lee to Theodore Roosevelt, November 15, 1908, Theodore Roosevelt Papers, Reel 86, Manuscript Division, Library of Congress.

77. Ibid.

78. Ibid.

79. Ibid.

80. Ellen B. Lee to William A. Anderson, December 21, 1910, in Anderson Papers, University of Virginia Special Collections; Anderson to Judge T.S. Garnett, February 22, 1911, in Anderson Papers, University of Virginia Special Collections; Ellen B. Lee to Anderson, April 17, 1911, University of Virginia Special Collections; Ellen B. Lee to Anderson, May 1, 1911, University of Virginia Special Collections; Theodore Garnett to Anderson, May 21, 1911, University of Virginia Special Collections; Anderson to Mrs. Lee, Care of Fitzhugh Lee, Jr., March 20, 1913, University of Virginia Special Collections; Clipping and Bill of Ames, Brownley & Hornthal, March 1, 1913, in Anderson Papers, University of Virginia Special Collections.

81. Theodore Roosevelt to Captain Fitzhugh Lee, March 13, 1915, Theodore Roosevelt Papers, Reel 385, Manuscripts Division, Library of Congress; Theodore Roosevelt to Captain Fitzhugh Lee, June 22, 1915, Theodore Roosevelt Papers, Reel 385, Manuscripts Division, Library of Congress; Fitzhugh Lee to Theodore Roosevelt, August 24, 1915, Theodore Roosevelt Papers, Reel 201, Manuscripts Division, Library of Congress; Theodore Roosevelt to Newton Diehl Baker, May 8, 1917, in Morison, ed., *Letters of Theodore Roosevelt*, 1187; Theodore Roosevelt to Charles Joseph Bonaparte, May 25, 1917, in *The Letters of Theodore Roosevelt*, 1194-1195.

82. Herbert Malloy Mason, Jr., *The Great Pursuit* (New York: Random House, 1970), Appendix C, 246; Ibid., 97-99; Fitzhugh Lee to Theodore Roosevelt, August 24, 1915, Theodore Roosevelt Papers, Reel 201, Manuscripts Division, Library of Congress; Fitz Lee to Theodore Roosevelt, May 18, 1917, Reel 233, Manuscripts Division, Library of Congress.

83. Lee to Roosevelt, May 18, 1917, Reel 233, Manuscripts Division, Library of Congress.

84. Theodore Roosevelt to Fitzhugh Lee, Jr., November 27, 1908, Theodore Roosevelt Papers, Manuscripts Division, Library of Congress.

85. Theodore Roosevelt to Fitzhugh Lee, Jr., July 23, 1907, Theodore Roosevelt Papers, Reel 346, Manuscripts Division, Library of Congress.

86. Fitzhugh Lee, Jr. to Kermit Roosevelt, Undated [ca 1907], Kermit Roosevelt Papers, Manuscripts Division, Library of Congress.

87. Col. Fitzhugh Lee, Jr. to Kermit Roosevelt, January 6, 1932, Kermit Roosevelt Papers, Manuscripts Division, Library of Congress.

88. *Fairfax Herald*, July 26, 1907; "Col. Fitzhugh Lee Dies," *New York Times*, November 14, 1954; Fitzhugh Lee, Jr. to Kermit Roosevelt, Undated, Kermit Roosevelt Papers, Manuscripts Division, Library of Congress; Fitzhugh Lee, Jr. to Kermit Roosevelt, Undated [ca. November 1927], Kermit Roosevelt Papers, Manuscripts Division,

Library of Congress; Kermit Roosevelt to Fitzhugh Lee, Jr., December 15, 1935, Kermit Roosevelt Papers, Manuscripts Division, Library of Congress.

89. Col. Fitzhugh Lee, Jr. to Kermit Roosevelt, January 6, 1932, Kermit Roosevelt Papers, Manuscripts Division, Library of Congress; Fitzhugh Lee, Jr. to Kermit Roosevelt, Undated [ca. Jan 7, 1933], Kermit Roosevelt Papers, Manuscripts Division, Library of Congress; "Lee's Widow Dies at her Home Here," *Alexandria Gazette*, June 19, 1933; "Col. Fitzhugh Lee Dies," *New York Times*, November 14, 1954.

90. "The Edmund Jennings Lee House (428 North Washington Street)," Leeland Collection, in the Society of the Lees of Virginia Collection, Special Collections, Alexandria Library, Box 264, File 26; "Henry Lee of Leesylvania," Society of the Lees of Virginia Collection, Special Collections, Alexandria Library, Box 264, File 38.

91. Published Obituary, "Mrs. Sally Lee," in Leeland Collection, Society of the Lees of Virginia Collection, Box 264, Z: 26, Special Collections, Alexandria Library.

92. "Edmund Jennings Lee House," Leeland Collection, Society of the Lees of Virginia Collection, Special Collections, Alexandria Library, Box 264, File 26; Lee, *Lee of Virginia*, 475.

93. Lee, *Lee of Virginia*, 472-473.

94. Ibid., 473.

95. Lee, *Lee of Virginia*, 473; Rebecca Burwell Lee, comp., *Lights and Shadows-Sketches of HARRY BEDINGER LEE-Confederate lad, schoolteacher, lawyer, minister of the Gospel; his wife LUCY MARSHALL and their CHILDREN* (n.p., 1952), 4; T. Michael Miller, "1837-Year of Death for the Lee Family," typescript copy in Society of the Lees of Virginia Collection, Special Collections, Alexandria Library, Box 264, M-37. T. Michael Miller is the author of many excellent sources on Alexandria and its families.

96. "Edmund Jennings Lee House," Leeland Collection, Society of the Lees of Virginia Collection, Special Collections, Alexandria Library; Will of Edmund J. Lee, Alexandria Wills, Book 4, Page 320, as copied by C.G. Lee, Jr., in Leeland Collection, Society of the Lees of Virginia Collection, Special Collections, Alexandria Library, Box 264, Z: 26.

97. Lee, *Light and Shadows*, 5; Helen Lee Goldsborough, "Leeland," *Magazine of the Jefferson County Historical Society*, December 1949, Volume 15, 11.

98. Goldsborough, "Leeland," *Magazine of the Jefferson County Historical Society*, December 1949, Volume 15, 11-13.

99. Goldsborough, "Leeland," *Magazine of the Jefferson County Historical Society*, December 1949, 12-13; Lee, *Lights and Shadows*, 5; Ibid., 12.

100. Netta Lee to Netta Goldsborough, March 4, 1887, in Leeland Collection, Society of the Lees of Virginia Collection, Special Collections, Alexandria Library.

101. Lee, *Lights and Shadows*, 7.

102. C.F. Lee to Edmund J. Lee Esq., May 1, 1850, Typed Copy in Society of the Lees of Virginia Collection, Leeland Collection, Special Collections, Alexandria Library, Box 264 Z: 24.

103. *Shepherdstown Register*, April 19, 1856, as noted in Goldsborough, "Leeland," *Magazine of the Jefferson County Historical Society*, December 1949, 14.

104. Goldsborough, "Leeland," *Magazine of the Jefferson County Historical Society*, December 1949, 14-15.

105. Lee, *Lee of Virginia*, 480-481; Lee, *Lights and Shadows*, 3.

106. Lee, *Lights and Shadows*, 16.

107. Alexandria Lee Levin to Ludwell [Lee?], May 17, 1964, Edwin Gray Lee Correspondence, Society of the Lees of Virginia Collection, Special Collections, Alexandria Library, Box 264: M: 40; Typed

page attached to letter, "Foreward for The Bell of Bedford." This appeared to be a working title.

108. Alexandra Lee Levin, "Who hid John H. Surratt, the Lincoln Conspiracy Case Figure?," *Maryland Historical Magazine*, Vol. 60, No. 2, June 1965, 175-177.

109. Levin to Ludwell [Lee?], May 17, 1964, Edwin Gray Lee Correspondence, Society of the Lees of Virginia Collection, Special Collections, Alexandria Library.

110. Lee, *Lee of Virginia*, 480-481; Lee, *Lights and Shadows*, 6; Ibid., 12-13.

111. Entry of Monday, July 15, Edwin Gray Lee Diary 1867-68 Transcription, Leeland Collection, Society of the Lees of Virginia, Special Collections, Alexandria Library, Box 264: Z: 30.

112. Ibid.

113. Entries of Friday, November 21, 1867 and Monday, November 11, 1867, in Lee Diary, Leeland Collection; E.G. Lee to E.J. Lee, Esq., November 24, 1869, Edwin Gray Lee Letters 1866-70, Society of the Lees in Virginia Collection, Special Collections, Alexandria Library, Box 264: Z: 32; E.G. Lee to Mother, July 16, 1870, Edwin Gray Lee Letters, Society of the Lees in Virginia Collection, Special Collection, Alexandria Library.

114. Lee, *Lights and Shadows*, 5; Ibid., 16; Goldsborough, "Leeland," *Magazine of the Jefferson County Historical Society*, December 1949, 15-16; Lee, *Lee of Virginia*, 511; Goldsborough, "Leeland," 16; Lucy Chaplin Lee, *An American Sojourn in China: Family Memories* (Annandale, VA: n.p., 1968), 5.

115. Lee, *An American Sojourn in China*, 5.

116. Lee, *An American Sojourn in China*, 31-33; Armistead Mason Lee, "Some Reminiscences of My Father, Edmund J. Lee, D.D., 1877-1962," 1, Typed Manuscript, 1981, in Society of the Lees of Virginia Collection, Leeland Collection, Special Collections, Alexandria

Library, Box 264, M-37.

117. Lee, *An American Sojourn in China*, 34; Armistead Lee, "Some Reminiscences," 2; Lee, *An American Sojourn in China*, 52; Ibid., 54.

118. Armistead Lee, "Some Reminiscences," 1-2.

119. Lee, *Lee of Virginia*, 404-405; Paul C. Nagel, *The Lees of Virginia* (New York: Oxford University Press, 1990), 198-199.

120. "Memoirs," in Charles Carter Lee Papers, Reel 11, Library of Virginia; Chas. Carter Lee to Edward Everett, September 4, 1856, in Charles Carter Lee Papers, Library of Virginia.

121. Charles C. Lee, *Virginia Georgics* (Richmond, VA: J. Woodhouse and Company, 1858), Title Page; Ethel Armes, *Stratford Hall: The Great House of the Lees* (Richmond, VA: Garrett & Massie, Inc., 1936), 496.

122. Portion of Charles Carter Lee, *Virginia Georgics*, 42 in Armes, *Stratford Hall*, 496. Note Two explains "the American Ulysses" is Light Horse Harry Lee.

123. H. Chamberlayne jr. to Charles Carter Lee, June 27, 1865, Charles Carter Lee Papers, Reel 11, Library of Virginia.

124. Charles Carter Lee to "Cousin," August 28, 1869, Charles Carter Lee, Reel 11, Library of Virginia; Lee, *Lee of Virginia*, 404.

125. Ibid., 404-405; Ibid., 488-489. A more detail perspective on the relationships to the Penn and Taylor families is detailed in a copy of a letter (in the hand of Lucy Penn Lee) of Cousin John Taylor to Miss Julia Taylor in Society of the Lees of Virginia Collection, Box 264: N: 13, Special Collections, Alexandria Library.

126. G.T. Lee to Cazenove Lee, July 1, 1929, Society of the Lees of Virginia Collection, Box 264: N: 19, Special Collections, Alexandria Library.

127. G.W.C. Lee to G.T. Lee, May 17, 1888, Society of the Lees of Virginia Collection, Box 264: N: 14, Special Collections, Alexandria Library.

128. "George Taylor Lee," 1933 clipping from unnamed paper, in Society of the Lees Collection, Box 264: N: 19, Special Collections, Alexandria Library.

129. G.T. Lee to Cazenove Lee, July 1, 1929, Society of the Lees of Virginia Collection, Box 264: N: 19, Special Collections, Alexandria Library.

130. G.T. Lee to Cazenove Lee, August 26, 1929, Society of the Lees of Virginia Collection, Box 264: N: 19, Special Collections, Alexandria Library.

131. Ibid.

132. Ibid.

133. Ibid.

134. George Taylor Lee to Capt. Henry Wise, May 12, 1909, Society of the Lees of Virginia Collection, Box 264, N: 19, Special Collections, Alexandria Library. The reference to the "house" was the Bushong House near the Valley Road. Lee refers to a fellow cadet.

135. Ibid.

136. Ibid.

137. G.T. Lee to Cazenove Lee, August 26, 1929, Society of the Lees of Virginia Collection, Box 264: N: 19, Special Collections, Alexandria Library; Author's Preface in George Taylor Lee, *The Puritan Maid* (New York: Broadway Publishing Company, c. 1904), vi-viii.

138. Lee, *Lee of Virginia*, 488-489; G.T. Lee to J.P. Lee, December 4, 1888, Reel 2, Charles Carter Lee Papers, Virginia State Library.

139. Lee, *Lee of Virginia*, 489; Lee to Wise, May 12, 1909, Society of the Lees Collection, Special Collections, Alexandria Library.

140. George Taylor Lee, *America's Vision-A Message to all Freemen of Every Name and Clime* (Fine Creek Mills, VA: 1918); George Taylor Lee, "Reminiscences of General Robert E. Lee, 1865-68," in *The South Atlantic Quarterly*, Volume XXVI, No. 3, July 1927, Duke University Press, 236-237.

141. George Taylor Lee, "Reminiscences of General Robert E. Lee, 1865-68," in *South Atlantic Quarterly*, Volume XXVI, No. 3, July 1927, Duke University Press, 237-239.

142. Ibid., 240-241.

143. Ibid., 251.

144. Ibid., 250.

145. Cazenove Lee to George Taylor Lee, June 7, 1929, in Society of the Lees of Virginia Collection, Box 264: N: 19, Special Collections, Alexandria Library.

146. George Taylor Lee to Cazenove Lee, February 27, 1930, in Society of the Lees of Virginia Collection, Box 264: N: 19, Special Collections, Alexandria Library; George Taylor Lee to Cazenove Lee, July 1, 1929, in Society of the Lees Collection, Box 264: N: 19, Special Collections, Alexandria Library.

147. Obituary, Unknown Newspaper, in Society of the Lees Collection, Box 264: N: 19, Special Collections, Alexandria Library "Dorothy Vandegrift Lee, Longtime D.C. Civic Leader," *[Washington] Evening Star and Daily News*, November 17, 1972.

148. Lee, *Lee of Virginia*, 405; Ibid., 489.

149. Alexander, *Stratford Hall and the Lees*, 195; Lee, *Lee of Virginia*, 405.

150. W.C. Lee to George Taylor Lee, November 18, 1880, in Society of the Lees of Virginia Collection, Box 264: N: 14, Special Collections, Alexandria Library; W.C. Lee to George Taylor Lee, Handwritten Copy, November 28, 1880, in Society of the Lees of Virginia, Box

264: N: 14, Special Collections, Alexandria Library.

151. C.R. Lee to George Taylor Lee, February 29, 1884, in Society of the Lees of Virginia, Box 264: N: 15, Special Collections, Alexandria Library. Explanatory Notes by "T.I.P." in C.R. Lee to George Taylor Lee, February 29, 1884.

152. C.R. Lee to George Taylor Lee, February 29, 1884, in Society of the Lees of Virginia Collection, Box 264: N: 15, Special Collections, Alexandria Library.

153. Ibid.

154. Ibid.

155. "John Penn Lee," in *History of Virginia*, 393; Will of Mary Custis Lee, February 9, 1918, District of Columbia Archives.

156. Lucy Penn Lee to George Taylor Lee, June 17, 1884, in Society of the Lees of Virginia Collection, Box 264: N: 15, Special Collections, Alexandria Library.

157. Lucy Penn Lee to Ella Lee, June 12, 1888, in Society of the Lees of Virginia Collection, Box 264: N: 16, Special Collections, Alexandria Library.

158. R.E. Lee, Jr. to George Taylor Lee, May 21, 1888, in Society of the Lees of Virginia Collection, Box 264: N: 16, Special Collections, Alexandria Library.

159. G.W.C. Lee to George T. Lee, Esq., 17 May 1888, in Society of the Lees of Virginia Collection, Box 264: N: 14, Special Collections, Alexandria Library.

160. "John Penn Lee," in *History of Virginia*, 393-394.

161. John Penn Lee to Ella Lee, December 30, 1888, in Society of the Lees of Virginia Collection, Box 264: N: 16, Special Collections, Alexandria Library.

162. "John Penn Lee," in *History of Virginia*, 394. Isabella Lee died in October 1927. The two young children who died in infancy were Lewis W. (1901) and Nancy S. (1904-05). Chiswell died in June 1945. Information from Franklin County Historical Society, *Cemetery Records of Franklin County, Virginia* (Baltimore, MD: Gateway Press, 1986), 186; Ibid., 199.

Legacy IV: Transition

1. Omer Hirst Interview, June 15, 1999.

2. "Perkins Herd Leads.," *Fairfax Herald*, November 7, 1930; Lee Hubbard Telephone Interview, May 18, 1999.

3. Cragg, *Memories of Ravensworth*.

4. "November Report," *Fairfax Herald*, December 4, 1931; Mayo Stuntz Phone Interview, October 10, 1999.

5. Elsie Sisson Interview, February 2, 2000; Cragg, *Memories of Ravensworth*.

6. Cragg, *Memories of Ravensworth*.

7. Ibid.

8. Cam Sheads Interview, Box 3-03A, Fairfax County Public Library.

9. "Bold Bootleggers," *Fairfax Herald*, January 27, 1922.

10. "Wilson M. Farr," in William T. Muse, ed., *Proceedings of the Sixty-Ninth Annual Meeting of the Virginia State Bar Association-Held at the Greenbrier White Sulphur Springs West Virginia August 6, 7, 8, 1959* (Richmond, VA: Keel-Williams Corporation, Printers, 1959), 99; "Captured Still," *Fairfax Herald*, April 16, 1926; "Election Day--Last Minute Work Now Being Done By Candidates,"*Fairfax Herald*, July 29, 1927; "Captured Whiskey Car," *Fairfax Herald*, November 25, 1927; "V. Williams of Fairfax Dies at 75," *Northern Virginia Sun*, November 16, 1968; "Wilson M. Farr," in Muse, ed., *Proceedings*, 99.

11. Cragg, *Memories of Ravensworth*.

12. "Dr. George B. Lee, Gynecologist, 75," *New York Times*, July 14, 1948.

13. Copy of letter, Dr. George B. Lee to Hazel Davis, April 23, 1932, in John W. Wayland, *Historic Homes of Northern Virginia* (Staunton, VA: McClure Co., Inc., 1937), 559.

14. *Fairfax Herald*, October 23, 1936.

15. Appendix With Chronology, in Wayland, *Robert E. Lee & His Family*, 90-91; Greenlee D. Letcher to Mr. Carter Lee, March 19, 1940, G.W.C. Lee Papers, Leyburn Library, Special Collections, Washington and Lee University.

16. L.M. Harris to Greenlee D. Letcher, April 14, 1940, G.W.C. Lee Papers, Leyburn Library, Special Collections, Washington and Lee University.

17. *New York Times*, July 14, 1948; Listing of Presidents of Society in *The Historical Society of Fairfax County, Virginia, Inc., Volume 13, 1973-1975*. Robert E. Lee IV served as President of the Historical Society of Fairfax County, Virginia, Inc. from June 1972 to June 1974.

18. "Nephew of R.E. Lee Dies Suddenly in Macon." *Macon Telegraph*, June 13, 1901; "Major John Mason Lee, C.S.A. 1839-1924," *Magazine of the Society of the Lees of Virginia*, Volume 11, Number 1, April 1924, 35; "Daniel Murray Lee," in *Confederate Veteran*, Volume 25, Number 1, 84; *Alexandria Gazette*, June 14, 1967; Marguerite Moncure Lamond, "Clement Conger Receives Historical Document," *Alexandrian Magazine*, January 1978. Note: The daughter of James and Ellen Rhea married Admiral John N. Opie. Their children were: John N., Fitzhugh Lee, Elizabeth, Margaret, and Barbara. Information from *Alexandria Gazette* obituary, "Mrs. Ellen Lee Rhea Dies in California," October 16, 1959.

19. Lee, *Lee of Virginia*, 517; "Noted Rector Slain by Shot From Dark," *New York Times*, February 7, 1938.

20. "Noted Rector Slain by Shot From Dark," *New York Times*, February 7, 1938.

21. "Noted Rector Slain by Shot From Dark," *New York Times*, February 7, 1938; "4 Held In Murder of Georgia Rector," *New York Times*, October 28, 1938.

22. "Noted Rector Slain by Shot from Dark," *New York Times*, February 7, 1938.

23. Ibid.; "4 Held In Murder of Georgia Rector," *New York Times*, October 28, 1938; "Convicted In Lee Murder," *New York Times*, January 23, 1939.

24. "Mayoralty Race Assured As Opie, Allen Announce Independent Candidacies," *Alexandria Gazette*, April 14, 1967; "Candidates At Rally Reaffirm Opposition To Open Housing," *Alexandria Gazette*, May 31, 1967; "Rivals Contest Sharply; Trade Charges, Jibes," *Alexandria Gazette,* June 2, 1967; "Final Primary Speeches Readied By Candidates Running For City Office," *Alexandria Gazette*, June 5, 1967; "Mayor-Elect Beatley Committed to Role of Team Chief; Stresses Land Use, Transit," *Alexandria Gazette*, June 14, 1967.

25. C.F. Lee Jr. to Mrs. Flora Johnson, September 16, 1871, in Society of the Lees of Virginia Collection, Grace Moulder Collection, Box 264: CCC, Folder 26, Special Collections, Alexandria Library; Lee, *Lee of Virginia*, 515.

26. Lee, *Lee of Virginia*, 515-516; Membership List 1921-82, Society of the Lees of Virginia Collection, Box 264: BBB: 7, Special Collections, Alexandria Library; Plaque in Elizabeth Barrett Branch, Alexandria Library. Cazenove further donated much to the study of Alexandria history.

27. "Story of the Establishment of the Robert E. Lee Memorial Foundation," Given by Mrs. Frank H. Griffin Before the Society of the Lees of Virginia at Stratford, Virginia May 4, 1963.

28. "Story of the Establishment," Given by Griffin; Freeman, *The Cornerstones of Stratford*, 3; Ibid, 5.

29. Introduction in Ethel Armes, *Stratford Hall: The Great House of the Lees* (Richmond, VA: Garrett & Massie, Inc., 1936); "Story of the Establishment," Given by Griffin.

30. Calvin Bragg Valentine to Eleanor Lee Templeman, June 21, 1963, Society of the Lees of Virginia Collection, Box 264: SS: 5, Special Collections, Alexandria Library.

31. Eleanor Lee Templeman to Mrs. Frank H. Griffin, typed copy, July 24, 1963, Society of the Lees of Virginia Collection, Box 264: SS: 5, Special Collections, Alexandria Library.

32. "Ravensworth," Commonwealth of Virginia, County of Fairfax, Historic Landmarks Survey #119, Date of Record 2/24/1972, Fairfax County Division of Planning.

33. "Fitzhugh Family Cemetery," *Cemeteries of Fairfax County, Virginia*, Cemetery FX143, Fairfax County Virginia Libraries.

34. "Historic Ravensworth Farm On Braddock Road Is Sold For Housing Development," *Alexandria Journal,* April 9, 1959. The information on using old brick from the Ravensworth estate was from Dan Cragg, who owns one of these homes in North Springfield.

35. "Mall site was part of historic 'Ravensworth,' *[Springfield] Independent*, February 28, 1973.

36. Ellen Anderson, "Ossian Hall: Decaying Relic of Pre Revolutionary Virginia," *Northern Virginia Sun*, July 15, 1957.

37. Joseph Q. Bristow to Mrs. E.L. Templeman, May 20, 1957, Society of the Lees of Virginia Collection Property Records, Ossian Hall, 264: PP: 12, Special Collections, Alexandria Library.

38. Joseph Q. Bristow to Mrs. E.L. Templeman, August 18, 1957, Society of the Lees of Virginia Collection Property Records, Ossian Hall, 264: PP: 12, Special Collections, Alexandria Library.

39. Virginia Fleming Dickens to Mrs. Eleanor Lee Templeman, December 12, 1957, in Society of the Lees of Virginia Collection Property Records, Ossian Hall, 264: PP: 12, Special Collections, Alexandria Library.

40. Agnes Miller to Mrs. R.M. Templeman, ca March 25, 1959, in Society of the Lees of Virginia Collection Property Records, Ossian Hall, 264: PP: 12, Special Collections, Alexandria Library; Muriel Guinn, "Development to Replace Historic Manor in Fairfax," *Washington Post*, September 1, 1959. Other historic properties connected with the Lees formerly available for tours have passed into private hands for lack of funding. The Robert E. Lee Boyhood Home in Alexandria is an example of this. Others, such as the Leesylvania House Site in Neabsco, Virginia, has mixed use as a park and marina.

41. Steve Parker,"His Faith In Lee Spurred Movement," *Alexandria Gazette*, May 5, 1975; "Annie Lee's Unlikely Homecoming: Lee's 'Little Raspberry' Fuels a War Between Two States," *Colonnade-The Alumni Magazine of Washington and Lee*, Vol. 69, Number 3, Fall 1994.

42. "Ravensworth Historical Marker Dedication Ceremony," Saturday, September 11, 1993 11:00 AM. Brochure.

Bibliography
Primary Sources-Interviews & E-Mail

Dove, Douglas, in Dan Cragg, comp. *Memories of Ravensworth-An Interview with Mr. Douglas Dove*, Fairfax County Public Library, September 1993.
Dove, Ernest. Telephone Interview, May 30, 1999.
Hirst, Omer L. Telephone Interview, June 15, 1999.
Hubbard, Lee. Telephone Interview, May 18, 1999.
Lee, IV, Robert E. Telephone Interview, June 8, 1999.
Moore, Virginia. Telephone Interview, May 12, 2000.
Oliver, Carolyn. Telephone Interviews, August 25, 1999 and August 29, 1999.
Sheads, Cam. Fairfax County Public Library, Interviewed by Roseann Birkenstock.
Sheads, Bill. Interview, Fairfax Station, Virginia, September 22, 1999.
Sisson, Elsie. Phone Interview, February 2, 2000.
Stephens, John. Phone Inteview, September 9, 1999.
Stuntz, Mayo. Phone Interview. October 1999.
Tyre, Mary. Telephone Interview, December 23, 2001.
Wilson, Donna Lee. E-Mail, May 3, 2000.
Wood, Hugh & Ethel. Interview, Waynesboro, Virginia, August 22, 1999.

Primary Sources-Manuscripts, Court Records and Directories

Alexandria, Virginia. *Hill's Alexandria Directory*, 1938.
Anderson, William A. Papers. University of Virginia Special Collections.
Berkeley County WV Register of Deaths. Berkeley County Courthouse.
Bristow, Joseph L. Papers. Kansas State Historical Society.
Case Files for Congressional Cases. Ann M. Fitzhugh's Exr. vs. U.S. Record Group 123. National Archives and Records Administration.
Dickins, Francis Asbury. Papers. Southern History Collections, University of North Carolina.
District of Columbia. *Boyd's Directory of the District of Columbia 1928*. R.L. Polk & Co.
Fairfax County Court Case, George B. v. Mary M. Lee. File C. Fairfax County Archives.

Fairfax County Court Case, Newman v. Newman. Fairfax County Archives.
Fairfax County Court Case CFF #6L. Fairfax County Archives.
Fairfax County Court Case CFF #48E. Fairfax County Archives.
Fairfax County Criminal Court Docket Book. Fairfax County Archives.
Fairfax County Death Registers. 1881, 1895, 1897. Fairfax County Archives.
Fairfax County Deed Book 958. Fairfax County Archives.
Fairfax County Division of Planning. "Ravensworth." Historic Landmarks Survey #119. Fairfax County Library.
Fairfax County General Register, 1902-03. Fairfax County Archives.
Fairfax County Indenture Liber I-6. Fairfax County Archives.
Fairfax County Indenture Liber W-4. Fairfax County Archives.
Fairfax County Minute Book 1807-08. Fairfax County Archives.
Fairfax County Minute Book 13. Fairfax County Archives.
Fairfax County Slave Schedules 1860. Fairfax County Archives.
Fairfax County Will Book 138. Fairfax County Archives.
Fitzhugh, Anna Maria. Bible Record. Virginia Historical Society.
Fitzhugh, Henry Accounts Book. Virginia Historical Society.
Fitzhugh, William H. Personal Papers. Alexandria Library Special Collections.
Fitzhugh, William H. to Mary Lee Custis, July 29, 1813. Letter. Virginia Historical Society.
Lee, Charles Carter. Collection. Library of Virginia.
Lee Family Papers. Virginia Historical Society.
Lee Family Papers. Special Collections, Leyburn Library. Washington & Lee University.
Lee, Fitzhugh. Papers. University of Virginia Special Collections.
Lee, Fitzhugh. Personal Papers. Virginia State Archives.
Lee, Fitzhugh to Unknown, July 27, 1904. Author's Collections.
Lee, Fitzhugh, Jr. to Dr. Douglas S. Freeman, November 24, 1931. Courtesy Donna Lee Wilson.
Lee, George Bolling. Papers. Virginia Historical Society.
Lee, G.W.C. Papers. Special Collections, Leyburn Library. Washington and Lee University.
Lee, Mary C. to Mary Macon, June 1870. Letter. Library of Virginia Archives.

Lee, Mary Custis. Will. District of Columbia Archives.
Lee, Mary M. Wills. District of Columbia Archives.
Lee, Mary Tabb. Will. District of Columbia Archives.
Lee, R.E. Papers. Duke University.
Magnolia Cemetery, Charleston, SC. Records of Magnolia Cemetery Trust.
Peniston, Captain Robert C. to R.W. Harris, October 30, 1979. Letter. Lee Chapel Files, Washington and Lee University.
Rockbridge Company. Papers. Special Collections, Leyburn Library, Washington and Lee University.
Roosevelt, Kermit. Papers. Manuscript Division, Library of Congress.
Roosevelt, Theodore. Papers. Manuscript Division, Library of Congress.
Sale of 711 Prince Street, Alexandria, Virginia. Flyer. Special Collections, Alexandria Public Library.
Sharon Cemetery, Alexandria, Virginia. Registers.
Society of the Lees in Virginia. Collections. Alexandria Library Special Collections.
Southern Claims Commission. Case File 14896. Records Group 233. National Archives and Records Administration.
U.S., 1920 Census. Alexandria, Virginia. National Archives and Records Administration.
U.S., 1910 Census. Charlottesville, Virginia. National Archives and Records Administration.
U.S., 1900 Census. Fairfax County. National Archives and Records Administration.
U.S., 1910 Census. Fairfax County. National Archives and Records Administration.
U.S. Court of Claims. Depositions of Anna Maria Fitzhugh and Daniel W. Lewis in Original Claim #14013. Case Files for Congressional Cases 1884-1952. Record Group 123, National Archives and Records Administration.
Virginia State Penitentiary. Index Cards to Penitentiary Inmates. Virginia State Archives.
Watt Papers. Virginia Historical Society.
Wickham, H.T. January 22, 1925. Notes. Virginia Historical Society.
Wood, Russell. Service Discharge Record. Berkeley County, WV.
Works Progress Administration. *Alphabetical Index Birth Records,*

Alexandria, Virginia, Dates Included 1853-1911-Appendix Dates Prior to 1853, Official Project 165-1-31-85, W.P. 5822.
Works Progress Administration. Alexandria, Virginia Death Records.

Newspapers

Alexandria Gazette.
Alexandria Journal.
Fairfax Herald.
Herndon News Observer.
Lexington Gazette.
Macon Telegraph.
Martinsburg Evening Journal.
New York Times.
Northern Virginia Sun.
Richmond News-Leader.
Shepherdstown Register.
Springfield [VA] Independent.
Washington Evening Star.
Washington Post.
Washington Star-News.

Published Letters

Calcott, Margaret Law, ed. *Mistress of Riversdale: The Plantation Letters of Rosalie Stier Calvert, 1795-1821.* Baltimore, MD: John Hopkins University Press, 1991.

DeButts, Mary Custis Lee, ed. *Growing Up in the 1850's-The Journal of Agnes Lee.* Chapel Hill, NC: University of North Carolina Press for the Robert E. Lee Association, Inc., 1984.

Dorchester County Historical Society Notebook.

Griffin, Frank. "Story of the Establishment of the Robert E. Lee Memorial Foundation." Speech. May 4, 1963.

Irwin, Will, ed. *Letters to Kermit from Theodore Roosevelt 1902-1908.* New York: Charles Scribner's Sons, 1946.

Jones, J. William, *Personal Reminiscences, Anecdotes, and Letters of Robert E. Lee.* New York: D. Appleton & Co., 1874.

Morison, Elting E., et al., eds. *The Letters of Theodore Roosevelt, Vol. 5: The Big Stick, 1905-1907,* Cambridge, MA: Harvard University Press, 1952, Renewed, 1980, by Elting E. Morrison.

Nevins, Allen, ed. *Letters of Grover Cleveland 1850-1908.* New York:

DaCapo Press, 1970.
Wilson, Clyde N. and Edwin Hemphill, ed., *The Papers of John C. Calhoun.* University of South Carolina, 1972.

Secondary Sources

250^t Anniversary of the Founding of King William County Virginia. Program. Circuit Court of King William County, 1952.

Alexander, Frederick Warren, comp. *Stratford Hall and the Lees Connected With Its History-Biographical, Genealogical, and Historical.* Oak Grove, VA: 1912.

Alexandrian Magazine. January 1978.

Andrews, Marietta Minnigerode. *Memoirs of a Poor Relation-Being the Story of a Post-War Southern Girl and her Battle With Destiny.* New York: E.P. Dutton & Co., Inc., 1927.

Arlington Historical Magazine. Volume 6, No. 2. October 1978.

Armes, Ethel. *Stratford Hall: The Great House of the Lees.* Richmond, VA: Garrett & Massie, Inc., 1936.

Bagby, Bathurst Brown, M.D. *"Recollections."* West Point, VA: The Tidewater Review, 1950.

Campbell, Judith A., comp. *Page County Virginia-Death Notices Volume 6.*

Capone, Audrey B. "Ravensworth: A Short History of Annandale, Virginia," *Annandale Community Directory*, 12th Edition, Annandale, VA: Annandale Chamber of Commerce, 1998.

Cemeteries of Fairfax County, Virginia. Virginia Room, Fairfax County Public Library, n.d.

Colonnade-The Alumni Magazine of Washington & Lee. Volume 69, Fall 1994.

Confederate Veteran. Volume 25.

Conner, E.R. III. *Railroading on the Washington Division.* Manassas, VA: REF Publishing, 1986.

Curious Story of a Tapestry Portrait of WASHINGTON Ceremonies Attending the Presentation of the COURTENAY FLAG. Walhalla, SC: The Keowee Courier Press, 1903.

Coulling, Mary P. *The Lee Girls*, Winston-Salem, NC: John F. Blair, Publisher, 1987.

Dewey, Adelbert M. *The Life and Letters of Admiral Dewey From Montpelier to Manila-Containing Reproductions in Fac-simile of Hitherto Unpublished Letters of George Dewey during the Admiral's Naval Career and Extracts from his Log-Book.* New

York: The Woolfall Company, 1898.

Eby, Jerrilynn. *They Called Stafford Home-The Development of Stafford County, Virginia from 1600 until 1865.* Bowie, MD: Heritage Books, Inc., 1997.

Edney, Kermit. *Kermit Edney Remembers-Where Fitz Left Off.* Alexander, NC: Worldcomm, 1979.

Evans, D'Anne. *Wakefield Chapel.* Fairfax, VA: Fairfax County Office of Comprehensive Planning, 1977.

Fairfax Chronicles. Volume IX.

Felsenthal, Carol. *Alice Roosevelt Longworth.* New York: G.P. Putnam's Sons, 1988.

Franklin County Historical Society, *Cemetery Records of Franklin County, Virginia.* Baltimore, MD: Gateway Press, 1986.

Freeman, Douglas Southall. *The Cornerstones of Stratford-Address at the Dedication of Stratford, October 12, 1935, by the Robert E. Lee Memorial Foundation.* Richmond, VA, 1935.

Geddes, Jean. *Fairfax County-Historical Highlights From 1607.* Middleburg, VA: Denlinger's Publishers, Ltd., 1967.

Gould, Lewis L. *The Spanish-American War and President McKinley.* Lawrence, KS: University Press of Kansas, 1982.

Harper's New Monthly Magazine. Volume XXIII.

Historical and Archeological Committee of Citizens to Serve Stafford. *Foundation Stones of Stafford County,Virginia Volume II.* Fredericksburg, VA: Fredericksburg Press, Inc., 1992.

History of Virginia-Volume VI-Virginia Biography. Chicago, IL: American Historical Society, 1924.

Historical Society of Fairfax County, Virginia, Inc. Yearbook. Volume 13, 1973-1975.

Kinsley, Ardyce, comp. *The Fitzhugh Lee Sampler.* Lively, VA: Brandylane Publishers, 1992.

Lawrence, Elizabeth Pugh. *Genealogical Chart of the Fitzhugh-Grymes Family at "Eagle's Nest," King George County, Virginia 1674-1940,* 1971.

Lee, Charles Carter. *Virginia Georgics.* Richmond, VA: J. Woodhouse and Company, 1858.

Lee, Edmund Jennings, M.D., ed. *Lee of Virginia 1642-1892 Biographical and Genealogical Sketches of the Descendants of Colonel Richard Lee with Brief Notes of the Related Families of Allerton, Armistead, Ashton, Aylett, Bedinger, Beverley, Bland, Bolling, Carroll, Carter, Chambers, Corbin, Custis, Digges, Fairfax, Fitzhugh, Gardner, Grymes, Hanson, Jenings, Jones, Ludwell, Marshall, Mason, Page, Randolph, Shepherd, Shippen, Tabb, Taylor, Turberville, Washington, and Others*. Baltimore, MD: Genealogical Publishing Company, Inc., 1974.

Lee, Fitzhugh, with Joseph Wheeler, Theodore Roosevelt, and Richard Wainwright. *Cuba's Struggle Against Spain*. New York: The American Historical Press, 1899.

Lee, Fitzhugh. *General Lee*. New York, NY: D. Appleton and Company, 1894.

Lee, George Taylor. *America's Vision-A Message to all Freeman of Every Name and Clime*. Fine Creek Mills, VA: 1918.

Lee, George Taylor. *The Puritan Maid*. New York, NY: Broadway Publishing Company, c. 1904.

Lee, Lucy Chaplin. *An American Sojourn in China: Family Memories*. Annandale, VA: 1968.

Lee, R.E. Jr. *My Father General Lee*. New York, NY: Doubleday & Company, 1960.

Lee, Rebecca Bedinger, comp. *Lights and Shadows-Sketches of HARRY BEDINGER LEE-Confederate lad, schoolteacher, lawyer, minister of the Gospel; his wife LUCY MARSHALL and their CHILDREN*. N.P., 1952.

Lindsey, Angela, Kristin Oliver, and Eileen Corrigan, *The Lees of Ravensworth "The Forgotten Generation,"* in Historical Society of Fairfax County, Virginia, Inc., Essay Awards 1991, Volume 1, No. 4.

Magazine of the Jefferson County Historical Society. Volume 15, December 1949.

Magazine of the Society of the Lees of Virginia. Volume II, April 1924.

Marshall, Nellie M., comp. *Tombstone Records of Dorchester County, Maryland 1678-1964, Volume I*. Cambridge, MD: Dorchester County Historical Society, Inc., 1993.

Maryland Historical Magazine. Volume 60, June 1965.

Mason, Herbert Malloy Jr. *The Great Pursuit*. New York: Random House, 1970.

Maxwell, Hu. *The History of Randolph County, West Virginia-From Its Earliest Settlement to the Present*. Morgantown, WV: Acme Publishing Company, 1898.

Memorial Addresses on the Life and Character of William H.F. Lee (A Representative from Virginia) Delivered in the House of Representatives and in the Senate, Fifty-Second Congress, First Session. Washington, D.C.: Government Printing Office, 1892.

Memorial of the Semi-Centennial Anniversary of the American Colonization Society, January 15, 1867. Washington, D.C.

Miller, Lynda Mundy-Norris. *Glasgow, Virginia: One-Hundred Years of Dreams*. Natural Bridge Station, VA: Rockbridge Publishing Company, 1992.

Munford, Robert Beverley, Jr. *Richmond Homes and Memories*. Richmond, VA: Garrett and Massie Inc., 1936.

Muse, William T., ed. *Proceedings of the Sixty-Ninth Annual Meeting of the Virginia State Bar Association-Held at the Greenbrier White Sulphur Springs West Virginia August 6, 7, 8, 1959*. Richmond, VA: Keel-Williams Corporation, Printers, 1959.

Nagel, Paul C. *The Lees of Virginia*. New York, NY: Oxford University Press, 1990.

Nichols, James L. *Fitzhugh Lee, A biography*. Lynchburg, VA: H.E. Howard, 1989.

Patton, Sandie Smithers. *Flat Rock-Little Charleston of the Mountains*. Asheville, NC: Church Printing Company.

Phinney, Lucy Walsh. *A History of a Name and a Place-The Story of the Mount Vernon Unitarian Church and Hollin Hall*. Evergreen Historical Associates, 1994.

Pippenger, Wesley E. *Alexandria, Virginia Life in 1850: The Diary of Ella Hooe Fowle (1832-1855)*. Arlington, VA, January 1999.

Proceedings of the Sixty-Eighth Annual Meeting of the Virginia State Bar Association. Richmond, VA: Virginia State Bar Association, 1959.

Proceedings of the Virginia Historical Society at its Annual Meeting Held in the Society's Building, December 19th, 1896, with the List of Officers and Members of the Society. Richmond, VA: Wm. Ellis Jones, Book and Job Printer, 1896.

Ramage, James A. *Gray Ghost-The Life of Colonel John Singleton Mosby*. Lexington, KY: University Press of Kentucky, 1999.

Ravensworth Farmer.

Ravensworth Historical Marker Dedication Ceremony. Brochure, September 11, 1993.

Readnour, Harry Warren. *General Fitzhugh Lee, 1835-1905: A Biographical Study*. Charlottesville, VA: 1971.

Samuels, Peggy and Harold. *Teddy Roosevelt at San Juan: The Making of a President*. College Station, TX: Texas A&M University, 1997.

Sargent, Winthrop, ed. *A History of an Expedition Against Fort Duquesne in 1755 Under Major-General Edward Braddock*. Arno Press.

Segeser, A. Bower. *Joseph L. Bristow: Kansas Progressive*. Lawrence, KS: University Press of Kansas, 1968.

Sifakis, Stewart. *Who Was Who in the Confederacy*. New York: Facts on File, 1988.

The Social List of Washington and Social Precedence in Washington.

Washington, D.C.: Carolyn Hagner Shaw, 1948.
South Atlantic Quarterly. Volume XXVI. 1927.
South Carolina Historical and Genealogical Magazine. Volume I. July 1900.
South Carolina Historical and Genealogical Magazine. Volume XXXIX. 1938.
Sprouse, Edith M., *Clermont: The Rest of the Story.* Typescript. Special Collections, Alexandria Public Library.
Staudenraus, P.J. *The African Colonization Movement 1816-1865.* New York: Columbia University Press, 1961.
Stuart, Alexander H.H. *A Narrative of the Leading Incidents of the Organization of the First Popular Movement in Virginia in 1865 to Re-Establish Peaceful Relations Between the Northern and Southern States, and of the Subsequent Efforts of the "Committee of Nine, in 1869, to Secure the Restoration of Virginia to the Union.* Richmond, VA: Wm. Ellis Jones, Book and Job Printer, 1888.
Templeman, Eleanor Lee. *Arlington Heritage-Vignettes of a Virginia County.* 195.
Templeman, Eleanor Lee. "Ravensworth," *Historical Society of Fairfax County, Inc., Vol. 7, 1960-61.*
Vance, Marguerite. *The Lees of Arlington: The Story of Mary and Robert E. Lee.* E.P. Dutton & Company. 1949.
Virginia Cavalcade. Volume V.
Virginia Magazine of History and Biography. Volume IV. 1897.
Virginia Magazine of History and Biography. Volume XXIII.
Virginia Magazine of History and Biography. Volume XLVII.
Wayland, John W. *Historic Homes of Northern Virginia and the Eastern Panhandle of West Virginia.* Staunton, VA: McClure Company, Inc., 1937.
Wayland, John W. *Robert E. Lee and His Family.* Staunton, VA: McClure Printing Company, 1951.
White, Henry Alexander. *Robert E. Lee and the Southern Confederacy, 1807-1870.* New York: G.P. Putnam Sons, 1897.

Index

Accotink Creek:		26, 27
Accotink Valley, VA:		36
Alexandria Theological Seminary:		52, 75, 100, 126
Alexandria, VA:		13, 14, 24, 36, 40, 44
		60-62, 67, 75, 80-82
		93, 99, 100-102, 103-
		104, 128, 132
Allen:	Roscoe	122
Altoona, PA:		93
American Colonization Society:		8
Anderson:	William A.	83, 91, 92-93, 95-97
Andrews:	Marietta Minnegerode	80
Anking, China:		107
Annandale, VA:		16, 20, 24, 132
Appomattox Courthouse, VA:		111, 114
Aquia Creek, VA:		82
Arlington House:		x, 6, 11, 13-15, 43-45
		50, 71, 81, 99, 121
		134
Armes:	Ethel	68-70, 71, 110, 130
Ashley:	Mabel	64
Atlantic City, NJ:		51
Auld:	George	25
Ayres:	Jonah	25, 122
	Samuel	25, 34, 57, 122
Bagby:	Dr. Bathurst	79-80
Baker:	Secretary of State Newton	97
Baldwin:	J.D.	128
Banks:	Major General Nathaniel	45
Battaile:	Ann Fitzhugh	17
	Sue	17-18
Bayless:	Alfred	13
Beatley:	Charles E.	128
Bedford:		103, 104, 106
Bedinger:	Daniel	103
Bellet:	Count du	105-106
Benjamin:	Judah	105
Black:	William	76
Blackmere:	Count Friedrich August de	63-64
Bolling:	George W.	14, 57

	Martha Nicholls	14
	Sarah Melville	25
Boston, MA:		91
Bowe:	N.W.	27
Bowman:	A. Smith	126
Boxer Rebellion:		89
Braddock:	Edward	24
Breckinridge:	General John C.	112
Bristow:	Edwin	32
	Joseph Little	1-2, 31-32, 36, 132
	Joseph (Son of Joseph Little)	132-133
Buckley:	R.R.	58
Burch:	R.W.	24
Burke:	George	13
	Taylor	60-61
Burke Station, VA:		24
Calhoun:	John C.	8
Calvert:	Maria	6
Cambridge, MD:		9
Campbell:	John L.	47-48
	William Walker	60-61
Capon Springs, WV:		109
Catoosa Springs, GA:		92
Charlestown, WV:		117
Charlottesville, VA:		35, 60, 72, 90, 95 117
Charleston, SC:		21, 43, 52, 64, 65 66
Chicago Land Company of Virginia:		84
Choctaw:		89
Christ Church, Alexandria, VA:		100
Church of the Good Shepherd, Annandale, VA:		33
Clay:	Clement	105
Clermont:		81-82
Cleveland:	President Grover	46, 85, 86-88
Cleyborn:George		128
Cofer:	Henry J.	127, 128
	W.H.	127, 128
Coffey:	Michael	20
College of William & Mary:		105
Cooke:	John Esten	126

Craik:	Anne Fitzhugh	5-6
	William	6-7
Culpeper, VA:		17
Custer:	General George A.	93
Custis:	Daniel Parke	48
	Family	ix, x, 36, 55
	George Washington Parke	6, 43, 54, 76
	Martha	48
	Mary Lee Fitzhugh	6, 7
	Nellie	48
Danville, VA:		89
Davis:	Haywood	3, 38, 40
	Hazel	124
	Jefferson	12, 79, 107
	Mrs. Jefferson	90
DeRenne:	W.J.	79
Derosier:	Charles	60
	Jessie	60-62
Dewey:	Admiral Thomas	88, 89
Dickins:	Albert	16
	Francis Asbury	10, 16-17, 133
	Frank	16
	Mrs. Francis Asbury	10-11, 16-17
	Randolph	16
Dillard:	Judge P.H.	118
Dodd:	Colonel George A.	97
Dove:	Douglas	1-2, 33, 122
"Dress Parade:"		121
Dreyhausen:	Hans	66
Dumfries, VA:		30
Duncan:	J.M.	1-2, 3, 39
du Pont:	Francis I.	64
Durand:	G.C.	127
Egbert:	Dr. E.H.	127
El Paso, TX:		98
Enchantment:		52, 63-65
Episcopal High School, Alexandria, VA:		23
Eutaw Springs, SC:		81
Fairfax, VA:		33, 59, 61, 62, 79
		123
Fairfax County Herd Association:		122
Falls Church, VA:		33

Falmouth, VA:		5
Farmville, VA:		114
Farr:	Wilson W.	3, 38, 123
Fendall:	Mary	100
	Philip	44-45
Fine Creek Mills:		109
Fitzhugh:	Anna Maria	xi, 7, 9-10, 12-14, 13-16, 30, 81, 82, 132
	Ann	30-31, 132
	Battaile	5
	David	17, 18
	Dolly	18
	Edwin	18
	Giles	5
	Henry	5
	Maria M.	17
	Martha Carter	6
	Mordecai	5
	Nicholas	5
	Richard	5, 17
	Col. William	4
	William(of Chatham)	4, 7, 132, 134
	William Henry	7-10, 82, 132
	William M.	17
Five Forks:	Battle of	82
Flat Rock, NC:		52, 63
Ford:	Henry	130
	President Gerald	133
Fort Bliss, TX:		99
Fort McPherson, GA:		99
Fort Riley, KS:		90
Fowle:	George Dashiell	82
Fox:	Dennis	31
Fredericksburg, VA:		5
Freeman:	Douglas Southall	67-68, 69-70, 79 125, 130
Garland:	Charlie	60
	Clarence	60
	Eva	60, 61-62
	Russell	60
Garnett:	Theodore S.	97
Gettysburg College:		124

Gibson:	Mrs. Charles Dana	130
Glasgow, VA:		83-84
Glass:	Carter	70
Godwin:	L.O.	128
Goldsborough:	Charles	7, 9-10
	Mary Caroline	7
	Robert H.	8
Grant:	President Ulysses S.	45
	Ulysses S. III	93, 124
Green:	B.W.	79
	John	44-45
Griffin:	Mrs. Frank	131
Gunston Hall:		81
Hamilton, Canada:		106
Hampton:	General Wade	21
Hancock:	Winfield S.	18
Harper:	Molly	104
Harris:	L.M.	125
Harvard College:		109
Hawkins:	Captain Charles	30-31
Hemphill:	Edwin	68
Hendrick:	Burton J.	67, 70-71
Herbert:	Upton	18
Hirst: Omer L.		1, 20, 121
Hollin Hall:		39-40, 42
Hot Springs, VA:		52
Houdon:	Antoine	64
Howard:	General Oliver O.	78
Howe:	Dr. James Lewis	125
Hunter:	General David	106
Hunton:	Mrs. Eppa	25
Ickes:	Harold	64
Ilda, VA:		24
Ingalls:	Lieutenant	45
Jackson:	General Thomas J.	83, 105
Jacksonville, FL:		89
Jamestown Exposition of 1907:		47, 90-92, 95-96, 97
Jasper, FL:		88
Jefferson:	Memorial Road	90
	President Thomas	90, 114
Jeffries:	Ben	30

Jennings:	John Melville	73
Jessup:	Sam	35
Johnson:	President Andrew	45, 46
Johnson City, TN:		114
Johnston:	Gen. Albert Sidney	12
	General Joseph	85
Jones:	Bolling	20
	Owen	20, 24-25, 33
	Raymond "Casey"	41
	Rev. J. William	77
Keith:	Thomas R.	59
Kendrick:	George W.	47
Kerr:	Charles	48
Kincheloe:	J.U.	58
Kirby:	Sheriff Eppa	40-41, 62
Kirby-Smith:	General Edmund	106
Lanier:	May	129-131
Lee:	Agnes	10, 15
	Ann Carter (Mother of Robert E.)	8, 9, 100
	Ann Carter (Dau of Robert E., Jr.)	77
	Anna Maria Mason	81, 84, 89
	Anne (Dau of Edmund Jennings)	100
	Annie (Dau of Robert E.)	10, 133
	Armistead	108
	Arthur	105
	Arthur (Son of William Fitzhugh)	101
	Bessie Read Nelson	107
	C. Carter (Son of John Penn)	67-69, 119
	Cassius Francis	100, 102, 104, 106
	Cassius Jr.	129
	Catherine D. Walker	119
	Catherine Randolph	117
	Cazenove	68-70, 111, 112, 115
		129, 131
	Charles Carter	9-10, 67, 108-110
		111, 116, 117, 120
		126
	Charles Henry	126-128
	Charlotte Haxall	76
	Charlotte Wickham	12
	Chiswell (Son of John Penn)	119
	Dan	92

Edmund Jennings	75, 78, 100-102, 120
	126, 129
Edmund Jennings II	102-105, 106, 107
Edmund Jennings III	103, 107
Edmund Jennings IV	108-109
Edwin Gray	103, 105-107
Eliza Shepherd	102-103
Ella G. Fletcher	111, 115, 119
Ellen Bernard Fowle	82, 88, 93, 95-96, 97
Fitzhugh	xi-xii, 74-75, 78
	80-93, 94, 119, 128
Fitzhugh Jr.	xii, 75, 92, 93-99
	119-120
George Dashiell	90, 91, 93, 96
George Bolling (Bolly)	ix-x, xi, 2-3, 14
	18-20, 28, 33, 34
	35, 39, 43, 47, 49
	50, 51, 52-53, 54
	55, 57-58, 59-60
	61-62, 65, 124-125
George Taylor	111-116, 117, 118
	120, 129
George Taylor III	126
George Washington Custis	ix, xi, 10, 16, 21
	25-29, 32, 37, 38
	46-51, 55, 77, 79
	84-85, 111, 114, 118
	125
Helen Keeney	34, 51, 57
Henrietta (Dau of Edm J II)	103
Henrietta Bedinger	103-104, 106
Henry (Half-Bro of Robert E.)	68, 109
Henry ("Light Horse Harry")	67-68, 69, 70, 76
	81, 83, 85, 93, 100
	108-109, 126
Henry (Son of Chas. Carter)	116
Henry (Son of John Penn)	69, 119
Ida	103
Isabella G. Walker	119
J. Collins	71
John Mason	126
John Penn	116, 117-119

Juliet Carter	77, 79
Kathre L. Burton	90
Lucy	102
Lucy Chapin (Mrs. Edm. J IV)	107
Lucy Penn Taylor	109, 111, 117, 118
Mary Catherine	101
Mary Custis (Mrs. Robert E.)	x, 6, 8, 10-11, 12 15-16, 37, 44-46 54, 57
Mary Custis (Dau of Robert E.)	10, 21-22, 27, 29, 44 46-47, 49-51, 54, 61 77, 117
Mary Custis (Dau. of Robert, Jr.)	77
Mary M. Pinckney	34, 43, 51-60, 63-66
Mary Tabb (Mrs. William Henry)	xi, 14, 16, 18-20, 24 25, 27, 29, 31, 32-34 49, 51, 53, 55, 56-58 59, 66
Mary Walker	52, 126
Mildred	10, 21-22, 29, 46, 76
Mildred (Dau. of Chas. Carter)	116
Mildred Washington	129
Nannie	93
Rebecca Rust	107
Richard (Son of John Penn)	119
Richard Bland	71
Richard Henry	100, 109
Richard Henry (Son of Edm J.)	105
Robert C.	84
Robert E.	ix, x, xi, xii, 2, 6, 7 9, 10, 11-12, 14, 15 29, 38, 45, 46, 54 55, 56, 57, 62, 64 65, 66, 67, 68, 69 71, 74, 75, 77-80 82, 84, 94, 99, 100 108, 110, 111, 114 115, 117, 119, 120 125, 126, 128, 129 130, 133, 134
Robert E. Jr.	xi, 10, 14, 27, 46, 47 49, 74, 76-80, 84, 119

	Robert E. III (Bob)	14, 18-19, 25-29, 33-34, 37, 39, 43, 49, 51-54, 58, 65, 124-125
	Robert E. IV	53, 126
	Robert Randolph	116
	Sally (Mrs. Edmund Jennings)	100, 101
	Susan Cooke	126
	Sydney Smith	9, 75, 80-81
	Thomas	ix
	Virginia	93
	William Fitzhugh (S of Edmund)	101-102
	William Henry Fitzhugh (Rooney)	xi, 10, 11, 12, 13-14 16, 18-23, 25, 28, 34 37, 38, 49, 53, 56-57 75, 76, 134
	Williams Carter	116-117
Lee Monument Association:		82
"Lee Rangers":		12
Leeland:		75, 102, 104, 105, 107
Letcher:	Greenlee D.	83, 125
Levin:	Alexandra Lee	105-106
Lewis:	Daniel W.	14
Lexington, VA:		14, 15, 16, 21, 26, 29 48, 50-51, 52, 53-54 76, 77, 83, 105, 111, 118
Lincoln:	Abraham	24, 65, 106
Link:	John N.	28
Little Rock, AR:		65
Logan:	John A.	45
Lonoke, AR:		113
Love:	Judge James M.	56-57
	Thomas R.	18
Lynchburg, VA:		119
Macon, GA:		126
Madden:	W.J.	84
Madison:	President James	72
Magnolia Cemetery, Charleston, SC:		65-66
Manassas:	Battle of	13, 31-32
"Man O'War:"		121
Marion Artillery:		52
Marshall:	John	109

	Mary	33
Martin:	Thomas Staples	85
Martinsburg, VA (WV):		6, 41
Mason:	George	40, 81
	John	81
Mathews:	John	4
Maynard:	Oscar	63, 65-66
McClellan:	General George B.	12
McKenney:	Torrey	72
McKinley:	President William	50, 87-88, 93
Memminger:	Christopher	52
Mercer:	Charles Fenton	8
Meredith:	Bob	77
	Sarah	77
Middleton:	Arthur	52
	Beverly M.	66
	Henry I.	51-52
	Ralph Izard (Nephew of Mary M.)	65, 66
	Virginia Memminger	51
Minaca, Mexico:		97
Minnegerode:	Charlie	80
Minter:	Matilda	60-62
	Raleigh	60
Moore:	Hon. R. Walton	59
Myers:	Barton	95
Nagel:	Paul	109
Napoleon:	Emperor Louis	106
Nash: Mrs. Ben		34
Nelson:	Andrew	3, 19-20, 22, 25, 27 33, 34, 36, 38-39 42, 60-62
New Market, VA: Battle of		111-112, 116
Newell:	Mrs. Emerson Root	70
Newman:	Elizabeth	30
	Glenn	31, 59
	John	20, 30
	Lilly	20, 25, 30
	Linwood	30, 38-39, 61-62
	Richard	30
Norfolk, VA:		47, 97
North American Company:		39
Oak Hill:		5, 17, 24, 30-31

Old Capitol Prison:		17
Olney:	Secretary of State Richard	86
Opie:	Fitzhugh Lee	128
Ossian Hall:		1, 5, 10, 16, 24
		31-32, 132, 133
		134
Page: Walter Hines		78-79
Parke:	Colonel Daniel	48, 54
Paulus Hook, NJ:		81
Pennsylvania Railroad:		93
Perkins:	Frances	64
Petersburg, VA:		14, 22
Pickett:	Charles	59
Pierce:	President Franklin	55
Pinckney:	Gustavus M.	52
Pittsburgh, PA:		24
Pittsburgh and Virginia Railroad:		83
Pohick Episcopal Church:		132
Pollard:	William	x
Ravensworth:		x, xi, 1-19, 21, 23
		24-39, 42, 43, 47
		49, 50, 51, 52, 53
		54-55, 56-60, 61
		64, 65, 66, 77
		79-80, 81, 104
		121-124, 132-134
Reading:	Alice Matilda	72
	Anna Washington	72
Rhea: Ellen Lee		90, 128
	James Cooper	90, 96
Richland:		82
Richmond, VA:		12, 13, 27, 32, 41
		57, 58-59, 72, 76
		79, 82-83, 84, 88
		92, 101, 109, 114
Ritchie:	Judge A.C.	58, 61
Roanoke, VA:		52, 114, 117
Robert E. Lee Memorial Foundation:		68-70, 124, 129-131
Rockbridge Company:		83-84
Rocky Mount, VA:		67, 117, 118, 119
Romancoke:		xi, 14, 74, 76, 78-80
Roosevelt:	Belle Willard	79-80

	Ethel	99
	Kermit	80, 94-95, 98-99
	President Franklin Delano	130
	President Theodore	35, 75, 80, 91, 93-95, 96, 97-98
Rosser:	Thomas	78, 81
"Rough Riders":		94, 97
Ruiz:	Ricardo	87
Rust:	Mary	72
Sanford:	General Charles W.	43
Scott: General Winfield		12
Segessenman: Frederick		2, 20, 33
Shanghai, China:		108
Sheads:	Arneita	32-33
	Edward Campbell	26, 30, 31, 33, 122-123
	John David	24
Shepherd:	Captain Abraham	102
Shepherdstown, WV:		75, 102-104, 107
Sheridan:	General Philip	82
Sherman:	General William Tecumseh	87
	Secretary of State John	87
Shively:	Frances	73
Smith:	Francis S.	44
	Judge Howard W.	40, 41, 62
Smith Island:		45
Society of the Lees of Virginia:		68, 70, 71, 73, 111, 115, 129, 131
South Boston Improvement Company:		83
Southern Claims Commission:		15
Spanish-American War:		75, 88-89, 93-94
Spotsylvania: Battle of		81
Sprague:	R.J.	122
Springfield Station, VA:		24
Staunton, VA:		112
St. Simons Island, GA:		126-128
Stephens:	John	40
	Virginia Letcher	34
Stetson:	Eugene	130
Stewart:	Kate	34
Stone Mountain, GA:		124

Stratford Hall:		xii, 67, 68, 69-70
		81, 109, 110, 130-131
Stuart:	General James Ewell Brown	81
Sully Foundation:		73
Sully Plantation:		71, 72, 73
Summerville, SC:		57
Surratt:	John H.	106
Taliaferro:	Sidney F.	55
Taylor:	Colonel Hancock	45
	John of Caroline	115-116
Templeton:	Eleanor Lee	5, 71-73, 131, 133
Thalheimer Brothers:		58-59
Thompson:	Jacob	105
Thompson Dairy:		39
"Thrasher:"		122
Tucker:	Henry St. George	95
Tucson, AZ:		99
Villa: Pancho		97-98
Virginia Constitutional Convention of 1829-30:		9
Virginia Historical Society:		73
Virginia Military Institute:		93, 111
Virginia State Penitentiary:		41
Ward:	Berkley	17
Washington:	Bushrod	8
	George	ix, x, xii, 2, 6, 37
		48, 54-55, 64, 67, 76
		125-126, 134
	John A.	47
	Joseph	23
	Martha	64, 67, 125
Washington & Lee University:		xi, 14, 21, 28, 37, 52
		53-54, 77, 117, 118
		121, 125
Washington City, Virginia Midland and Great Southern Railroad:		26
Washington, DC:		27, 28, 32, 33-34, 51
		55, 58, 60, 70, 77, 79
		80, 87, 88, 90, 103
		106, 109

Washington Railway and Electric Company:		39
Watt:	Elizabeth	17-18, 21, 33
	William	21, 24, 33
Waycross, GA:		88
Wayland:	John W.	49
Weitzel:	Dr. John	71
	Marie W.	71-72, 73
Wheeler:	General Joseph	81, 90
	Laura	25
White:	Dr. Henry A.	77
White House, VA:		x-xi, 14, 16, 59 76
Willard:	Family	79
	Joseph E.	33
Williams:	Virgil	3, 38, 123
Wilson:	Harley	39
	President Woodrow	97
Winchester:	Battle of	82
Windsor Forest:		109, 116
Wood:	Carl	35-36, 42
	Davis	35
	Elizabeth McCauley	35
	Grace Marrs	35, 42
	Oscar	35, 39-40, 42
	Russell	3, 35-36, 38, 39 40-42, 123
Wytheville, VA:		59

www.ingramcontent.com/pod-product-compliance
Lightning Source LLC
Chambersburg PA
CBHW071436150426
43191CB00008B/1140